D1180509

A BIBLIOGRAPHY OF WORD FORMATION
IN THE GERMANIC LANGUAGES

A BIBLIOGRAPHY OF WORD FORMATION
IN THE GERMANIC LANGUAGES

Richard K. Seymour

Duke University Press   Durham, N. C.   1968

ACKNOWLEDGMENTS

The author gratefully acknowledges the support of the Council on Research of Duke University which made the compilation of this bibliography possible. Research assistants Susan Oehl, Paul Alexander, and Michael Elzay aided the author greatly by doing much of the mechanical and clerical work.

TABLE OF CONTENTS

INTRODUCTORY COMMENTS

The compilation of this bibliography came about because of the lack of any quasi-complete, unified listing of articles and monographs dealing with the rather broad field of word formation in Germanic. Any scholar endeavoring to do research in this area has at one time or another experienced irritation at the loss of time and effort spent in tracking down references to work already done on a particular aspect of word formation. Inter-dialect comparative work, both synchronic and diachronic, for example, suffers considerably from this lack. To be sure, there exist, at least for German and English, certain standard works[1] which are comprehensive in nature but in terms of accessibility of their bibliography neither well organized nor complete.

With the aim of at least partially filling this rather large gap the effort has been made here to bring together in one place a listing by author of all articles and monographs dealing with word formation in Germanic that could be uncovered. Certain obstacles presented themselves from the outset, the most problematical being the precise defining of the term *word formation*. The difficulty is actually not so much one of a theoretical definition, but rather that of determining which items to include and which to exclude from the listing. Essentially, the question posed is when or at what point is a particular item so peripheral or marginal that it does not warrant inclusion. Thus there arose at the outset the necessity of limiting the scope of the compilation. The following three major categories have been omitted owing to the existing, rather extensive bibliography: loan words and borrowings, place name studies, and personal name studies. Treatments of borrowings, for example, are often etymological in nature; however, certain items which deal with principles or specific features of word formation that have become generally productive in the receiving language have been included. Often a suffix prevalent in the formation of place names enjoys a degree of currency in the formation of other types of words. A similar situation obtains for certain features of personal name formation. If works dealing with place and

---

1. For English, among others: Herbert Koziol, *Handbuch der englischen Wortbildungslehre* (Heidelberg, 1937), and Hans Marchand, *The Categories and Types of Present-day English Word-Formation: A Synchronic-Diachronic Approach* (Wiesbaden, 1960). For German, among others: Walter Henzen, *Deutsche Wortbildung*, 3. Aufl. (Tübingen, 1965), and W. Wilmanns, *Deutsche Grammatik* (Strassburg, 1899), Vol. II.

personal names were, as indicated, somewhat general or broad in scope, they were included. Obviously the basis of selection of such items is open to criticism.

In general, dictionaries, glossaries, and word lists have not been incorporated unless there appeared to be a sufficiently valid reason to do so. Existing comprehensive bibliographies of various lexicons can easily be consulted.[2] Included in this bibliography are only those dictionaries, etc., which present the vocabulary or a selection of the word inventory of an area which has undergone but limited investigation, if any. Again, the selection of dictionaries and the like is open to criticism, but the user should keep in mind that those listed may be valuable source material or may not be listed elsewhere.

A quick glance at the indexes will point up the fact that although an effort was made to be quite selective in the matter of dictionaries, borrowings, etymologies, place and personal names, etc., a rather considerable number of entries is indexed. It seemed better to err on the liberal side than to eliminate material to the point of narrowness. The primary emphasis in the compilation rests on "general word formation" with the inclusion of as many marginal and peripheral items as was deemed warranted.

The majority of the items listed deal with compounding, derivation by prefixes, suffixes and infixes, gradation, onomatopoeia, root formants, back formations, etc. No restriction was made in regard to grammatical categories (nouns, verbs, etc.). Items dealing with semantic development are listed insofar as they relate to word formation per se.

Index 4, Languages, gives a complete list of all languages dealt with. There is little point in repeating here the many languages (and dialects) included under the heading Germanic, but mention should be made of the non-Germanic languages. Works dealing with Latin, Greek, French, etc., have been included if they discuss or treat, for example, a suffix borrowed into Germanic or one of the Germanic languages and the subsequent development of that suffix. This kind of listing can, at best, fall short of being exhaustive.

No bibliography can claim to be complete or thoroughly up-to-date. Certainly the present bibliography makes no such claim. Nonetheless, within the framework of the restrictions outlined above the user will find the listing as complete and exhaustive as was possible. It is hoped that nothing of value has been omitted through the year 1964. Owing to the time lag in the acquisition of journals and new books the entries for 1965 and 1966 are admittedly incomplete.

---

2. Wolfram Zaunmüller, *Bibliographisches Handbuch der Sprachwörterbücher, ein internationales Verzeichnis von 5,600 Wörterbüchern der Jahre 1460–1958 für mehr als 500 Sprachen und Dialekte* (Stuttgart, 1958), among others.

NOTES ON USING THE BIBLIOGRAPHY

Each item is entered in the Alphabetical Listing by the author's surname. In the case of joint authorship the item is listed under the name of the first author. Abbreviations of journals, series, languages, etc., are given on pp. *xiii–xv*.

Occasionally an entire entry is enclosed in brackets. This is done to indicate that the monograph or article was not available for inspection—in most instances not available in the United States. Such entries are naturally only as accurate as the source from which they were taken and could not be verified for pertinence, etc.

Brackets are also used within entries to enclose information concerning reviews of the prime entry, e.g.:

> 14. Ahlsson, Lars-Erik, *Die altfriesischen Abstraktbildungen*, Uppsala, 1960. [Dietrich Hofmann, *AfdA* 73 (1962) 87–92.]

Since some titles do not clearly indicate their content or scope, comments have been appended. When these appear, they are preceded by the symbol ¶:

> 84. Bech, Fedor, "Kleine Beiträge: Nr. 1 Gebeinze, geborgze, gebuscheze," *Germania* 10 (1865) 395–398. ¶ Formations in *-eze, -ze*; prefix *ge-*; these correspond to Low Ger. and Du. words in *-ete, -te*; many examples.

With certain exceptions such comments avoid being value judgments since the worth of any item depends entirely on the purpose or intent of the user.

The order of modified vowels in the alphabetical listing is:

$$\text{å} = \text{aa} \qquad \text{ä} = \text{ae} \qquad \text{ö, ø} = \text{oe} \qquad \text{ü} = \text{ue}$$

The Indexes, six in number, prefaced by a list of abbreviations, are self-explanatory locator aids. All numbers refer to the numbered entries in the Alphabetical Listing by Authors.

ABBREVIATIONS

I. JOURNALS AND SERIES

AASF	*Annales Academiae Scientiarum Fennicae*, Series B
AfdA	*Anzeiger für deutsches Altertum*
AJPh.	*American Journal of Philology*
Alemannia	*Alemannia. Zeitschrift für Sprache, Litteratur und Volkskunde des Elsasses und Oberrheins*
Allg.Ztg.Beil.	*Allgemeine Zeitung, Beilage*
AmSp.	*American Speech*
APhS	*Acta Philologica Scandinavica*
Arkiv	*Arkiv för nordisk filologi*
Beitr.z.Schweizerd. Grammatik	*Beiträge zur Schweizerdeutschen Grammatik*
Ber. der Kgl. Sächs. Ges. der Wsch. zu Leipzig, phil.-hist. Klasse	*Berichte der Königlichen Sächsischen Gesellschaft der Wissenschaften zu Leipzig, philologisch-historische Klasse*
Bezzenberger Beiträge	*Beiträge zur Kunde der indogermanischen Sprachen*
CMLR	*Canadian Modern Language Review*
DA	*Dissertation Abstracts*
De Gids	*De Gids, Algemeen Cultureel Maandblad*
Deutscher Sprachwart	*Deutscher Sprachwart. Zeitschrift für Kunde und Kunst der Sprache*
Engl.Stud.	*Englische Studien*
Folksmaalsstudier	*Folksmaalsstudier. Meddelanden fraan föreningen för nordisk filologi i Helsingfors*
GQ	*German Quarterly*
GR	*Germanic Review*
GRM	*Germanisch-Romanische Monatsschrift*
Herrigs Archiv	*Archiv für das Studium der Neueren Sprachen*
IF	*Indogermanische Forschungen*
JEGP	*Journal of English and Germanic Philology*

MLN	*Modern Language Notes*
MLQ	*Modern Language Quarterly*
MLR	*Modern Language Review*
Mod.Phil.	*Modern Philology*
NdJb.	*Niederdeutsches Jahrbuch (Jahrbuch des Vereins für niederdeutsche Sprachforschung)*
NdKbl.	*Niederdeutsches Korrespondenzblatt (Korrespondenzblatt des Vereins für niederdeutsche Sprachforschung)*
NdMitt.	*Niederdeutsche Mitteilungen*
Neuphil.Mitt.	*Neuphilologische Mitteilungen*
Nordisk Tidsskrift	*Nordisk Tidsskrift for Filologie*
PBB	*Beiträge zur Geschichte der deutschen Sprache und Literatur*
PMLA	*Publications of the Modern Language Association of America*
SN	*Studia Neophilologica*
SPE	*Society for Pure English*
SSN	*Scandinavian Studies and Notes*
Tijdschrift	*Tijdschrift voor Nederlandsche taal- en letterkunde*
Word	*Word: Journal of the Linguistic Circle of New York*
ZddSprv.	*Zeitschrift des deutschen Sprachvereins*
ZfdA	*Zeitschrift für deutsches Altertum*
ZfdBildung	*Zeitschrift für deutsche Bildung*
ZfddtU	*Zeitschrift für den deutschen Unterricht*
ZfdMaa.	*Zeitschrift für deutsche Mundarten*
ZfdPh.	*Zeitschrift für deutsche Philologie*
ZfdW	*Zeitschrift für deutsche Wortforschung*
ZffrzSpruLit.	*Zeitschrift für französische Sprache und Literatur*
ZfhdMaa.	*Zeitschrift für hochdeutsche Mundarten*
ZfMaa.	*Zeitschrift für Mundarten*
ZfMdaf.	*Zeitschrift für Mundartforschung*
ZfOrthographie	*Zeitschrift für Orthographie*
ZfrPh.	*Zeitschrift für romanische Philologie*
ZfvglSpr.	*Zeitschrift für vergleichende Sprachforschung*

II. OTHER

ae.	altenglisch		Eng.	English
ahd.	althochdeutsch		Ger.	German
diss.	dissertation		Gmc.	Germanic
Du.	Dutch		Go.	Gothic

hebr.	hebräisch	nhd.	neuhochdeutsch
hochd.	hochdeutsch	n.r.	nieuwe reeks
IE	Indo-European	OE	Old English
Lat.	Latin	OF	Old French
masc.	masculine	OHG	Old High German
ME	Middle English	OIcel.	Old Icelandic
mhd.	mittelhochdeutsch	Sp.	Spanish
MHG	Middle High German	Sw.	Swedish
MLG	Middle Low German	wf	word formation
ndl.	niederländisch	Zt.	Zeitschrift
N.F.	Neue Folge		

ALPHABETICAL LISTING BY AUTHORS

1. Aakerlund, Walter, *Studier över adjektiv- och adverb-bildningen medelst suf-fixen -liker och -lika i fornsvenskan*, Lund, 1929. [*Neophilologus* 16 (1931) 229–230.]

2. Aakermalm, Aake, "Fast sammansättning och lös förbindelse," *Ny-svenska studier* 41 (1961 [1962]) 174–196. ¶ Compound verbs and verbal groups in Sw.

3. ——, *Fornnordiska verb med substantivisk förled. Ett bidrag till nordisk ord-bildningslära*, diss., Lund, 1955 (= *Stockholm Studies in Scandinavian Philology* 12). ¶ Deals with Old Scandinavian compound verbs with a substantive as the first part.

4. ——, "Om termerna avledning och retrograd avledning," *Arkiv* 71 (1956) 66–69. ¶ Concerned with the terms "derivation" and "back-formation" in reference to T. Johannisson's article "Om sammansätta verb i svenskan," *q.v.*

5. ——, "Om verbet *atombomba* och liknande bildningar i nutida svensk dagspress," *Nysvenska studier* 32 (1954) 8–46.

6. Abrahamson, E., "Ett par bohuslänska växtnamn," *Namn och bygd* 24 (1936) 37–43 (= *Nomina Germanica. Hyllningsskrift till Bengt Ivar Hes-selman*). ¶ Verb + adjective yielding substantival adjective.

[7. Achmanova, O. S., "O primenenii sravnitel'no-istoričeskogo metoda v oblasti slovoobrazovanija (Na materiale germanskich jazykov)," in *Sbornik statej po jazykoznaniju. Pamjati zaslužennogo dejatelja nauki pro-fessora Maksima Vladimiroviča Sergievskogo*, Moscow, 1961, 60–73. ¶ Deals with the use of the method of historical comparison in Gmc. wf.]

8. Adamus, Marian, *On the Participles, Finite Verbs and Adjectives of the Germanic Languages*, Warsaw, 1962. ¶ Marginal.

9. Adler, H. G., "Zusammengesetzte Wörter," *Muttersprache* (1960) 72–75.

10. Adler-Mesnard, M., *Traité de la formation des mots allemands*, Paris, 1841. ¶ Rare book available in the Bonaparte Collection of the Newberry Library; deals with derivatives and compounds.

11. Adolphi, Paul, *Doppelsuffixbildung und Suffixwechsel im Englischen mit besonderer Rücksicht auf das lateinisch-romanische Element*, diss., Marburg, 1910. ¶ Part I: double suffixes (nouns, adverbs): *-let, -erer, -ancy, -ency, -ery, -ry, -stress*; Part II: "Suffixwechsel" (nouns, adjectives) *-eous, -ious, -able, -ible*, etc., (adverbs; foreign suffixes [Lat., OF, Gmc.]) *-ster, -ile, -ine.*

12. Aeolus, *Originations of Words with a Digressional Treatise on the Scale AEI Leading to a View of the Scale of Colours*, Paris, 1843. ¶ Bonaparte Col-lection, Newberry Library; interesting but of little value.

13. Ahldén, Tage, *der-* = *er-, Geschichte und Geographie*, Göteborg, 1953 (= *Acta Universitatis Gotoburgensis. Göteborgs högskolas aarsskrift* 59, 5). ¶ Verb prefix; Ger. dialects.

14. Ahlsson, Lars-Erik, *Die altfriesischen Abstraktbildungen*, Uppsala, 1960. [Dietrich Hofmann, *AfdA* 73 (1962) 87–92.]

15. Alanne, Eero, "Das Fortleben der mhd. Ausdrücke für den Weinberg, die Weinbergsarbeiten und die Weinbehandlung in Österreich und Südtirol," *Neuphil.Mitt.* 59 (1958) 110–150.

16. ——, "Das Fortleben des mhd. *íchen* und seiner Synonyme am Oberrhein," *Neuphil.Mitt.* 55 (1954) 275–289.

17. ——, "Das Fortleben einiger mhd. Ausdrücke für den Weinhandel und Gefäßnamen in Österreich und Südtirol," *Neuphil.Mitt.* 60 (1959) 231–266.

18. ——, "Das Fortleben einiger mhd. Bezeichnungen für den Weinhandel am Oberrhein," *Neuphil.Mitt.* 56 (1955) 178–193.

19. ——, "Das Fortleben einiger mhd. Gefäß- und Handwerkernamen am Oberrhein," *Neuphil.Mitt.* 56 (1955) 193–230.

20. Albrecht, Erich A., "New German Words in Popular English Dictionaries," *GQ* 22, 1 (1949) 10–16.

21. Aldrich, Ruth I., " '-en'; '-lon,' " *AmSp.* 33 (1958) 147–148. ¶ Trade names.

22. ——, "-mobile," *AmSp.* 39 (1964) 77–79.

23. Alexander, Henry, "The Particle *ing* in Placenames," *Essays and Studies* 2 (1911) 158–182. ¶ Although dealing with place names, of general interest for the suffix *-ing*.

24. Alexander, L. H., *Participial Substantives of the -ata Type in Romance Languages with Special Reference to French*, New York, 1912. ¶ Valuable as it relates to OHG *-âta*.

25. Andersen, Harry, "Om Ordet *Honning* i Gammeldansk," *APhS* 6 (1931) 203–206. ¶ *Honning* and the suffix *-ung, -ing*.

26. Anderson, George, "The þis-Compounds in Gothic," *JEGP* 35 (1936) 27–43.

27. Anderson, W., "Zum Lehnwort im Baltendeutsch," *ZfMaa.* 14 (1938) 146. ¶ Of peripheral interest to wf as such.

28. Andersson, Alfons, "Amerikansk-engelska laanord i Esse-maalet (Österb.)," *Folkmaalsstudier* 2 (1934) 137–140.

29. Andreas, Willy, "Wilhelmisch oder Wilhelminisch?" *Historische Zt.* 161, 2 (1940) 324. ¶ Adjective formation from proper names.

30. Andreson, K. G., "Imperativnamen," *Herrigs Archiv* 43 (1868) 393–404.

31. Andrews, A. L., "Old Norse Notes," *MLN* 29 (1915) 133–136. ¶ Masc. *-ill-*.

32. Andrews, Charles M., "The *-ing* Suffix in English Place-names," *Nation* 69 (1899) 427.

33. Anika, Hans, "Wortbildende Kräfte in der englischen Pressesprache des letzten Jahrzehnts," diss., Hamburg, 1951.

34. Annerholm, Hjalmar, *Studier över die inkoativa verben paa na(n) i gotiskan och de nordiska fornspraaken*, Stockholm, 1956 (= *Stockholm Studies in Scandinavian Philology* 14). ¶ With Ger. summary.

35. Ansteinsson, John, "Sekundær *t* etter *er*-suffiks," *Norske videnskabersselskabs forhandlinger* 13 (1940) 24–26.

36. Antrim, Harry T., "An Instance of a -*Wise* Adverb from 1920," *AmSp.* 37 (1962) 159.

[37. Arakin, V. D., "Vozniknovenie kornevogo, ili bessuffiksl'nogo sposoba slovoobrazovanija v anglijskom jazyke," in *Sbornik statej po jazykoznaniju. Pamjati zaslužennogo dejatelja nauki professora Maksima Vladimiroviča Sergievskogo*, Moscow, 1961, 43–50. ¶ *Book>to book*, etc., in Eng.]

38. Arendal, Isaia van, "Über die Kosenamen auf -*eles*," *Allg.Ztg.Beil.* 86 (1900) 3–5. ¶ Although referring to personal names, of interest for diminutive formations and -*es* suffix.

39. Armstrong, J. L., "The Gerund in Nineteenth-Century English," *PMLA* 7 (1892) 200–211.

40. Arnesen, Martin, "Namen auf -*bern* im Friesischen und Nordgermanischen," *ZfvglSpr.* 22 (1874) 93–94.

41. Arnold, Robert Franz, "Die englischen Lehn- und Fremdwörter im gegenwärtigen Nhd.," *Zt. für die deutsch-österreichischen Gymnasien* (1904) 91 ff.

42. ——, "Wortgeschichtliche Zeugnisse," *ZfdW* 8 (1906–1907) 1–28. ¶ Many compounds.

43. Arntz, Helmut, "Deutsche Grammatik," in *Festschrift für Otto Behaghel*, Heidelberg, 1934, 75–109. ¶ Part IV, pp. 97–99, deals with wf in general.

44. ——, "Gemeingermanisch," in *Germanen und Indogermanen. Volkstum, Sprache, Heimat, Kultur: Festschrift für Hermann Hirt*, 2 vols., ed. Helmut Arntz, Heidelberg, 1936, II, 433 ff.

45. ——, "Urgermanisch, Gotisch und Nordisch," *Festschrift für Otto Behaghel*, Heidelberg, 1934, 29–74. ¶ Sec. 11 deals with wf in general.

46. Aronstein, Philipp, *Englische Wortkunde*, Leipzig and Berlin, 1925. ¶ Almost entirely the many aspects of wf: derivation, compounding, onomatopœia, etc.

47. Arvesen, Ole Peder, *Tre spraak i Norge?*, Oslo, 1948. ¶ Fear of Danish elements; in passing mentions the endings -*else*, -*ing* for -*ni*, -*ning*.

48. Bach, Adolf, *Deutsche Mundartforschung*, 2nd ed., Heidelberg, 1950. [*AfdA* 66 (1952–1953) 29.]

49. ——, *Deutsche Namenkunde*, I, 1 and 2 *Personennamen*, II, 1 and 2 *Ortsnamen*, Heidelberg, 1952–1954. [Emil Öhman, *Neuphil.Mitt.* 56 (1955) 60–62.]

50. ——, "Die deutschen Namen auf *-ing-* in ihrer geschichtlichen und räumlichen Entwicklung," *Rheinische Vierteljahrsblätter* 10 (1940) 77–90. ¶ Deals with *-ing* in general.

51. ——, *Die deutschen Personennamen,* Berlin, 1943. [H. Schmoecke, *NdKbl.* 56 (1943–1949) 63] ¶ *-mann, -er, -brink, -lon, -holt, -horst, -kamp, -hof, -hus, -hövel; -a, -ma, -ker, -tjer,* etc.

52. ——, *Geschichte der deutschen Sprache,* 8th ed., Heidelberg, 1965.

53. ——, "Lateinisch *mons* in deutschen Ortsnamen," *Beiträge zur Namenforschung* 1 (1948–1950) 170–180.

54. ——, "Die Ortsnamen auf *-heim* im Südwesten des deutschen Sprachgebiets," *Wörter und Sachen* 8 (1928) 142–175.

55. ——, "Über die lateinisch-romanischen Elemente im Wortschatz der nassauischen Mundarten," *Nassauische Annalen* 42 (1939) 82 ff.

56. Bachmann, F., "Ortsnamen auf *-sĕke, -rode, -rade,*" *NdKbl.* 16 (1892) 41.

57. Back, Elisabeth, *Wesen und Wert der Lehnübersetzung,* Gießen, 1935 (= *Gießener Beiträge* 40).

58. Badstüber, Hubert, *Die Nomina agentis auf -ære bei Wolfram und Gottfried,* diss., Leipzig, 1901. ¶ Pp. 10–11 list all the words; pp. 12 ff. go into detail.

59. Bahder, Karl von, "Nhd. *e* als Fugenvocal in Zusammensetzungen," *PBB* 53 (1929) 1 ff.

60. ——, *Die Verbalabstracta in den germanischen Sprachen,* Halle, 1880.

61. ——, *Zur Wortwahl in der frühneuhochdeutschen Schriftsprache,* Heidelberg, 1925. [Hugo Suolahti, *Neuphil.Mitt.* 28 (1927) 108–110.]

62. Bahlow, H., "Beiträge zur Geschichte der deutschen Familiennamen," *Teuthonista* 3 (1926–1927) 33–38.

63. Bakker, J. J. M., "Chambrette," *De Nieuwe Taalgids* 54 (1961) 42–43. ¶ Neologisms in *-ette.*

64. Baldinger, Kurt, *Kollektivsuffixe und Kollektivbegriffe,* Berlin, 1950 (= *Veröffentlichungen des Instituts für romanische Sprachwissenschaft* 1).

65. Ball, Alice Morton, *The Compounding and Hyphenation of English Words,* New York, 1951. ¶ Introductory chapter of some value, otherwise a dictionary-like handbook.

66. ——, *Compounding in the English Language,* New York, 1939. ¶ Dictionary usefulness.

67. ——, "Uncle Sam and the Compounding of Words," *AmSp.* 13 (1938) 169–174. ¶ Primarily stylistic, but with some insight into the process of compounding.

68. Barber, Charles Clyde, *Die vorgeschichtliche Betonung der germanischen Substantiva und Adjektiva,* Heidelberg, 1932 (= *Indogermanische Bibliothek,* 3. Abteilung, 12. Band). ¶ Often gives historical information on (IE) suffixes and prefixes in terms of stress.

69. Bardeleben, [no initial], von, "Die Betonung zusammengesetzter Zeit-wörter," *ZddSprv.* (1925) 261–266.

[70. Bareš, Karel, "On the Transformation of Morphemes in Present-Day English," *Philologica Pragensia* 8 (1965) 124–131.]

71. Barker, Howard F., "Surnames in -is," *AmSp.* 2 (1926–1927) 316–318.

72. Barnow, A. J., "Note Concerning the Diminutive in Dutch," *Nether-land-America Foundation Monthly Letter* (March 1928).

73. Bartlett, Adeline C., "Full-word Compounds in Modern English," *AmSp.* 15 (1940) 243–249.

74. Bartz, Wilhelm, *Fremdwort und Sprachreinigung bei Friedrich Ludwig Jahn,* diss., Greifswald, 1936. ¶ Part 5 gives a glossary of neologisms coined by Jahn for foreign words.

75. Basler, Otto, "Die Sprache des modernen Arbeiters," *ZfdW* 15 (1914) 246–270. ¶ General.

76. Bathe, M., "Die Ortsnamen auf *-leben* als sprachliches Problem," *NdKbl.* 63 (1956) 24.

77. Bauerle, Richard F., "The Highly Productive Suffix *-ville*," *AmSp.* 35 (1960) 312–314.

78. Baum, S. V., "The Acronym, Pure and Impure," *AmSp.* 37 (1962) 48–50.

79. Baumann, Friedrich Herbert, *Die Adjektivabstrakta im älteren Westger-manischen,* diss., Freiburg i. Br., 1914. ¶ Derivation, pp. 4–71: *-î, -ida, -nis, -injo, -odi*; compounding, pp. 71–77: *-heit, -tuom, -scaf*; substantiva-tion, pp. 77–96.

80. Baumgarten, Bruno, "Über steigernde Zusammensetzungen," *ZfddtU* 22 (1908) 273–299.

81. Baumgartner, Eugen, *Die nhd. Adverbia auf* -lings. . . , Strassburg, 1904.

82. Baur, Arthur, *Das Adjektiv in Notkers Boethius: unter besonderer Berück-sichtigung seiner Verhältnisse zur lateinischen Vorlage,* diss., Zürich, 1940. ¶ Part I, A: formation of adjective; Part II: relation of Lat. and Ger. adjectives.

83. Bech, F., "De Døvstummes egne Ord- og Saetningsdannelser," *Ber-lingske Tidende* (Sept. 6, 1930). ¶ Examples of different wf's with deaf mutes.

84. Bech, Fedor, "Kleine Beiträge: Nr. 1 Gebeinze, geborgze, gebuscheze," *Germania* 10 (1865) 395–398. ¶ Formations in *-eze, -ze*; prefix *ge-*; these correspond to LowGer. and Du. words in *-ete, -te*; many ex-amples.

85. ——, "Wortformen auf *-eze*," *Germania* 14 (1869) 431–432. ¶ Supple-ment to *Germania* 10; see no. 84.

86. ——, "Wortformen auf *-eze*," *Germania* 22 (1877) 290–293, *Germania* 28 (1883) 296–301.

87. Bechler, Karl, *Das Präfix -to- im Verlaufe der englischen Sprachgeschichte*, diss., Königsberg, 1909.

88. Becker, Dietrich, "Shakespeares Präfixbildungen. Ein Beitrag zur Erforschung der sprachlichen Neuprägungen Shakespeares," diss., Münster, 1950.

89. Becker, Friedrich, "Die Guttural-Deminution in den alemannischen Mundarten. Ein kleiner Beitrag zum Schweizerischen Idioticon," *Neues Schweizerisches Museum* Jg. 6 (1866) 93–98.

90. Beckmann, E., "Über die doppelformigen englischen Adjektiv-Adverbien," *Herrigs Archiv* 64 (1880) 25–70.

91. Beckmann, Paul, "Reste der alten Diminutivendung -*ke*, -*ken* im Mecklenburgischen," *NdJb.* 85 (1962) 126–128.

92. Beek, P. van, "The *be*-Prefix in Verbs of King Alfred's Translation of Boethius' De consolatione philosophiae," *University of Iowa Doctoral Dissertations: Abstracts and References* (1900–1937) 1 (1940) 161–175.

93. Behaghel, Otto, "Bebildern-bebeistanden," *Muttersprache* 51 (1936) 273 f.

94. ——, *Die deutsche Sprache*, 3rd ed., Leipzig, 1904. ¶ Besonderer Teil: sechster Abschnitt: wf, pp. 252–294; derivation, compounding.

95. ——, *Geschichte der deutschen Sprache*, 3rd ed., Strassburg, 1911 (= *Pauls Grundriß*, vol. 3). [Hugo Soulahti, *Neuphil.Mitt.* 13 (1911) 131–133.]

96. ——, "Giesser oder Giessener," *ZdallgdSprv.* 19 (1904) 8–10.

97. ——, "*Metze*," *ZfdW* 3 (1902) 218 f.

98. ——, "Nachtrag zu den 'Imperativnamen'," *Neuphil.Mitt.* 26 (1925) 26.

99. ——, "Neue -*isten*," *ZdallgdSprv.* 28 (1913) 272.

100. ——, "Die neuhochdeutschen Zwillingswörter," *Germania* 23 (1878) 257–292.

101. ——, "Zeitwörter, die von Hauptwörtern abgeleitet sind," *ZfdW* 1 (1901) 1–3.

102. ——, "Zur Bildungssilbe -*er*," *ZfdW* 1 (1901) 63–64.

103. ——, "Zur Lehre von der deutschen Wortbildung," *Wissenschaftliche Beihefte zur ZdallgdSprv.* 14–15 (1898) 137–147.

104. ——, "Zur Lehre von der Zusammensetzung," *ZdallgdSprv.* 31 (1916) 278–283.

105. ——, "Zusammensetzung?" *Muttersprache* 51 (1936) 344 f.

106. Behr, Ursula, *Wortkontaminationen in der neuenglischen Schriftsprache*, diss., Würzburg, 1935.

107. Behre, Frank, "Middle English *rochine*," *SN* 11 (1938) 251–256. ¶ Derivation type ME *rochine* "rock" (*roche* + *in*[*e*]), patterned after OF *wastine, desertine*.

108. Behrens, D., "Zur Geschichte der französischen Sprache in England: Französische Elemente im Englischen," in *Pauls Grundriß*, 950–989.

109. Bein, Alex, "Zionismus," *ZfdW* 19 (1963) 178–179.
110. Beke, Ö., "Deutsche Fisch- und Pflanzennamen," *IF* 52 (1934) 137–141.
111. Belanner, Ivar, "Naagra utvecklingstendenser i svenskan," *Skola och samhälle* 29 (1948) 229–236. ¶ Verb formations of the type *rekordsaalde, friluftade*, etc.; long noun compounds, etc.
112. Belden, Henry Marvin, "Perfective *ge-* in Old English *bringan* and *gebringan*," *Engl.Stud.* 32 (1903) 366–370.
[113. Belopol'skaja, A. P., "Adverbializovannoe pričastie v sovremennom nemeckom jazyke," in *Voprosy sintaksisa romano-germanskich jazykov*, Leningrad, 1961, 19–34. ¶ Adverbialized participle in Ger.]
114. Bengtsson, Elna, *Studies on Passive Nouns with a Concrete Sense in English*, Lund, 1927. ¶ Meaning-oriented, but deals with certain suffixes, etc.
115. Bennett, William H., "The Parent Suffix in Germanic Weak Verbs of Class III," *Language* 38 (1962) 135–141.
116. Bense, J. F., *A Dictionary of the Low Dutch Element in the English Vocabulary*, The Hague, 1926 ff.
117. Benson, Sven, *Studier över adjektivsuffixet -ot i svenskan*, Lund, 1951 (= *Skrifter utg. genom Landsmaalsarkivet i Lund* 8).
118. Benveniste, Emile, "Fonctions suffixales en gotique," *Bulletin de la Société de Linguistique de Paris* 56, 1 (1961) 21–45.
119. ——, "Les noms abstraits en *-ti-* du gotique," *Die Sprache* 6 (1960) 166–171.
120. ——, *Origines de la formation des noms en indo-européen*, Vol. I, Paris, 1935; Vol. II, *Noms d'agent et noms d'action en indo-européen*, Paris, 1948.
121. Berg, B. van den, "De accentuatie van Nederlandse samenstellingen en afleidingen," *De Nieuwe Taalgids* 46 (1953) 254–260.
122. Bergener, Carl, *A Contribution to the Study of the Conversion of Adjectives into Nouns in English*, diss., Lund, 1928.
123. Berger, Vilhelm, "Svensk-amerikanska spraaket. Ett bidrag till kännedomen om engelska spraakets inflytande paa svenska spraaket i Amerika," *Nysvenska studier* 15 (1935) 1–37. ¶ Part 4 of a listing of examples, gives neologisms.
124. Bergman, Gösta, "Det lämpliga utrycket," *Nysvenska studier* 31 (1953) 126–135. ¶ Part VII deals with compounds in Sw. in which the first component ends in *-a*; Part VIII with mass-words in *-on*; Part IX with verbal derivatives in *-era*.
125. ——, *A Short History of the Swedish Language*, trans. and adapted by F. P. Magoun, Jr., and Helge Kökeritz, Stockholm, 1947. ¶ Deals briefly with wf.

126. ——, *Skolpojksslang*, Stockholm, 1934. ¶ Chap. 6 deals with the origin of slang words.

127. ——, "Västgötaknallarna och deras hemliga spraak, maansing," *Nysvenska studier* 9 (1930) 153–238. ¶ Lat. suffixes *is, es, us, um.*

128. Bergmann, Karl, *Die gegenseitigen Beziehungen der deutschen, englischen und französischen Sprache auf lexikologischem Gebiete*, Dresden and Leipzig, 1912 (= *Neusprachliche Abhandlungen aus den Gebieten der Phraseologie, Realien, Stilistik und Synonymik* Heft 18).

129. Bergsten, Nils, *A Study on Compound Substantives in English*, Uppsala, 1911.

130. Bergström, G. A., *On Blendings of Synonymous or Cognate Expressions in English: A Contribution to the Study of Contamination*, diss., Lund, 1906.

131. Bergstrøm-Nielsen, Henrik, "Die Kurzwörter im heutigen Deutsch," *Moderna Spraak* 46 (1952) 12–22. ¶ Esp. pp. 20–22; clipped words, alphabet words, etc.

132. Berman, J. M., "Contribution on Blending," *Zt. für Angl. und Am.* 9 (1961) 278–281.

133. Berner, Nils, *Die mit der Partikel ge- gebildeten Wörter im Hêliand*, diss., Lund, 1900.

134. Bernhardt, E., "Die Partikel *ga-* als Hilfsmittel bei der gothischen Conjugation," *ZfdPh.* 2 (1870) 158–166.

135. Bernhardt, J., "Dänischer Einfluß auf das Hochdeutsch in Schleswig-Holstein," *NdKbl.* 17 (1893) 80 f.

136. Berrer, Julie, *Verbale Bildungsmittel zur Intensivierung im Alem.*, diss., Tübingen, 1934. ¶ By means of sound alternation, *n-* infix, "Verstärkung des Auslautes."

137. Berrey, Lester V., "Newly-wedded Words," *AmSp.* 14 (1939) 3–10. ¶ Blends.

138. Berulfsen, Bjarne, "Er suffikset *-else* upoetisk?" *Maal og Minne* (1957) 47–76.

139. Berz, F., *Der Kompositionstypus steinreich*, diss., Bern, 1952.

140. Best, Karl, *Die persöhnlichen Konkreta des Altenglischen nach ihren Suffixen geordnet*, diss., Strassburg, 1905.

141. Betthmann, Hermann, "Nd. Adjektive auf *-ern*," *NdKbl.* 32 (1911) 40.

142. Betz, Werner, *Deutsch und Lateinisch; die Lehnbildungen der ahd. Benediktinerregel*, Bonn, 1949.

143. ——, *Der Einfluss des Lateinischen auf den ahd. Sprachschatz: Der Abrogans*, Heidelberg, 1936.

144. ——, "Lateinisch und Deutsch," *Der Deutschunterricht* Heft 1 (1951) 21 ff. ¶ Germanizing of Lat. words—unit for unit—Lehnbildung (derivation, compounding).

145. ——, "Die Lehnbildungen und der abendländische Sprachenausgleich,"
     PBB 67 (1944) 275 ff.
146. Beyer, E., "Gestaltende Kräfte bei den Wortbildungen des amerikan-
     ischen Sportslang," *Die Lebenden Fremdsprachen* 3 (1951) 205–208.
     ¶ Metaphors, alliteration, assonance, short forms, suffixes (*-ler, -ite*,
     etc.).
147. Bezzenberger, Adalbert, *Untersuchungen über die gotischen Adverbien und
     Partikeln*, Halle, 1873.
148. Bezzola, Reto Roberto, *Abbozzo di una storia dei Gallicismi italiani nei
     primi secoli*, Heidelberg, 1925. ¶ Certain suffixes which also occur
     in Ger.
149. Biener, Clemens, "Die Steigerungsadverbia bei Adjektiven," *PBB* 64
     (1940) 165 ff.
150. Biese, Y. M., "Neuenglisch *tick-tack* und Verwandtes," *Neuphil.Mitt.*
     40 (1939) 146–205.
151. ——, "Notes on the Compound Participle in the Works of Shake-
     speare and his Contemporaries," *AASF* B 63, 2 (1950) 1–18.
152. ——, "Origin and Development of Conversions in English," *AASF*
     B 45, 2 (1938) 1–490.
153. Birlinger, A., "Sprachvergleichende Studien im Alemannischen und
     Schwäbischen," *ZfvglSpr.* 15 (1866) 191 ff.
154. ——, "Zur deutschen Wortforschung *mûch-, mauch-*," *ZfvglSpr.* 20
     (1872) 316–320.
155. Bizer, H., "Schwäbische Prädikative und Adverbien nach der Art *a
     graesse* 'sehr groß,'" *Teuthonista* 9 (1933) 117 ff.
156. Bjerre, Birger, *Nordiska konjunktionsbildningar med temporal innebörd*,
     Lund, 1935 (= *Lunds universitets aarsskrift* N.F. avd. 1, vol. 31, 3).
157. Björkman, Erik, "Ae. *weʒ—lā, weʒ—la—weʒ*, me. *wei—la—wei* etc.,"
     Herrigs Archiv 114 (1905) 164 ff. ¶ Contamination form.
158. ——, "Die Pflanzennamen der althochdeutschen Glossen," *ZfdW* 2
     (1901) 202 ff., *ZfdW* 3 (1902) 263 f.
159. ——, *Scandinavian Loan-Words in Middle English*, 2 parts, Halle, 1900,
     1902 (= *Studien zur Englischen Philologie* 7, 11). [G. Binz, *ZfdPh.* 34,
     4; Flom, *MLN* 17, 6; M. Förster, *Anglia Beibl.* 9 (1900) 240–243;
     Horn, *Literaturblatt* 25, 11; K. Luick, *Literar. Centralblatt* 35 (1903)
     and *Herrigs Archiv* 109.]
160. ——, "Zur dialektischen Provenienz der nordischen Lehnwörter im
     Englischen," *Spraakvetenskapliga sällskapets i Uppsala förhandlingar*
     Sept. 1897–May 1900 (Uppsala, 1901) Bilaga A (= *Uppsala universi-
     tets aarsskrift* 3, 4).
161. Blackwell, James Shannon, *A Manual of German Prefixes and Suffixes*,
     New York, 1888.

162. Bladin, Vilhelm, *Studies on Denominative Verbs in English*, diss., Uppsala, 1911.

163. Blaisdell, Foster W., Jr., *Preposition-Adverbs in Old Icelandic*, Berkeley, 1959 (= *University of California Publications in Linguistics* 17). ¶ Origin of prepositions; bibliography, pp. 67–70.

164. Bloomfield, Leonard, "Etymologisches," *PBB* 37 (1911) 245–261. ¶ Suffixes -*t*, -*l*, etc.

165. ——, *Language*, New York, 1933.

166. ——, "Notes on Germanic Compounds," in *Mélanges Linguistiques offerts à M. Holger Pedersen à l'occasion de son soixante-dixiéme anniversaire: 7 Avril 1937*, Aarhus, 1937, 303–307 (= *Acta Jutlandica Aarsskrift for Aarhus Universitet* 9, 1).

167. ——, "Notes on the Preverb *ge*- in Alfredian English," in *Studies in English Philology: A Miscellany in Honor of Frederick Klaeber*, ed. Kemp Malone and Martin B. Ruud, Minneapolis, 1929, 79–102.

168. Bloomfield, Maurice, "On Adaptation of Suffixes in Congeneric Classes of Substantives," *AJPh.* 12, 1 (1891) 1–29.

169. Bloomfield, Morton W., "Final Root-Forming Morphemes," *AmSp.* 28 (1953) 158–164. ¶ -*ash* as in *bash*, *gash*, etc.

170. Blümel, Adolf, "Von 'abat-jour' bis 'Zeitvertreib': Wortbildung durch Imperativ und direktes Objekt," *Die Neueren Sprachen* 14 (1965) 82–87.

171. Blume, Johannes Rudolf, *Über den Ursprung und die Entwicklung des Gerundiums im Englischen*, Bremen, 1880.

172. Blumer, J., *Zum Geschlechtswandel der Lehn- und Fremdwörter im Hochdeutschen*, Leipzig, 1891.

173. Bock, Alfred, *Das französische Element in den neuenglischen Dialekten*, diss., Frankfurt a/M, 1911. ¶ The anglicizing of agricultural, botanical, and animal terms.

174. Bock, Karl Nielsen, *Niederdeutsch auf dänischem Substrat: Studien zur Dialektgeographie Südostschleswigs*, Kopenhagen, 1933 (= *Universitets-Jubilæts danske Samfund 299* and *Deutsche Dialektgeographie 34*). ¶ Deals in part with adverb formations.

175. Bödtker, A. Trampe, "Französische Einflüsse im Englischen," *Anglia Beibl.* 21 (1910) 56–58.

176. ——, "French Words in English after 1066," *MLN* 24 (1909) 214–217.

177. Böhtlingk, O., "Die Komposita der Typen *Bindfaden* und *Bindewort*," *Ber. der Kgl. Sächs. Ges. der Wsch. zu Leipzig, philol.-hist. Klasse* 52 (1900) 201–207.

178. Böning, H., "Wörter auf -*els*," *NdKbl.* 53 (1940) 13.

179. Boesch, Bruno, "Die Gruppenbildung in altalemannischen Ortsnamen," *Beiträge zur Namenforschung* 3 (1951–1952) 256–286. ¶ -*ingen*-, -*ikon*-, -*wil*-, etc.

180. Bogner, Artur, *Die Verbalvorsilbe* bi- *im Althochdeutschen*, diss., Hamburg, 1933.

181. Bohnenberger, Karl, "Auslautend *g* im Oberdeutschen," *PBB* 31 (1906) 393–428. ¶ Deals primarily with the pronunciation of -*g*, but also with how it occurs in suffixes.

182. ——, "Die heim- und weiler-Namen Alemanniens mit einem Anhang über die ingen-Namen," *Württembergische Vierteljahrshefte für Landesgeschichte, Neue Folge* 31 (1922–1924) 1–28.

183. Bohner, P. Theodor, "Die Adjektiva auf -weise," *ZfdW* 5 (1903–1904) 237–239.

184. ——, "Präfix *un*- bei Goethe," *ZfdW* 6 (1905) 37–140.

185. Bolinger, Dwight, "Rime, Assonance, and Morpheme Analysis," *Word* 6 (1950) 117 ff.

186. ——, "Word Affinities," *AmSp.* 15 (1940) 62–73. ¶ Sound symbolism (Jespersen); onomatopoeia in reverse, accretions due to sound, words with imitative elements, word constellations.

187. Bont, A. P. de, "Een achtervoegsel -*kaar*," *Driemaandelijksche Bladen* 2 (1950) 55–56. ¶ The dialect suffix -*kaar* and its etymology.

188. Booker, John M., *The French "inchoative" Suffix* -iss *and the French* -ir *Conjugation in Middle English*, diss., Chapel Hill, N.C., 1912 (= *Studies in Philology* 9).

189. Borowski, Bruno, *Lautdubletten im Altenglischen*, Halle, 1924. ¶ Based on free forms that have become bound; see Part I: -*red*, -*erd*; -*wulf*, -*ulf*; -*foest*, -*fest*; -*wold*, -*wald*, etc.

190. Borst, Eugen, *Die Gradadverbien im Englischen*, Heidelberg, 1902 (= *Anglistische Forschungen* 10).

191. Bosch, J. H. van den, "Over samenstellingen," *Taal en Letteren* 1 (1891) 281–284 and 3 (1893) 11–20, 145–152.

192. Both, M., *Die konsonantischen Suffixe altenglischer Konkreta und Kollektiva*, diss., Kiel, 1909.

193. Boult, Joseph, "On the Syllable '-ing' in Names of Places in the British Isles," *Walford's Antiquarian Magazine and Bibliographer* 1 (1882) 295–298.

194. Bourciez, E., *Eléments de linguistique romane*, 3rd ed., Paris, 1930. ¶ Of value in tracing Gmc. suffixes of Romance origin.

195. Brady, Caroline, "The Old English Nominal Compounds in -*rǽd*," *PMLA* 67 (1952) 538–571.

196. Bradley, Francis Wright, *German Word Formation*, Columbia, S.C., 1915 (= *University of South Carolina Bulletin* 43, 4).

197. ——, "The Onomatopoeia of the German Verbal Suffix -tschen," *Mod. Phil.* 26 (1929) 401–414.

198. ——, *The Semantic Development of the German Verbal Suffix* -zen, Columbia, S.C., 1926.

199. ——, "The Verbal *-zen* in Germanic," diss., Chicago, 1926.

200. Bradley, H., *The Making of English*, 10th ed., New York, 1904. ¶ Pp. 123 ff.

201. Brandenstein, Wilhelm, "Die Vorsilbe 'un-' in Theorie und Anwendung," *Sprachforum* 2 (1956–1957) 231-232. ¶ Types: *Unlust, Ungewitter, Unmut.*

202. Brandstätter, Franz August, *Die Gallicismen in der deutschen Schriftsprache*, Leipzig, 1874. ¶ Pp. 70–121 list Gallicisms (French) with literal translation in Ger.: loan translation.

203. Brandstetter, Renward, *Drei Abhandlungen über das Lehnwort*, Luzern, 1900 (= *Wissenschaftliche Beilage zum Jahresbericht über die Höhere Lehranstalt in Luzern für das Schuljahr 1899/1900*). ¶ I. Das Lehnwort in der Luzerner Mundart; II. Das Lehnwort in der bugischen Sprache; III. Die Lehnwörter, welche der Luzerner Mundart und der bugischen Sprache gemeinsam angehören.

204. Brandt, Martha, *Beiträge zur mittelhochdeutschen Wortforschung*, diss., Köln, 1928. ¶ Part II, pp. 55–86: MHG compounds with *-var.*

205. Branky, F., "Zu den Substantiven auf *-ling*," *ZfdW* 5 (1903–1904) 270–275.

206. Brate, E., "Nordische Lehnwörter im Orrmulum," *PBB* 10 (1885) 580 ff. ¶ Additions and corrections.

207. Brattegard, Olav, "Über die deutschen Lehnwörter des Tischlerhandwerks in Norwegen," *NdMitt.* 3 (1947) 18–28. ¶ Compounds in *-sag*, etc.

208. Braune, Wilhelm, *Abriß der althochdeutschen Grammatik mit Berücksichtigung des Altsächsischen*, 11th ed., Tübingen, 1959.

209. ——, *Althochdeutsche Grammatik*, ed. W. Mitzka, 9th ed., Tübingen, 1959.

210. ——, "Über die Quantität der althochdeutschen Endsilben," *PBB* 2 (1876) 125 ff.

211. Brechenmacher, J. K., "Schwäbische Sprachschöpfung," *Muttersprache* 41 (1926) 298 ff.

212. Briegleb, O., "Die Hauptfälle des Zwischen-*s* der Zusammensetzung," *Sprachecke des Deutschen Sprachvereins, Zweig Hannover* 49 (1937) 6th col.

213. ——, "Vom zusammengesetzten Haupwort," *Muttersprache* 49 (1934) 8–9.

214. Brilioth, B., "Intensiva och iterativa verb bildade genom affix i Engelskan," *Nordisk Tidsskrift* (3rd ser.) 20 (1911) 117–120.

215. Brink, Bernhard ten, "Das altenglische Suffix *-ere*," *Anglia* 5 (1882) 1–4.

216. ——, *Chaucers Sprache und Verskunst*, Leipzig, 1884. ¶ Occasional notes on wf in chap. 2 ("Von der Flexion").

217. Brinkmann, Hennig, "Der Austausch zwischen den Wortarten im Deutschen," in *Die Wissenschaft von deutscher Sprache und Dichtung: Methoden, Probleme, Aufgaben (Festschrift für Friedrich Maurer, zum 65. Geburtstag am 5. Januar 1963)*, ed. Siegfried Gutenbrunner, Hugo Moser, Walther Rehm, and Heinz Rupp, Stuttgart, 1963, 3–24. ¶ Transfer of nouns, adjectives, and verbs to other classes.

218. ——, "Das deutsche Adjektiv in synchronischer und diachronischer Sicht," *Wirkendes Wort* 14 (1964) 94–104.

219. ——, "Die Zusammensetzung im Deutschen," *Sprachforum* 2 (1956–1957) 222–230.

220. Brockmanns, A. L., *Untersuchungen zu den Haustiernamen des Rheinlands*, Bonn, 1939 (= *Rheinisches Archiv* 34).

221. Brocks, A., "Lehnwörter, Erbwörter, Fremdwörter," *Neue westpreußische Mitteilungen* (Nov. 16, 1894). ¶ Lecture.

222. Brøndum-Nielsen, J., "Trykforholdene ved Afledningsendelsen -agtig i Dansk," *Danske Studier* (1917) 35–39.

223. Brown, Augustus F., "The Derivation of English Adjectives Ending -ful," *DA* 19 (1958) 803–804.

224. Brown, Roland Wilbur, *Composition of Scientific Words: A Manual of Methods and a Lexicon of Materials for the Practice of Logotechnics*, [n.p.], 1954. ¶ Revised edition of the next item.

225. ——, *Materials for Word-Study: A Manual of Roots, Prefixes, Suffixes and Derivatives in the English Language*, New Haven, Conn., 1927.

226. Brown, Thomas Richard, *A Treatise on the English Terminations of Words; with a List of the most common Prefixes, and their usual Significations: to which is appended a Practical Vocabulary*, London, 1838.

227. Brüll, Hugo, *Untergegangene und veraltete Worte des Französischen im heutigen Englisch, Beiträge zur französischen und englischen Wortforschung*, Halle, 1913.

228. Bruggencate, K. ten, "On the Use and Formation of Substantives," *Taalstudie* 7 (1886) 348–352.

229. Brugmann, Karl, "Ahd. henna ags. hen," *IF* 37 (1916–1917) 249–253.

230. ——, "Das Genus der Deminutivbildungen," *IF* 19 (1906) 215–216.

231. ——, *Grundriß der vergleichenden Grammatik der indogermanischen Sprachen*, 2. Band: *Wortbildungslehre*, 1. Hälfte, Strassburg, 1889.

232. ——, *Kurze vergleichende Grammatik der indogermanischen Sprachen*, Strassburg, 1902–1904. ¶ Esp. pp. 296 ff.

233. ——, "Über das Wesen der sogenannten Wortzusammensetzung, eine sprachpsychologische Studie," *Ber. der Kgl. Sächs. Ges. der Wsch. zu Leipzig, philol.-hist. Klasse* (1900) 359–401.

234. ——, "Zur Geschichte der Nominalsuffixe -as-, -jas- und -vas-," *Zfvgl-Spr.* 24 (1879) 1–99.

235. ——, "Zur nominalen Stammbildung der germanischen Sprachen," *IF* 33 (1913–1914) 300–313. ¶ 1. Gothic *faírra*, OHG *ferro*; 2. Gothic *hulundi* and *nt* formations.

236. ——, "Zur Wortzusammensetzung in den idg. Sprachen," *IF* 18 (1905–1906) 59–76.

237. Buchanan, Charles D., *Substantivized Adjectives in Old Norse*, diss., Philadelphia, 1933 (= *Language Dissertations* 15).

238. Buchholz, Erich, *Das Verbum Substantivum im Mittelenglischen*, diss., Berlin, 1936.

239. Buck, C. D., *Comparative Grammar of Greek and Latin*, Chicago, 1933.

240. Buck, M. R., "Die Endung -er, -ern, (-erren) in oberdeutschen Mundarten," *Alemannia* 13 (1885) 215–224.

241. ——, "Oberdeutsche Familiennamen auf -ler, -eler," *Alemannia* 9 (1881) 25–29.

242. ——, "Sammlung oberdeutscher personifizierter Lokalnamen auf -ler," *Alemannia* 9 (1881) 29–30.

243. Budde, E. H., "Randbemerkungen zum i-Umlaut im Deutschen," *Muttersprache* (1957) 175–178. ¶ Concerns adjectives in -*isch*, -*ig*, -*lich*.

244. Buffington, A. F., " 'Dunnerwedder' Compounds," *Allentown Morning Call*, March 17, 1945.

245. Bugge, Sophus, "Zur altgermanischen Sprachgeschichte. Germanisch *ug* aus *uw*," *PBB* 13 (1888) 504–515. ¶ Compounds in Old Norse in -*huð*, -*uð*, etc., adjectives in -*ūðigr*; in *hugdig* in Old Saxon, *hūdig* in OE.

246. Burchkardt, F., *Untersuchungen zu den griechischen und lateinisch-romanischen Lehnwörtern in der ahd. Sprache*, diss., Berlin, 1905.

247. Burnham, Josephine M., "Three hard-worked Suffixes," *AmSp.* 2 (1926–1927) 244–246. ¶ -*dom*, -*ster*, -*itis*.

248. Bußmann, E., "-*ing* als Bezeichnung der Ortszugehörigkeit," *NdKbl.* 42 (1928–1929) 9.

249. Buwalda, H. S., "De dimunitiva yn it Bildts," *Us Wurk* 7 (1958) 62–65. ¶ Dialect of Het Bildt (Frisia).

250. Bzędga, Andrzej, "Hauptprobleme der Reduplikation im Deutschen," *Zeszyty naukowe Uniwersytetu im. Adama Mickiewicza w Poznaniu* 9 (1957) 117–130 (= *Filologia* 1).

[251. ——, "Struktura zdwojenia (na materiale germańkim)," *Biuletyn polskiego towarzystwa językoznawczego* 21 (1962) 115–125. ¶ Reduplication in Gmc.]

252. Cahen, Maurice, "Remarque sur le stile des adjectifes gotiques en -*kunds*," in *Mélanges linguistiques offerts à M. J. Vendryes*, Paris, 1925, 75 ff.

253. Calfisch-Einicher, Emma, *Die lateinischen Elemente in der mittelhochdeutschen Epik des 13. Jahrhunderts*, Reichenberg, 1936.
254. Callaway, Morgan, Jr., "Concerning the Origin of the Gerund in English," in *Studies in English Philology: a Miscellany in Honor of Frederick Klaeber*, ed. Kemp Malone and Martin B. Ruud, Minneapolis, 1929, 32–49.
255. Callewaert, P., "De verkleinwoorden in het Kortrijks," *Taal en Tongval* 15 (1963) 45–57.
256. Cameron, Kenneth, *English Place Names*, London, 1961. ¶ Chap. 2, Types; chap. 8, preposition + adverb in place names; chap. 9, affixes in place names.
257. Carl, Helmut, "Tiernamen bilden Verben," *Wirkendes Wort* 8 (1957–1958) 352–357.
258. Carlson, Harold G., "Recent American Loan Words from German," *AmSp.* 15 (1940) 205 ff.
259. Carr, Charles Telford, *The German Influence on the English Vocabulary*, Oxford, 1934 (= *SPE Tract* 42). ¶ Loanwords by period and field.
260. ——, *Nominal Compounds in Germanic*, London, 1939 (= *St. Andrews University Publication* 41).
261. ——, "Some Notes on German Loan Words in English," *MLR* 35 (1940) 69–71. ¶ Including a discussion of the word "word-building."
262. Carr, Elizabeth Ball, "Notes Concerning Language Names," *AmSp.* 28 (1953) 62–64. ¶ -ish, -ic, -an, etc.
263. ——, "Trends in Word Compounding in American Speech," *Speech Monographs* 21 (1954) 143 (= *Abstract of Ph.D. Theses, St. Louis University* 1953).
264. ——, "Word-Compounding in American Speech," *Speech Monographs* 26 (1959) 1–20.
265. Carstensen, Broder, "Bemerkungen zu Wörtern auf '-er,' " *Muttersprache* (1963) 172–177.
266. ——, "Zur Struktur des englischen Wortverbandes," *Die Neueren Sprachen* 13 (1964) 305–328. ¶ Substantivierung, pp. 313–314.
267. Cassidy, Frederic G., "Iteration as a Word-Forming Device in Jamaican Folk Speech," *AmSp.* 32 (1957) 49–53.
268. Cate-Silfwerbrand, R. B. ten, *Vlees, Bloed en Been: Synoniemvergelijkend onderzoek van drie Germaanse woordformaties*, Assen, 1958 (= *Studia Germanica* no. 1). ¶ Eng. and Ger. summaries.
269. Cederschiöld, Gustaf, "För riksspraaket nya verb, som bildats genom avledning," *Spraak och Stil* 10 (1910) 211–228.
270. ——, "Naagra Anmärkningar over Verbal Abstraterna paa -ande (resp. -ende)," *Spraak och Stil* 15 (1915) 129–143.

271. ——, "Om Komparationen af fornisländska Adjektiva paa -*legr* (-*ligr*) och Adverb paa -*lega* (-*liga*)," *Arkiv* 9 (1893) 95–97.

272. ——, *Studier öfver verbalabstrakterna i nutida svenska*, Göteborg, 1908 (= *Göteborgs högskolas aarsskrift, part 3*, 1908). ¶ Suffixes: -*ande*, -*ende*, -*ning*, -*ing*, -*era*, -*ara*, -*eri*, -*an*, -*else*, -*sel*, -*nad*, -*a*, -*e*, -*d*, -*t*, -*est*, -*el*, -*la*, -*ra*.

273. Chamberlain, A. F., "The Use of Diminutives in -*ing* by Some Writers in Low German Dialects," *PMLA* 7 (1892) 212–219.

274. Chapin, Alonzo Bowen, *An Inquiry into the Origin and Meaning of English Suffixes*, New Haven (England), 1843.

275. Chapman, Robert W., *Adjectives from Proper Names*, Oxford, 1939 (= *SPE Tract 52*). ¶ -*ad*, -*id*, -*ic*, -*ite*, -*ist*, -*eque*, -*ish*, -*ese*, -*ene*, -*ote*, Lat. names, etc.

276. Chidekel', S. S., "O složnoprojizvodnych slovach v sovremennon anglijskom jazyke," *Trudy vojennogo instituta inostrannych jazykov* 2 (1953) 46–64. ¶ Compound derivatives in modern Eng.

277. Chrétien, C. D., "Indo-European Final **-s* in Germanic," *University of California Publications in Modern Philology* 25 (1941) 1–10. ¶ **-s* and **-z* considered as proto-Gmc. variants.

278. Christiansen, Hallfrid, "De germanske uaksentuerte prefikser i nordisk," *Norsk Tidsskrift for Sprogvidenskap* (1960) 340–382.

279. ——, "En studie over nordnorske husdyrnavn," *Norsk Tidsskrift for Sprogvidenskap* 10 (1938) 291–360. ¶ Domestic animals: suffixes -*lin*, -*a*, -*i*, -*e*.

280. ——, "Suffikset -*nad* in nordnorsk," *Norsk Tidsskrift for Sprogvidenskap* 8 (1937) 469–475.

281. Christiansen, Reidar Th., "Sudrøy-Norn," *Maal og Minne* (1938) 1–27. ¶ Norwegian loanwords in the dialect of the island of Lewis (Outer Hebrides).

[282. Christmann, E., "Ein seltenes Ableitungssuffix in der nordwestlichen Pfalz (sə)," *Pfälzisches Museum* 42, *Pfälzische Heimatkunde* 21, 296 f.]

[283. ——, "*Mackes, Muppes, Schnokes* und andere -*es*," *Pfälzische Heimat, Sonntags-Beilage zur Pfälzischen Rundschau* 29.6 (1924).]

[284. ——, "Namen der männlichen Gans," *Bayerische Wochenschrift für Pflege von Heimat und Volkstum* 10. Jg. (1932).]

[285. ——, " 'Reinhard' der Fuchs und 'Gerhard' der Gänserich—wie kamen Tiere zu solchen Menschennamen?" *Hessische Blätter für Volkskunde* 41 (1950).]

286. ——, "Sinn und Alter der nordwestpfälzischen Siedlungsnamen auf ahd. -*hûsen* und -*bûr*," *ZfdA* 84 (1952–1953) 84 ff.

287. Clark, G. N., *The Dutch Influence on the English Vocabulary*, Oxford, 1935 (= *SPE Tract 44*).

288. Clement, Knut Jong Bohn, "Eigenthümliche Elemente der frisischen Sprache," *Herrigs Archiv* 9 (1851) 179–187; *Herrigs Archiv* 10 (1852) 136–147; and *Herrigs Archiv* 12 (1853) 71–81. ¶ 1. The endings *ens* and *lis*, pp. 179–183; 2. Diminutive, Ablaut, pp. 136–143.

289. Clodius, P., "Die Funktion des Adjektivs in den neueren Sprachen, insbes. im Franz., zur Bildung zusammengesetzter Begriffe," *Programm*, Rastenburg, 1900.

290. Coard, Robert L., "The Verb Menagerie," *Georgia Review* 19 (1965) 77–80. ¶ Verbs drawn from animal names.

291. Coetsem, F. van, "Het suffix *-erse* in het Geraardsbergse dialect," *Taal en Tongval* 11 (1959) 253–257. ¶ Dialect of Grammont (Flandre-Orientale).

292. Coffin, H. C., "Back-formations," *Words* 1 (1935) 7–8.

293. Cohen, A., "Het Nederlands diminutiefsuffix: een morfonologische proeve," *De Nieuwe Taalgids* 51 (1958) 40–45.

294. Coleman, Evelyn S., "Die Lehnbildungen in Notker Labeos *Consulatio*-Übersetzung: ein Beitrag zur Lehngutforschung," diss., Cambridge, Mass., 1963. ¶ Lehnbildungen with suffixes, prefixes; compounding; pp. 301 ff., summary list; excellent bibliography.

295. Coleridge, Herbert, "On Diminutives in '*let*,'" *Trans. Phil. Soc.* (1857) 93–115.

296. Collin, Carl, "Än en Gaang Abstrakter och Konkreter," *Filologiska Föreningen i Lund, Spraakliga Uppsatser* 4 (1916) 19–33.

297. ——, "Semasiologiska Studier över Abstrakter och Konkreter," *Filologiska Föreningen i Lund, Spraakliga Uppsatser* 3 (1951) 225–261.

298. Collitz, Klara H., "Accentuation of Prefixes in English," *Engl. Stud.* 43 (1910–1911) 252–260.

299. ——, "The Suffix *-ei* in Modern German," *GR* 3 (1928) 55–70.

300. Cooper, F. T., *Word Formation in the Roman sermo plebeius*, New York, 1895. ¶ Applies directly only to Lat., but indirectly of interest are Lat. suffixes in other languages, since it carries a full compilation of these suffixes; also an excellent bibliography.

301. Cooper, L., "Pleonastic Compounds in Coleridge," *MLN* 19 (1904) 223–234.

302. Cortelyou, John van Zandt, *Die altenglischen Namen der Insekten, Spinnen und Krustentiere*, Heidelberg, 1906 (= *Anglistische Forschungen* 19).

303. Cortsen, S. P., "Folkelig Omdannelse af Fremmedord," *Extrabladet København* (Oct. 25, 1930). ¶ Examples of Umbildung.

304. Cosijn, P. J., *Nederlandsche spraakkunst: Etymologie*, 8th ed., ed. Jan te Winkel, Haarlem, 1893. ¶ Part III: Leer der Woordvorming: nouns, adjectives, verbs, particles, pp. 123 ff.; derivation and composition.

305. ——, "Die substantivierten Partizipia präsentia des Urgermanischen," *IF* 10 (1899) 112 ff.

306. Craigie, William A., *The Growth of American English I, II*, Oxford, 1940 (= *SPE Tracts* 56 and 57).

307. ——, *Northern Words in Modern English*, Oxford, 1937 (= *SPE Tract* 5). ¶ Words from northern Great Britain.

308. Curme, George O., "The Development of Verbal Compounds in Germanic," *PBB* 39 (1914) 320 ff.

309. ——, "The Gerund in Old English and German," *Anglia* 38 (1914) 491–498.

310. ——, *A Grammar of the German Language*, 2nd ed., New York, 1952.

311. ——, "History of the English Gerund," *Engl.Stud.* 45 (1912) 348–380.

312. ——, "The Old English Gerund Again," *Engl.Stud.* 49 (1916) 323.

313. Curtius, G., "Individualisirende Suffixe," *ZfvglSpr.* 4 (1855) 211 ff.

314. Czeizel, J., "Zur Mundart von Deutschproben in der Slowakei," *ZfMdaf.* 15 (1939) 152–159. ¶ Fate of *l*, *r*, and diminutive formation.

315. Dahlberg, T., *Die Mundart von Dorste*, Lund and Kopenhagen, 1934 (= *Lunder germanistische Forschungen* 2, 1).

316. Dahlberg, Torsten, "Mittelniederdeutsche Suffixabstrakta: Einige Bemerkungen zur Wortbildung und Lexikographie," in *Worte und Werte, Bruno Markwardt zum 60. Geburtstag*, ed. Gustav Erdmann and Alfons Eichstaedt, Berlin, 1961, 51–59.

317. ——, *Mittelniederdeutsche Suffixabstrakta: Lexikalische und wortgeographische Randbemerkungen*, Göteborg, 1962 (= *Göteborger germ. Forschungen* 6).

318. Dahlström, A. H., "The Germanic K-Formations in the Scandinavian Languages," diss., Chicago, 1928. ¶ Some 739 nouns, verbs, and adjectives with the suffix.

319. ——, "Scandinavian *k*-suffixal Epithets with Pejorative Meaning," *SSN* 10 (1928) 56–59.

320. Dahm, Karl, *Der Gebrauch von gi- zur Unterscheidung perfectiver und imperfectiver Actionsart im Tatian und in Notkers Boethius*, diss., Leipzig, 1909. [V. E. Mourek, *AfdA* 34 (1910) 182.]

321. Dal, Ingerid, *Ursprung und Verwendung der altnordischen "Expletivpartikel" of, um*, Oslo, 1929 (= *Avhandlingar utg. af Det norske Videnskaps-Akad. i Oslo, II. Hist.-filos. Klasse* 5).

322. ——, "Zur Entstehung des englischen Participium Praesentis auf *-ing*," *Norsk tidsskrift for sprogvidenskap* 16 (1952) 5–116. ¶ II. present participle in Gmc.; III. verbal abstracts in *-ungō /*-ingō* in OE; IV. origin of Eng. gerund.

323. ——, "Zur Geschichte der schwachtonigen Präfixe im Nordischen," *Norsk tidsskrift for sprogvidenskap* 4 (1930) 179–210. ¶ um, of, ga.

324. Dam, Jan van, *Handbuch der deutschen Sprache*, II *Wortlehre*, 2nd ed., Groningen, 1944.

325. Damköhler, Ed., "Deminutiva in der Mundart von Cattenstedt," *NdJb.* 32 (1906) 129–133. ¶ The area is Blankenburg am Harz.

326. ——, "G in der Cattenstedter Mundart," *NdKbl.* 42 (1928–1929) 13 ff. ¶ *-barsch* = *-burgisch*; *je-* (participial) missing after infinitive.

327. ——, "Zur deutschen Wortbildung," *ZfddtU* 20 (1906) 196. ¶ *-ari* in place names for inhabitants.

328. Daniels, Karlheinz, *Substantivierungstendenzen in der deutschen Gegenwartssprache: Nominaler Ausbau des verbalen Denkkreises*, Düsseldorf, 1963 (= *Sprache und Gemeinschaft, Abt. Studien* 3). ¶ Investigates the process of circumlocutions for verbs: *Auftrag erteilen* for *beauftragen*, *zum Ausdruck bringen* for *ausdrücken*, etc.

329. Danielsson, B., *Studies on the Accentuation of Polysyllabic Latin Greek, and Romance Loan-Words in English, with special reference to those ending in -able, -ate, -ator, -ible, -ic, -ical, and -ize*, Stockholm, 1948 (= *Stockholm Studies in English* 3).

330. Darmesteter, A., *Traité de la Formation des Mots Composés*, Paris, 1875. ¶ General.

331. David, E., "Die Wortbildung der Mundart von Krofdorf," *Germania* 37 (1892) 377 ff.

332. Davis, C. G., "Die deutschen Substantiva auf *-ling* im 18. Jahrhundert," *ZfdW* 4 (1903) 161 ff.

333. Debus, Friedhelm, "Die deutschen Bezeichnungen für die Heiratsverwandtschaft," *Beiträge zur deutschen Philologie* 19–23 (1958) 1–116. ¶ Part IV: feminine suffixes *-in*, *-sche*; Part V: compounds; Part VI: affektbedingte und individualsprachliche Wortbildungen.

334. Delbrück, B., *Die indogermanischen Verwandtschaftsnamen: Ein Beitrag zur vergleichenden Altertumskunde*, Leipzig, 1889 (= *Abhandlungen der Königlichen Sächsischen Gesellschaft der Wissenschaften, phil.-hist. Klasse* 11, 5).

335. Dellit, Otto, *Über lateinische Elemente im Mittelenglischen: Beiträge zur Geschichte des englischen Wortschatzes*, Marburg, 1906 (= *Marburger Studien zur englischen Philologie* 11). ¶ II. Kultureller Charakter der Lehnwörter; III. Die Wortformen (Wortbildung): prefixes, suffixes.

336. Derocquigny, Jules, *A Contribution to the Study of the French Element in English*, Lille, 1904. ¶ Primarily a list, with quotes and explanations, of Eng. words and their French counterparts.

337. Deter, Herbert, *Alte Partizipia auf -en, -ed und -ate, die im modernen Englisch zu Adjektiven geworden sind*, diss., Saalfeld, 1934.

338. Deutschbein, Max, "Geographie der Wortbildung der germanischen Völkernamen nach angelsächsischer Überlieferung," *ZfMdaf.* 16 (1940) 113–122.

339. De Vries, Tieman, *Holland's Influence on English Language and Literature*, Chicago, 1916. ¶ Loanwords. Part II: influence on Eng. language, pp. 55–142.

340. Dey, William M., "A Note on the Old French *por-* in English," *Studies in Philology* 17 (1920) 111–112.

341. Diemer, L[udwig], *Die Substantivierung des Adjektivs im Althochdeutschen*, diss., Freiburg i. Br., 1911.

342. Diez, F., *Grammatik der romanischen Sprachen*, Bonn, 1882. ¶ Of historical and comparative value in borrowed derivational elements.

343. Dike, Edwin B., "The Suffix *-ess*, etc.," *JEGP* 36 (1937) 29–34.

344. Dillon, Myles, "Linguistic Borrowing and Historical Evidence," *Language* 21 (1945) 12 ff. ¶ Problem of linguistic borrowing in general, based primarily on Irish.

345. Dilthey, K., "Das lateinische Element der deutschen Sprache," *Herrigs Archiv* 3 (1847) 33–50. ¶ Lat. loans.

346. Dittrich, J. Bruno, "Das Kind als Wortbildner," *Muttersprache* 43 (1928) 245. ¶ *Pferdnis*, etc.

347. Dittrich, Ottmar, "Über Wortzusammensetzung, auf Grund der neufranzösischen Schriftsprache," *ZfrPh.* 22 (1898) 305–330, 441–464; 23 (1899) 288–312; 24 (1900) 465–488; 29 (1905) 129–176, 257–292. ¶ Theoretical.

348. Dodge, D. K., "The Gender of English Loan-words in Danish," *Americana Germanica* 2 (1898) 27–32.

349. Dorfeld, Carl, *Über die Function des Präfixes* ge- (got. ga-) *in der Composition mit Verben, Teil I: Das Präfix bei Ulfilas und Tatian*, diss., Halle 1885. [O. Erdmann, *AfdA* 12 (1886) 178–179.]

350. Dornseiff, Franz, *Die griechischen Wörter im Deutschen*, Berlin, 1950.

351. ——, "Der *-ismus*," *Die Wandlung* 3 (1948) 346–350. ¶ Origin and history of formations in *-ismus*.

352. ——, "Das Zugehörigkeitsadjektiv und das Fremdwort," *GRM* 9 (1921) 193 ff.

353. Downs, L. G., "Intensive Adverbs and Intensive Prefixes in the West Germanic Dialects: A Lexical and Semantic Investigation," *University of Minnesota Summaries of Ph.D. Theses* 1 (1940) 168–172.

354. Draat, P. Fijn van, "A Dutch Diminutive," *Neophilologus* 21 (1956) 35 ff.

355. ——, "The Loss of the Prefix *ge-* in the Modern English Verb and some of its Consequences," *Engl.Stud.* 31 (1902) 353–384 and 32 (1902) 371–388.

356. ——, "Reduplicatory Emphasis," *Engl.Stud.* 74 (1941) 156–167. ¶ Reduplicated compounds.

357. Drechsler, P., "Zu den Wortzusammensetzungen im Schlesischen," *Mitteilungen der schlesischen Gesellschaft für Volkskunde* 5 (1902) 67–92. ¶ *-mann, -ding.*

358. ——, "Zur Wortbildung im Schlesischen," *Mitteilungen der schlesischen Gesellschaft für Volkskunde* 9 (1906) 115 ff. ¶ Stammbildung.

[359. Dudek, J. B., "Czech Influence upon the American Vocabulary," *Student Life* (Lisle, Ill.) 18, 8 (1928) 6–19.]

360. Dückert, Joachim, "'*Wider*' und '*wieder*' im Neuhochdeutschen," *Wissenschaftliche Zeitschrift der Humboldt-Universität, Berlin, Gesellschafts- und sprachwissenschaftliche Reihe* 7 (1957–1958) 403. ¶ Summary of a Humboldt diss.

361. Düntzer, Heinrich, "Die sprachwidrige Zusammensetzung mit 'ich,'" *ZfddtU* 11 (1897) 603–606. ¶ *Ichroman*, etc.

362. Dyboski, R., "Über Wortbildung und Wortgebrauch bei Tennyson," *Bausteine* 1 (1906) 165–223. ¶ Erster Abschnitt: Wortbildung: derivatives, pp. 165–200; compounds, pp. 200–223.

363. ——, "Zur Wortbildung in Tennysons Jugendgedichten," *Bausteine* 1 (1906) 239–241. ¶ Derivatives and compounds.

364. E. W., "The Stress of the uns," *The Academy* 56 (1899) 385. ¶ Prefix *un-*.

365. Ebel, H., "Gothische Studien: Das gothische Passivum; die Abstractsuffixe *-ni* und *-ani*; die starke Adjectivflexion; die beiden Comparativformen," *ZfvglSpr.* 5 (1856) 300 ff.

366. ——, "Das Suffix *-ant* und Verwandtes," *ZfvglSpr.* 4 (1855) 321 ff. ¶ Essentially Lat. and Greek, but some reference to Ger.

367. Eckhardt, Eduard, *Die angelsächsischen Deminutivbildungen*, Habilitationsschrift, Freiburg, 1903 (= *Engl.Stud.* 32 [1903] 325–366). ¶ *-ing, -ling; -el, -ul, -la, -le, -ele-; -ca, -ce, -uc, -oc, -ic, -ec, -c; -in, -en, -oþ, -od, -ed, -ot, -et, -t, -etu; -et, -ete, -ette; -incel, -uncel;* others.

368. ——, "Die neuenglische Verkürzung langer Tonsilbenvokale in abgeleiteten und zusammengesetzten Wörtern," *Engl.Stud.* 50 (1916–1917) 199–299.

369. ——, "Nordische Bestandteile in der schottischen Mundart," *Herrigs Archiv* 184 (1944) 73 ff.

370. ——, *Das Präfix ge- in verbalen Zusammensetzungen bei Berthold von Regensburg*, Leipzig, 1889.

371. ——, "Reim und Stabreim im Dienste der neuenglischen Wortbildung," *Engl.Stud.* 72 (1937–1938) 161–191.

372. Egge, Albert E., "Inchoative or *N*-Verbs in Gothic, etc.," *AJPh.* 7 (1886) 38–45.

373. Ehrentreich, Alfred, "Sprachliche Spielereien im Amerikanischen," *Die Neueren Sprachen*, N.F. 3 (1954) 362 f. ¶ Blends.

374. Ehrismann, G., "Die Vorsilben *miß-* und *voll-* im Germanischen," *Germania* 37 (1892) 435–439.

375. ——, "Die Wurzelvariationen *s-teud-, s-teub, s-teug-* im Germanischen," *PBB* 18 (1894) 215 ff.

376. Eichholz, Hermann, *Die Zusammenbildungen im Mittel- und Neuhoch-deutschen*, Giessen, 1924. ¶ Seven-page abstract of his diss., 1918.

377. Eickhoff, P., "*-ithi, -ede, -ethe,*" *NdKbl.* 18 (1894–1895) 39.

378. ——, "*-menni,*" *NdKbl.* 18 (1894–1895) 40.

379. Eilenberger, R., *Pennälersprache*, Strassburg, 1910.

380. Einarsson, Stefán, "Compounds of the *mann-skratti* Type," in *Studies in Honor of Albert Morey Sturtevant*, Lawrence, Kan., 1952, 47–56 (= *University of Kansas Publications, Humanistic Studies* 29). ¶ "A devil of a man"; (O)Icel. with comparable compounds in Sw.

381. Einenkel, Eugen, "Die Entwicklung des englischen Gerundiums," *Anglia* 38 (1914) 1–76.

382. ——, *Geschichte der englischen Sprache*, II. *Historische Syntax*, 3rd ed., Strassburg, 1916. ¶ Eng. gerund.

383. ——, "Nachträge zum Gerundium," *Anglia* 38 (1914) 212.

384. ——, "Neues aus dem Gebiete der historischen Syntax," *Anglia* 47 (1923) 274–286. ¶ Eng. gerund.

385. ——, "Zur Geschichte des englischen Gerundiums," *Anglia* 37 (1913) 382–392.

386. ——, "Zur Herkunft des englischen Gerundiums," *Anglia* 38 (1914) 499–504.

387. Eitrem, H., "Stress in English verb + adverb groups," *Engl.Stud.* 32 (1903) 69–77.

388. Ejder, Bertil, *Adjektivändelsen -er i de nordiska spraaken särskilt i svenskan*, diss., Lund, 1945 (= *Lunda studier i nordisk spraakvetenskap* 3).

389. Ejskjær, Inger, "Stød i andet sammensætningsled i typen fortis-semi-fortis i danske ømaal," *APhS* 27 (1965) 19–67.

390. Ekblom, R., "Germ. *kuningaz* 'König,'" *SN* 17 (1944–1945) 1–24.

391. Ekwall, Eilert, "The English place-names Etchells, Nechells," in *Mélanges de philologie offerts à M. Johan Vising par ses élèves et ses amis scandinaves à l'occasion du soixante-dixième anniversaire de sa naissance le 20 avril 1925*, Göteborg, 1925, 104–106. ¶ Suffix *-isla.*

392. ——, *Street Names of the City of London*, Oxford, 1954. ¶ Derivation and composition.

393. ——, *Suffixet* ja *i senare leden af sammansatta substantiv inom de germanska spraaken*, Uppsala, 1904 (= *Uppsala universitets aarsskrift* 1904).

394. Elis, Carl, *Über die Fremdworte und fremden Eigennamen in der gotischen Bibel-Übersetzung in grammatischer und archäologischer Hinsicht*, diss., Einbeck, 1903.

395. Ellinger, "Über die Betonung der aus Verb + Adverb bestehenden englischen Wortgruppen," *Programm der Franz-Joseph-Realschule,* Wien, 1910.

396. Ellinger, Johann, "Die mit Präpositionen zusammengesetzten Adverbien *here, there, where,*" *Engl.Stud.* 73 (1939) 334–343. ¶ *Hereafter, thereafter,* etc.

397. ——, "Über die mit *that* zusammengesetzten Bindewörter im neueren Englisch," *Anglia* 58 (1935) 410–444.

398. Emeneau, M. B., "Some Neologisms in '-ize'," *AmSp.* 22 (1947) 71–72.

399. Erämetsä, Erik, *Englische Lehnprägungen in der deutschen Empfindsamkeit des 18. Jahrhunderts,* Helsinki, 1955 (= *AASF* B 98). ¶ Part II: Lehnbildungen *et al.*; Part III, in particular, deals with derivation and compounding.

400. ——, "Über den englischen Einfluss auf den deutschen Wortvorrat des 18. Jahrhunderts," *Neuphil.Mitt.* 59 (1958) 34–40.

401. ——, "Über die Ländernamen auf *-ie* und *-ien* im Kontinentalgermanischen," *Neuphil.Mitt.* 57 (1956) 224–227.

402. Erben, Johannes, "Deutsche Wortbildung in synchronischer und diachronischer Sicht," *Wirkendes Wort* 14 (1964) 83–93.

403. Erdmann, Axel, *Essay on the History and Modern Use of the Verbal Forms in -ing in the English Language, Part I: Old Anglo-Saxon Period,* Stockholm, 1871. ¶ *-ing-* as present participle, its history, composition. Personal nouns in *-e-nd.* The abstract noun in *-ung (-ing).*

404. Erdmann, J., "Beiträge zur Kenntnis der Mundart von Bingen-Stadt und Bingen-Land," *ZfdMaa.* (1906) 146 ff., 231 ff.

405. Ericson, E. E., "Our American Blend-habit," *Words* 17 (1941) 12–14.

406. Eriksson, Birgit, "Avledningssuffixen och deras funktioner hos substantiven i Nagumaalet," Helsinki, 1945 (*Studier i nordisk filologi* 31–32, 10). ¶ Suffixes of nouns and their functions in the Sw. dialect of Nagu.

407. Estrich, R. M., and Sperber, H., *Three Keys to Language,* New York, 1952. ¶ Pp. 276 ff. deal with the tendency toward playing with sound.

408. Étienne, E., *Essai de grammaire de l'ancien français (IXe-XIVe siècles),* Paris, 1895. ¶ Excellent summary of Lat. suffixes in French, useful for loan studies.

409. Ewald, F., *Die Entwicklung des k-Suffixes in den germanischen Sprachen,* Heidelberg, 1924.

410. Fabian, Erich, *Das exozentrische Kompositum im Deutschen,* Leipzig, 1931 (=*Form und Geist* 20).

411. Fabricius, W., "Zur Studentensprache," *ZfdW* 3 (1902) 91–101. ¶ Few observations on wf; glossary.

412. Fahrner, Rudolf, *Wortsinn und Wortschöpfung bei Meister Eckehart*, Marburg, 1929. ¶ Substantivized infinitives, pp. 79–121.

413. Falk, Hjalmar, "Anmälan av 'T. E. Karsten: *Studier öfver de nordiska spraakens primära nominalbildning I*,' Exkurs: verbalabstrakter paa -o- og -i- som förste kompositionsled," *Arkiv* 13 (1897) 196 ff.; exkurs 202 ff.

414. ——, "Die nomina agentis der altnordischen Sprache," *PBB* 14 (1889) 1–52. ¶ I. the suffix *-o*, p. 7; II. the suffix *-n*, p. 14; III. agent nouns in *-ir*, p. 20; IV. agent nouns in *-uhr*, p. 32; V. agent nouns in *-ari*, p. 36; VI. suffixes *-alo, -ilo, -ulo*, p. 37; VII. present participle, p. 41; VIII. agent adjectives in *-inn* and *-br*, p. 44; and IX. participia necessitatis, p. 48.

415. ——, "Prefiks-studier," in *Festskrift til Finnur Jónsson*, Copenhagen, 1928, 339–350. ¶ *au-, aur-, á-*.

416. Faltenbacher, H., *Die romanischen, spez. französ. und lateinischen (bezw. latinisierten) Lehnwörter bei Caxton*, diss., Munich, 1907.

417. Feist, Sigmund, *Vergleichendes Wörterbuch der gotischen Sprache*, 3rd ed., Leiden, 1939.

418. Feldmann, Wilhelm, "Fremdwörter und Verdeutschungen des 18. Jahrhunderts," *ZfdW* 8 (1906–1907) 49–99.

419. ——, "Substantiva auf *-ling*," *ZfdW* 12 (1910) 115–130, 269–271.

420. ——, "Zwitterworte: Kleine Beiträge zum neuhochdeutschen Geschlechtswandel," *ZfdW* 7 (1905–1906) 49–58.

421. Fettig, Adolf, *Die Gradadverbien im Mittelenglischen*, Heidelberg, 1935 (= *Anglistische Forschungen* 79). ¶ Specifically pp. 53 ff.: adverbs in *-e, -unge, -liche*.

[422. Feuerstein, Alfred, *Die neuhochdeutschen Verba mit der Bedeutung 'riechen und schmecken nach etwas' und verwandte Wortgruppen*, diss., Freiburg, 1922.]

423. Few, W. P., "Verbal Nouns in *-inde* in Middle-English and the Participial *-ing* Suffix," *Harvard Studies and Notes in Philology and Literature* 5 (1898) 269–276.

424. Fick, Aug., "Zu den Secundärsuffixen *-an, -ina, -inja, -tā, -tva, -vant*," *ZfvglSpr.* 18 (1869) 453–456. ¶ Pertains principally to Iranian, but some reference to Gmc. languages.

425. F
ičeva, N. I., "O verbalizirujuščej funkcii glagol'nych prefiksov v sovremennom nemeckom jazyke," *Vestnik Moskovskogo Universiteta, Serija 7: Filologija* No. 2 (1961) 43–53. ¶ Deals with the verbalizing function of verbal prefixes in present-day Ger.

426. Fischer, E. L., *Grammatik und Wortschatz der plattdeutschen Mundart im preußischen Samlande*, Halle, 1896. [*NdKbl.* 18 (1894–1895) 95.] ¶ *-sche*=NHG *-in*; diminutives in *-ke*.

427. ——, "Verba nominalia," *Engl.Stud.* 23 (1897) 70–73.

428. Fischer, Frank, *Die Lehnwörter des Altwestnordischen*, Berlin, 1909 (= *Palaestra* 85). ¶ Primarily treatment of loanwords, but introduction discusses most suffixes and prefixes as well as compounding.

429. Fischer, Hermann, *Geographie der schwäbischen Mundart*, Tübingen, 1895.

430. ——, *Schwäbisches Wörterbuch*, I–VI, VII (*Nachträge*). Tübingen, 1904–1936.

431. Fischer, Maja, "Die Diminutive im Deutschen und im Französischen: ein Vergleich von Gottfried Kellers Erzählungen *Die Leute von* Seldwyla mit ihren französischen Übersetzungen," *Muttersprache* 73 (1963) 129–138.

432. Flasdieck, H. M., "Untersuchung über die germanischen schwachen Verben III. Klasse," *Anglia* 59 (1935) 1–192. ¶ Heavy on derivation.

433. Fleece, J. A., "Words in '-fu,'" *AmSp.* 21 (1946) 70–72. ¶ Formations in analogy with *snafu*.

434. Fleischer, Ida, "Das Accentuationssystem Notkers in seinem Boethius," *ZfdPh.* 14 (1882) 129 ff.

435. ——, *Die Wortbildung bei Notker und in den verwandten Werken, eine Untersuchung der Sprache Notkers mit besonderer Rücksicht auf die Neubildungen*, Göttingen, 1901.

436. Flom, George T., "The Dialect Provenience of Scandinavian Loanwords in English, with Special Reference to Lowland Scotch," *PMLA* 15 (1900) [*Proceedings for 1899*] lxxvii. ¶ Abstract of a paper read.

437. ——, "The Gender of English Loan Nouns in Norse Dialects in America," *JEGP* 5 (1903) 1 ff.

438. ——, "A List of English Dialect Verbs with the Suffix *-l*," *Dialect Notes* 2 (1900–1904) 404–415. ¶ Consists of a list of about 375 verbs together with a few introductory remarks on the meaning of the suffix.

[439. Flury, Robert, "Zur Geschichte von -BAR, -SAM, -HAFT," diss., Zürich, 1965.]

440. Förstemann, E., "Die Zusammensetzung altdeutscher Personennamen," *ZfvglSpr.* 1 (1852) 97–116.

441. Förster, [no initial], "Erklärung eines scheinbaren Sprachfehlers in der neuhochdeutschen Wortbildung," *Deutscher Sprachwart* 1 (1858) 3–5; also *Deutscher Sprachwart* N.F. 4 (1869) 130–132. ¶ Feminine compounds with genitive *-s*.

442. Förster, Max, *Keltisches Wortgut im Englischen: eine sprachliche Untersuchung*, Halle, 1921. ¶ Derivation, compounding, borrowing. Specific sections deal with brittische Lehnwörter des Ae., altirische Lehnwörter im Ae., unhaltbare und bedenkliche Ableitungen, Personennamen, keltische Ortsnamen im Eng.

443. Fokkema, K., "Het Friese suffix -*ens* bij abstracta," *Taal en Tongval* 9 (1957) 194–197.
444. Fowler, H. W., *Dictionary of Modern English Usage*, Oxford, 1950.
445. Francescato, Giuseppe, "On Italian Loan-words in German," *Neophilologus* 42 (1958) 152–154. ¶ Essentially a review of Wis, Marjatta, *q.v.*
446. Franck, J., *Altfränkische Grammatik*, Göttingen, 1909. [Primus Lessiak, *AfdA* 34 (1910) 193–222.]
447. ——, "Over woordafleiding, haar doel en hare taak," *Taal en Letteren* 1 (1891) 131–148.
448. Francke, W., "Über Wortbildung und Wortgebrauch im Englischen und Amerikanischen der Gegenwart," *Neuphilologische Zeitschrift* 2 (1950) 12–21. ¶ General.
449. Franke, Karl, "Die obersächsische Hauptmundart," in Robert Wuttke, *Sächsische Volkskunde*, 2nd ed., Dresden, 1900, 275–295. ¶ Adverbial -*e*, p. 287; -*ig*, -*icht*, p. 288.
450. Franz, Wilhelm, *Die lateinisch-romanischen Elemente im Althochdeutschen*, diss., Strassburg, 1883. ¶ Formenlehre: A. Geschlecht und Flexion der Substantive, pp. 60–65, e.g., Lat. nouns in -*um*> masc.
451. ——, *Orthographie, Lautgebung und Wortbildung in den Werken Shakespeares mit Ausspracheproben*, Heidelberg, 1905. ¶ Paras. 72–89, prefixes; 70–132, suffixes; 133–147, composition; 148, substantivation of verbs.
452. ——, *Die Sprache Shakespeares in Vers und Prosa*, 4th ed., Halle, 1939. ¶ Wf: prefixes, pp. 100–113; suffixes, pp. 113–144; composition, pp. 144–152; substantivation, back-formations, etc., pp. 152–153.
453. ——, "Die Wortbildung bei Shakespeare," *Engl.Stud.* 35 (1905) 34–85. ¶ Derivation and compounding.
454. Friederici, Georg, *Hilfswörterbuch für den Amerikanisten*, Halle, 1926. ¶ "The chief value of Friederici lies in the documentation, especially of the relevant Spanish sources" (from *Short Notices* in *MLR* 23 [1928] 119).|
455. Friedrich, Johannes, *Deminutivbildungen mit nicht deminutiver Bedeutung*, diss., Leipzig, 1916.
456. Frings, Theodor, "Ingwäonisches in den Bezeichnungen der Zehnerzahlen. Von England über Friesland an den Niederrhein," *PBB* (Halle) 84 (1962) 1–66. ¶ Reprinted in *Fryske stúdzjes, oanbean oan Prof. Dr. J. H. Brouwer op syn sechstichste jierdei 23 augustus 1960*, ed. K. Dykstra, K. Heeroma, W. Kok, H. T. J. Miedema, Assen, 1960, pp. 7–39, with the addition of three appendixes of which the first is pertinent: Gertraud Müller, "-zo-, -zug, -zog, -zig, -zeg in den Zahlen 20–100," pp. 43–48.

457. ——, *Germania Romana*, Halle, 1932 (= *Teuthonista Beiheft* 4, 2). ¶ Loanwords from French.

458. ——, "Die Ortsnamen auf -*lar* und die ndl. Baumnamen des Typus *Hazelaar* 'Haselnußstrauch'," *ZfdA* 66 (1929) 46 ff.

459. ——, "Persönliche Feminina im Westergermanischen," *PBB* 56 (1932) 23 ff.

460. Frisk, Hjalmar, *Substantiva privativa im Indogermanischen: eine morphologisch-stilistische Studie*, Göteborg, 1948 (= *Göteborgs högskolas aarsskrift* 53, 3 [1947]).

461. ——, *Suffixales -th- im Indogermanischen*, Göteborg, 1936 (= *Göteborgs högskolas aarsskrift* 42, 2).

462. ——, *Über den Gebrauch des Privativpräfixes im indogermanischen Adjektiva*, Göteborg, 1941 (= *Göteborgs högskolas aarsskrift* 11).

463. Fröhlich, A., "Zusammenhang zwischen Lautform und Bedeutung bei englischen Wörtern," *Die Neueren Sprachen* 33 (1925) 27 ff. and 127 ff. ¶ Words in -*mp*, -*lp*, -*sp*, -*l*, -*b*, -*r*, etc.

464. Fry, Danby P., "On the Last Syllable in the Words *knowledge, revelach* and *wedlock*," *Trans.Phil.Soc.* (1860–1861) 75–89 and (1862–1863) 33–47. ¶ OE -*lac*.

465. Funke, Otto, *Englische Sprachkunde: ein Überblick ab 1935*, Bern, 1950 (= *Wissenschaftliche Forschungsberichte, Geisteswissenschaftliche Reihe* 10). ¶ Chap. 9: Wortbildung, pp. 123–129.

466. ——, *Die gelehrten lateinischen Lehn- und Fremdwörter in der altenglischen Literatur*, Halle, 1914. ¶ Wortbildung, pp. 130–134.

467. ——, "Zum Problem 'Sprachkörper und Sprachfunktion,' " in *Neusprachliche Studien: Festgabe Karl Luick zu seinem sechzigsten Geburtstage dargebracht von Freunden und Schülern*, Marburg, 1925, 102–121 (= *Die Neueren Sprachen Beiheft* 6). ¶ Wilhelm Horn's thesis: weakening of function may cause change in phonetic form of a word. Para. 5 takes up the problem in relation to compounds and personal names.

468. ——, "Zur Wortgeschichte der französischen Elemente im Englischen," *Engl.Stud.* 55 (1921) 1–25.

469. Gadde, Frederik, *On the History and Use of the Suffixes* -ery (-ry), -age *and* -ment *in English*, diss., Lund, 1910.

470. Galinsky, Hans, "Gedanken zu einer neuen Darstellung der englischen Wortbildung," *Die Neueren Sprachen* 11 (1962) 97–121. ¶ Review article of Hans Marchand (1960).

471. ——, *Die Sprache des Amerikaners*, II. *Wortschatz und Wortbildung*, 2nd ed., Heidelberg, 1959. ¶ Chap. 6: Wortbildung, pp. 61–119: compounding, conversion, derivation; back-formation, "Umformungen, Wortmischungen," compounding by prefixes; root formation, "Aufspaltung."

472. Gallée, J. H., "*henne, hunne* en *hune* en hunne samenstellingen," *Tijdschrift* 20 (1901) 46–58.

473. Gamillscheg, Ernst, *Etymologisches Wörterbuch der französischen Sprache,* Heidelberg, 1928.

474. ——, *Die romanischen Elemente in der deutschen Mundart von Lusern,* Halle, 1912 (= *Beihefte zur ZfrPh.* 43). ¶ Esp. part I (pp. 4–14): change of function and meaning, compounding, oldest loanwords.

475. Ganz, Peter F., *Der Einfluss des Englischen auf den deutschen Wortschatz,* Berlin, 1957. [Erik Erämetsä, *Neuphil.Mitt.* 59 (1958) 59–62.]

476. ——, "Seventeenth-Century English Loan-words in German," *JEGP* 54 (1955) 80–90.

477. ——, "Some English Loanwords in German," *MLR* 49 (1954) 478 ff. ¶ Considers *Redingote, Reporter, Review, Schal, Schrapnell, Sherry, Speech, Standard, Steward, Toast, Twist, Viadukt.*

478. Garke, H., "*-ei* in Ortsnamen," *NdKbl.* 39 (1924) 39.

[479. Garncarz, J., "Die Lehnbildungen in der Sprache Otfrids," Staatsexamensarbeit (Maschinenschrift), Bonn, 1951.]

480. Garnett, Richard, "On the Derivation of Words from Pronominal and Prepositional Roots," *Proc.Phil.Soc.* 2 (1844–1846) 205–215.

481. ——, "On the Formation of Words by Further Modification of Inflected Cases," *Proc.Phil.Soc.* 8 (1846–1848) 9–15, 19–29. ¶ Covers many languages, not all IE.

482. Garnier, Katharine von, *Die Präposition als sinnverstärkendes Präfix im Rigveda, in den homerischen Gedichten und in den Lustspielen des Plautus und Terenz,* diss., Leipzig, 1906. ¶ Related to Gmc.

483. Gartner, Theodor, "Trennbar zusammengesetzte Zeitwörter," *ZdallgdSprv.* (1902) 121, 186; (1903) 158; (1905) 169; (1906) 135 ff., 357 ff.; (1918) 29, 229; (1922) 153 ff.

484. Gartner, Thomas, "Fremdes im Wortschatz der Wiener Mundart," *ZfhdMaa.* 3 (1902) 127–151, 184–210, 274–276; 4 (1903) 118 ff., 252 ff.; 5 (1904) 29 ff.

485. ——, "Die Nachsilben *-chen* und *-lein,*" *Wiss. Beih. zur ZdallgdSprv.* 14–15 (1898) 167–176.

486. Gāters, Alfrēds, "Indogermanische Suffixe der Komparation und Deminutivbildung," *ZfvglSpr.* 72 (1954) 47–63. ¶ Only slight reference to Gmc.

487. Gay, Lucy M., "Anglo-French Words in English," *MLN* 14, 2 (1899) 80 ff.

488. Gelbe, Theodor, "Zusammengesetzte Wörter nach Betonung und Bedeutung," *Deutscher Sprachwart* N.F. 6 (1872) 242–247.

489. Geldner, Johann, *Untersuchungen einiger altenglischer Krankheitsnamen,* diss., Braunschweig, 1906. ¶ Under each sickness word derivatives and compounds are given.

490. Genthe, A., *Deutsches Slang*, Strassburg, 1892.

491. Gerbenzon, P., "Verfriesing en vernederlandsing van de Griekse, Latijnse en Franse leenwoorden in het Fries," *Us Wurk* 11 (1962) 40–48.

492. Gerber, Eduard, *Die Substantivierung des Adjektivs im XV. und XVI. Jahrhundert mit besonderer Berücksichtigung des zu Adjektiven hinzutretenden* one, Göttingen, 1895.

493. Gerbet, E., *Grammatik der Mundart des Vogtlandes*, Leipzig, 1908.

494. ——, "Westerzgebirgisch und Südostthüringisch," *ZfhdMaa.* 1 (1900) 113–132. ¶ Wortbildung, pp. 127–128; Fremdwort, pp. 130–131.

495. Gerckens, J., *Zur Entstehungsgeschichte der ti-Abstrakta*, diss., Borna-Leipzig, 1923. [E. Ochs, *ZfMaa.* 1 (1924–1925) 236.]

496. Gerhard, E. S., "A Few 'isms,' " *Word Study* 13, 4 (1938) 5–6. ¶ Sixty words in *-ism*.

497. Gerland, Georg, "Das deutsche *-tsch-*," *ZfvglSpr.* 21 (1873) 67–73.

498. ——, *Intensiva und Iterativa und ihr Verhältnis zu einander: eine sprachwissenschaftliche Abhandlung*, Leipzig, 1869. ¶ Intensives: IE., Ger., Semitic, uninflected languages; interatives: IE.

499. Gibbs, J. W., "English Prefixes Derived from the Greek," *American Journal of Science and Arts* 6 (1848) 206–209. ¶ List with comparative information on prefixes, followed by Eng. meaning and use; largely in reference to language of science.

500. Gibbs, Josiah, *The Formation of Teutonic Words in the English Language*, New Haven, Conn., 1860.

501. Gibson, T. A. and G. M., *Etymological Geography; being a Classified List of Terms and Epithets of most Frequent Occurrence, entering, as Postfixes or Prefixes into the Composition of Geographical Names*, 2nd ed., London, 1840.

502. Giesecke, G. E., "The Loan Translation in German as the Linguistic Conquest of Foreign Semantic Fields," *Stanford University Abstracts of (Doctoral) Dissertations* 14 (1939) 52–55.

503. Ginneken, J. van, "De nederlandsche samenstellingen met *-stof, -goed* enz.," *Onze Taaltuin* 8 (1939–1940) 130–132.

504. Glattes, Lothar, *Wortbildung im oberen Markgräflerischen*, diss., Freiburg, 1934. [W. Will, *ZfMaa.* 12 (1936) 108.]

505. Gloël, Heinrich, "Tautologien in der Wortbildung," *ZfddtU* 10 (1876) 76 ff.

506. Gneuss, Helmut, *Lehnbildungen und Lehnbedeutungen im Altenglischen*, Berlin, 1955. [K. Brunner, *Anglia* 75 (1957) 347.]

507. Goebel, Julius, "The Germanic Suffix *-ar-ja*," *PMLA* 15 (1900) 321–325.

508. Goedders, Christian, *Zur Analogiebildung im Mittel- und Neuenglischen*, diss., Kiel, 1884. ¶ II. Die Wirkung der Analogie in der Neubildung

(Nominalbildung und Verbalbildung, derivation and composition), III. Die Wirkung der Analogie in der Umbildung: der Laut als Ursache der Umbildung, die Form als Ursache der Umbildung (suffixale, praefixale Umbildung, Formübertragung).

509. Göpfert, E., "Aus dem Wortschatz eines erzgebirgischen Chronisten," *ZfhdMaa.* 1 (1900) 37–68. ¶ Vocabulary: etymologies, source words.

[510. ——, "Dialectisches aus dem Erzgebirge," *29. Bericht über die Progymnasial- und Realschulanstalt zu Annaberg*, Annaberg, 1872.]

511. ——, "Zur Wortbildung in der Mundart des sächsischen Erzgebirges," *ZfhdMaa.* 6 (1905) 9 ff. ¶ Verbs, nouns, adjectives, adverbs, and interjections.

512. Goergens, Ludwig, *Beiträge zur Poetik Otfrids, insbesondere die formelhaften Redewendungen und Reimwörter*, diss., Strassburg, 1910.

513. Götze, Alfred, "Alemannische Namenrätsel," in *Festschrift Friedrich Kluge zum 70. Geburtstage am 21. Juni 1926 dargebracht*, Tübingen, 1926.

514. ——, "Freundschaft," *ZfdW* 12 (1910) 93.

515. ——, "Wilhelminisch oder wilhelmisch?" *Muttersprache* 55 (1940) 119.

516. ——, *Zur Geschichte der Adjektive auf* -isch, diss., Leipzig, 1899.

517. ——, "Zur Geschichte der Adjectiva auf -*isch*," *PBB* 24 (1899) 464–522.

[518. Gonda, J., "Some Remarks on Onomatopoeia, Sound-symbolism and Word-Formation à propos of the Theories of C. N. Maxwell," *Tijdschrift voor Indische taal-, land- en volkenkunde* 80 (1940) 133–211.]

519. Goodloe, J. F., *Nomina Agentis auf* -el *im Neuhochdeutschen*, Göttingen, 1929 (= *Hesperia* 18).

520. Gottschald, N., *Deutsche Namenkunde*, München, 1932.

521. Gravow, [no initial], *Hat die Schreibung* -ieren *in Fremdwörtern etymologischen Wert?* Oppeln, 1881 (= *Separatabdruck aus ZfOrthographie*).

522. Gréb, J., "Eine eigenartige Gründler (Unterzipser) Verkleinerungsbildung: -*chenk*," *ZfMaa.* 14 (1938) 224–227.

523. Greenough, James Bradstreet, and Kittredge, George Lyman, *Words and Their Ways in English Speech*, New York, 1930. ¶ Esp. chaps. 13 and 14.

524. Grein, C. W. M., *Ablaut, Reduplication und secundäre Wurzeln der starken Verba im Deutschen nebst einem Exkurs über die Verba* dôn *und* iddja, Cassel and Göttingen, 1862.

525. Grewolds, Heinrich, "Die gotischen Komposita in ihrem Verhältnis zu denen der griechischen Vorlage," *ZfvglSpr.* 60 (1933) 1–153 (verbal), 61 (1934) 45–179 (nominal).

526. Grienberger, T. von, "Die germanischen Runennamen," *PBB* 22 (1896) 185–224. ¶ P. 220, diminutive animal names in -*uh*, (-*oh*), -*ah*.

527. Grigorovitza, E., "Rumänische Elemente und Einflüsse in der Sprache der Siebenbürger Deutschen," *ZfhdMaa.* 2 (1909) 58–73, 161–175. ¶ Dictionary.

528. Grimm, Jacob, *Deutsche Grammatik*, I–IV (parts 1 and 2), Berlin, 1870 ff.

529. ———, "Das -er örtlicher Appelative unadjektivisch," *ZfdA* 2 (1842) 191–192.

530. ———, "Über die zusammengesetzten Zahlen," *Germania* 1 (1856) 18–33.

531. ———, and Grimm, Wilhelm, *Deutsches Wörterbuch*, Leipzig, 1854 ff.

532. Grimme, H., *Plattdeutsche Mundarten*, 4th ed., Leipzig, 1922. ¶ Wortbildungslehre, pp. 120–125.

533. Gröger, Otto, *Die althochdeutsche und altsächsische Kompositionsfuge mit Verzeichnis der althochdeutschen und altsächsischen Composita*, diss., Zürich, 1910 (= *Gesellschaft für deutsche Sprache in Zürich* 11).

534. Groom, Bernard, *The Formation and Use of Compound Epithets in English Poetry from 1579*, Oxford, 1937 (=*SPE Tract* 49).

535. Groot, A. W. de, "De Interjectie," in *Studies op het gebied van het hedendaagse Nederlands*, The Hague, 1963, 13–22. ¶ P. 19 deals with compound interjections.

536. ———, "Wort und Wortstruktur," *Neophilologus* 24 (1939) 221–233. ¶ 1. Das Wort, 2. Die Wortstruktur, 3. Als Glied der Satzstruktur.

537. Gross, Erna von, *Bildung des Adverbs bei Chaucer*, diss., Berlin, 1921. ¶ Derivation from adjectives and nouns; composition.

538. Grosse, Siegfried, "Durative Verben und präfigierte Perfektiva im Deutschen," *Der Deutschunterricht* 15 (1963) 95–105.

539. Gruber, Hans, *Das adverbale uz-Präfix im Gotischen und Althochdeutschen, ein Beitrag zum Problem der Präfixkomposition*, Jena, 1930 (= *Jenaer germanistische Forschungen* 13). [*Neophilologus* 17 (1932) 310.]

540. Grunewald, Gottfried, *Die mittelniederdeutschen Abstraktsuffixe*, diss., Lund, 1944 (= *Lunder germanistische Forschungen* 13).

[541. Grzebieniowski, Tadeusz, "Słownictwo angielskie od imion własnych," *Sprawozdania z czynności i posiedzeń Łódzkiego Towarzystwa Naukowego* 16 (1961) 1–14. ¶ Eng. words derived from proper names.]

542. Gubler, H., *Die Liquid- und Nasalsuffixe in der schweizerdeutschen Substantivbildung*, diss., Basel, 1920.

543. ———, "Zur schweizerdeutschen Wortbildung," *ZfMaa.* 14 (1938) 193 ff. ¶ Noun suffixes -ori, -öri; -uri; -eri; -ari, -äri; -oli, -öli; -ali.

544. Gülzow, Erich, "Badener, doch Wiesbader," *Muttersprache* 55 (1940) 135–136. ¶ -er with place names ending in -en.

545. ———, "Hauptwörter auf -els," *NdKbl.* 50 (1937) 54.

546. ———, "Wörter auf -els," *NdKbl.* 53 (1940) 13.

547. Gürtler, Hans, "Die Abstraktbildungen des Althochdeutschen," *Neuphil.Mitt.* 24 (1923) 105–109.

548. ——, "Anomale Pluralbildungen der Diminutiva im Frühneuhochdeutschen," *ZfdW* 12 (1910) 135–138.

549. ——, *Das Diminutivsuffix -chen im Frühneuhochdeutschen*, diss., Freiburg,
1909.

550. ——, " Materialien zur Geschichte des Diminutivs auf *-chen* im Frühneuhochdeutschen," *ZfdW* 11 (1909) 181 ff.

551. Güte, Johannes, *Die produktiven Suffixe der persönlichen Konkreta im
Mittelenglischen*, Strassburg, 1908. ¶ Two parts: Gmc. and foreign
suffixes.

552. Haag, Karl, "Schwabensprache," *Muttersprache* 41 (1926) 295 f.

553. ——, "Zusammensetzung oder Ableitung," *Muttersprache* 51 (1936)
265–266.

554. Haensch, Günther, "Abkürzungswörter und 'Zahlwörter,' " *Lebende
Sprachen* 4 (1959) 21.

555. Haeringen, C. B. van, "*-aar* of *-er*," *De Nieuwe Taalgids* 44 (1951) 260–
266. ¶ The distribution of the suffixes *-aar* and *-er* in agent nouns
and nouns derived from place names.

556. ——, "Afleidingen en samenstellingen van *doen, gaan, slaan, staan* en
zien," *Tijdschrift* 63 (1944) 215–225.

557. ——, "Bij en om het prefix *her-*," *De Nieuwe Taalgids* 55 (1962) 313–
321.

558. ——, "Concentratie door Diminuering," *De Nieuwe Taalgids* 45 (1952)
194–199. ¶ Elliptical diminutive of words or phrases not necessarily
known as simplex.

559. ——, "Ingekorte samenstellingen," *De Nieuwe Taalgids* 41 (1948) 220–
222. ¶ Examples of the type *bootsmaat* for *bootsmansmaat*.

560. Hahne, F., "Bärbeißig—Rucksack—Stadtbad," *Muttersprache* 54 (1939)
184–188.

561. Hakamies, Reino, *Etude sur l'origine et l'évolution du diminutif latin et sa
survie dans les langues romanes*, Helsinki, 1951 (= *AASF* B 71). ¶ Related material.

562. Haldeman, S. S., *Affixes in their Origin and Application, exhibiting the
Etymologic Structure of English Words*, Philadelphia, 1865; rev. ed.
Philadelphia, 1871.

563. Hall, Fitzedward, *On English Adjectives in -able with Special Reference to
Reliable*, London, 1877.

564. Haltenhoff, Julius, *Zur Geschichte des nhd. Adjektivsuffixes -icht und seiner
Verwandten*, diss., Heidelberg, 1904.

565. Hammerich, L. L., "Hvorledes Ordene rejser fra Holland til Dan-
mark," *Gads danske Magasin* (1931) 653–660. ¶ Dutch loanwords
and how they came into Danish.

566. Hansen, A., "Zu den mittelniederländischen Wörtern in der Mark
Brandenburg," *NdKbl.* 42 (1928–1929) 44. ¶ *-ster* (*mähster*).

567. ——, "Wörter auf -els," NdKbl. 53 (1940) 12.

568. Hansen, Aage, "Om Lydudviklingen i Sammensætninger," in Studier tilegnede Verner Dahlerup paa Femog halvfjerdsaarsdagen d. 31. Oktober, 1934, Aarhus, 1934, 224–230.

569. Hansen, Laus, "Reim- und Ablautverdoppelungen," Zt. für Angl. und Am. 7 (1964) 5–31. ¶ On constructions such as face lace, drape shape.

570. Harder, Kelsie B., "I. The Suffix ee. II. Luxe," AmSp. 39 (1964) 294–296.

571. Harding, Erik, "Om naagra forna verbalprefix i Þrymskviða, före-trädda av ersättningspartikeln of (um)," Arkiv 73 (1958) 258–260. ¶ "Ancient verbal prefixes in the Þrymskviða, preceded by the sub-stitute particle of (um)."

572. ——, Urnordisk grammatik, Häfte 1–2, Lund, 1932. ¶ Part II deals, among other things, with vocalism in Proto-Norse suffix and prefix syllables.

573. Hargreaves, Henry, "English Abbreviations in Speech," Die Neueren Sprachen N.F. 6 (1957) 177–181. ¶ Many abbreviations used as words, e.g., R.A.F. (raf).

574. Harrison, Henry, Origin of "Yankee," London, 1913, 1917. ¶ Du. word: suffix -ke discussed on p. 3.

575. Harrison, Thomas P., The Separable Prefixes in Anglo-Saxon Prose, diss., Baltimore, 1892.

576. Harry, J. E., "Ology," Words 4 (1938) 120. ¶ Suffix is -logy, not -ology.

577. Harwood, F. W., and Wright, Alison M., "Statistical Study of English Word Formation," Language 32 (1956) 260 ff.

[578. Hasselhoff, Walter, Das Verbum substantivum im Frühmittelenglischen, diss., Münster, 1915.]

579. Hasselrot, Bengt, "Om diminutiver—ute och hemma," Nysvenska stu-dier 33 (1954) 139–154.

580. Hastenpflug, Fritz, Das Diminutiv in der deutschen Originalliteratur des 12. und 13. Jahrhunderts, diss., Marburg, 1914.

581. Hatcher, Anna Granville, "Bahuvrîhi in Sears-Roebuck," MLN 59 (1944) 515–526.

582. ——, "An Introduction to the Analysis of English Noun Compounds," Word 16 (1960) 356–373.

583. ——, "Modern Appositional Compounds of Inanimate Reference," AmSp. 27 (1952) 3–15.

584. ——, Modern English Word-Formation and Neo-Latin: A Study of the Ori-gins of English (French, Italian, German) Copulative Compounds, Balti-more, 1951. [Tauno Nurmela, Neuphil.Mitt. 57 (1956) 60–68.] ¶ Excellent notes.

585. Haugen, Einar, "The Analysis of Linguistic Borrowing," *Language* 26 (1956) 214 ff. ¶ Actually word borrowing.

586. Hauschild, Oskar, "Die Bedeutung der Assonanz und des Ablautes für die Wortbildung im Niederdeutschen," *NdKbl.* 21 (1899–1900) 3–9.

587. ——, *Die verstärkende Zusammensetzung der Eigenschaftswörter im Deutschen*, Ostern, 1899 (= *Wissenschaftliche Beilage zum Jahresbericht des Wilhelm-Gymnasiums in Hamburg*) [W. Kahl, *ZfhdMaa.* 1 (1900) 352]; supplemented by the following articles: *ZfdW* 4 (1903) 315–320, 5 (1903–1904) 242–248, and 6 (1904–1905) 198–211. ¶ Deals essentially with dialects.

588. Hauser, C., "Zur Wortforschung in Vorarlberg," *Alemannia* 18 (1890) 134–138.

589. Hausser, Eberhard, "Abstrakta im Schwäbischen," diss. (Maschinenschrift), Tübingen, 1959.

590. Havers, Wilhelm, *Handbuch der erklärenden Syntax*, Heidelberg, 1931. ¶ Pp. 257–258 gives a full list of references to ellipsis (clipping).

591. Hechtenberg, K., *Das Fremdwort im Deutschen*, 2nd rev. ed., Leipzig, 1900.

592. Heck, Casius, "Die Quantitäten der Accentvokale in neuenglischen offenen Silben mehrsilbiger nichtgermanischer Lehnwörter," *Anglia* 29 (1905) 1 ff.

593. ——, *Zur Geschichte der nichtgermanischen Lehnwörter im Englischen*, Offenbach, 1904.

594. Heeroma, K., "Aantekeningen bij 'het prefix in het verleden deelwoord,'" *Tijdschrift* 61 (1941) 13–23.

595. Hehn, Victor, *Kulturpflanzen und Haustiere*, 7th rev. ed., O. Schrader, Berlin, 1902.

596. Heikel, Ivar A., *Huru spraaket utvecklat sig*, Stockholm, 1936. ¶ Sec. 3: new words, wf in Sw.

597. Heilborn, Ernst, *Der Wortschatz der sogenannten ersten schlesischen Dichterschule in Wortbildung und Wortzusammensetzung dargestellt, I. Teil Wortbildung*, diss., Berlin, 1890.

598. Heinertz, N. Otto, "*Drottning* und *käring* (mit einam Nachtrag über das Wort *konungr*), ein Beitrag zur germanischen Kulturgeschichte," *APhS* 10 (1935) 146–162. ¶ *-ing*.

599. ——, "Kritische Wortstudien 1. Das germanische Präfix *ô-*," *SN* 20 (1947–1948) 103–138.

600. Heintze, H., and Cascorbi, P., *Die deutschen Familiennamen geschichtlich, geographisch, sprachlich*, 5th ed., Halle, 1922.

601. Heinzel, Richard, "Über die Endsilben der altnordischen Sprache," *Sitzungsberichte der philosophisch-historischen Classe der Kaiserlichen Akademie der Wissenschaften Wien* 87 (1877) 343–484.

602. ——, "Wortschatz und Sprachformen der Wiener Notkerhandschrift," *Sitzungsberichte der philosophisch-historischen Classe der Kaiserlichen Akademie der Wissenschaften Wien* 81, 2 (1876) 203–350. ¶ Vowels of derivations and endings.

603. Heinzerling, J., *Fremdwörter unter deutschen und englischen Tiernamen*, Siegen, 1889. ¶ Primarily etymological, with passing remarks on composition and suffixes.

604. Hekket, B. J., "De uitgang *-ster*," *Driemaandelijkse Bladen* 14 (1962) 49–50.

605. Hellpach, Willy, "*Tum*- Gemeinschaften," *ZfdBildung* 9 (1933) 620–625. ¶ *-tum, -tümlich*; *Kaisertum, Tumeigen, urtümlich*, etc.

606. Hellquist, Elof, *Bidrag till Läran om den nordiska Nominalbildningen*, Lund, 1890.

607. ——, "Bidrag till läran om den nordiska nominalbildningen," *Arkiv* 7 (1891) 1 ff.

608. ——, "Om fornnordiska sammansättningar med kortstafvigt verb till första sammansättningsled," *Arkiv* 15 (1899) 230–239.

609. ——, "Om nordiska verb paa suffixalt *-k, -l, -r, -s* ocht *-t* samt af dem bildade nomina," *Arkiv* 14 (1898) 1–46, 136–194.

610. ——, "Om uppkomsten af de fsv. adjektiven paa *-likin*," *Arkiv* 22 (1906) 359–362.

611. ——, "Ordbildning," in *Svensk etymologisk ordbok*, Lund, 1922, i–lxxiii. ¶ Derivation, listing all suffixes with illustrations, and compounding.

612. ——, *Svensk ordbildningslära fraan historik synpunkt*, Lund, 1922. ¶ General.

613. ——, *De svenska ordförraadets aalder och ursprung, en översikt* II, Lund, 1930. ¶ Discusses loanwords.

614. Helten, William L. van, *Altostfriesische Grammatik*, Leeuwarden, 1890. ¶ Vowels in the prefixes *gi-, bi-, ti-*, pp. 69–72; formation of adverbs, pp. 181–183.

615. ——, "Bijdragen tot de Dietsche Grammatica: IV. Iets over Dietsche adjectieven of *-e*," *Tijdschrift* 2 (1882) 55–61.

616. ——, "Grammatisches· XXII: Zu den Comparativsuffixen der Adjectiva und Adverbia im Germanischen," *PBB* 17 (1893) 550–554.

617. ——, "Das *þ* in got. *kunþa, kunþ* und das Suffix *st*," *ZfdA* 23 (1879) 418–432.

618. ——, "Über die westgermanischen Entsprechungen von altem **-nassuz*, **-Xaiðuz, *-skapi*," *PBB* 17 (1893) 297–302.

619. ——, *Über die Wurzel* lu *im Germanischen*, Rotterdam, 1873.

620. ——, "Zu (-)laus, (-)los," *ZfdW* 11 (1909) 56–57.

621. ——, "Zur Entwickelung der germanischen Comparativ- und Superlativsuffixe," *IF* 16 (1904) 63–71.

622. ——, *Zur Lexicologie des Altostfriesischen*, Amsterdam, 1907 (= *Verhandelingen der Koninklijke Akademie van Wetenschappen te Amsterdam Afdeeling Letterkunde nieuwe reeks* Deel 9). ¶ Strictly a dictionary, but individual articles (see p. 385 the suffix *-ire*) yield information on wf.

623. Hemken, Emil Wilhelm, *Das Aussterben alter Substantiva im Verlaufe der englischen Sprachgeschichte*, diss., Kiel, 1906. ¶ Derivatives and compounds purposely omitted with few exceptions; see p. 26.

624. Hemme, Adolf, *Das lateinische Sprachmaterial im Wortschatze der deutschen, französischen und englischen Sprache*, Leipzig, 1904. ¶ Introductory comments on wf, borrowing, etc. Dictionary of Lat. words and their reflexes in Ger., French, and Eng.

625. Hendrickson, John R., *Old English Prepositional Compounds in Relationship to their Latin Originals*, diss., Philadelphia, 1947.

626. Henke, Ingeborg, "Die Verbalkomposita mit *vol-*, *volle-* und *vollen-* im Frühmittelhochdeutschen," *PBB* (Halle) 79 (1957), Sonderband 461–488.

627. Hennemann, Hermann, "Die Mundart der sog. Grunddörfer in der Grafschaft Mansfeld," *ZfhdMaa.* 2 (1901) 176–225. ¶ Derivational suffixes, pp. 221–222.

628. Hennig, R., "Wilhelminisch oder Wilhelmisch?" *Historische Zt.* 162 (1940) 111.

629. Henrici, E., "Über die substantivische Anwendung der Bildungen mit *-lîh* in der Bedeutung 'jeder' bis zum 11. Jahrhundert," *PBB* 5 (1879) 51 ff.

630. Hentrich, Konrad, "Deutsches Partizip auf *-ing*," *ZfhdMaa.* 6 (1905) 372.

631. ——, "Gerundialpartizipien auf *-ing* im Nordwestthüringischen," *ZfdMaa.* (1907) 274–275.

632. Henzen, Walter, *Deutsche Wortbildung*, 3rd rev. ed., Tübingen, 1965. ¶ General.

633. ——, "Fortleben der schwachen Konjugationen im Lötschental," *PBB* 64 (1940) 271–308. ¶ Derivation; groups of weak verbs.

634. ——, "Der heutige Bestand der Verben mit *ver-*; Vorstudie zu einer Erforschung der Wortschatzbewegungen," *Veröffentlichungen des Instituts für deutsche Sprache und Literatur, Deutsche Akademie der Wissenschaften zu Berlin* 8 (1956) 173–189.

635. ——, "Inhaltsbezogene Wortbildung," *Herrigs Archiv* 194 (1957–1958) 4 ff.

636. ——, "Wortbedeutung und Wortnatur," in *Sprachgeschichte und Wortbedeutung: Festschrift Albert Debrunner gewidmet von Schülern, Freunden und Kollegen*, Bern, 1954, 179–194. ¶ Particularly pp. 188 ff., compounding.

637. Hermann, E., "Einige Beobachtungen an den idg. Verwandtschafts-
     namen," *IF* 53 (1935) 97 ff.
638. Hermann, Walter, "Verbalendung *-ize* oder *-ise*?" *Die Neueren Sprachen*
     N.F. 3 (1954) 552–554. ¶ Essentially a matter of spelling, but goes
     into origin.
639. Hertel, L., *Die Salzunger Mundart*, Weiningen, 1888.
640. Hertel, Oskar and Ludwig, "Die Pfersdorfer Mundart," *ZfhdMaa.* 3
     (1902) 96–120. ¶ P. 114, Wortbildung.
641. Hertrampf, Alfons, *Die Entstehung von Substantiven aus Verben im Neu-
     englischen*, Breslau, 1932. ¶ I: by suffixes, prefixes, general deriva-
     tion; II: tabulation and semantic considerations.
642. Hesse, Hugo, *Perfektive und imperfektive Aktionsart im Altenglischen*, diss.,
     Münster, 1906. [Karl Jost, *Anglia Beibl.* 18 (1907) 133–144.] ¶ Based
     on *Bede*; *ge-* prefix.
643. Hesseling, D. C., "De woorden op *-loos*," *De Nieuwe Taalgids* 2 (1908)
     249–253. ¶ On *-loos*, with and without connecting *-e-*.
644. Hettema, F. Buitenrust, "Woordvorming," *Taal en Letteren* 2 (1892)
     334 ff. ¶ Deals with noun + adjective compounds, e.g., *bloedrood*.
645. Heusler, A., *Altisländisches Elementarbuch*, 4th ed., Heidelberg, 1950.
646. Hicks, Fred Cole, "Strengthening Modifiers of Adjectives and Adverbs
     in Middle High German," *JEGP* 4 (1902) 267–347. ¶ *MHG vil,
     harte, gar, rehte, al,* etc.
647. Hieble, Jacob, "Compound Words in German," *GQ* 30 (1957) 187–
     190.
648. ——, "Foreign Nouns in German," *GQ* 31 (1958) 269–271. ¶ List of
     foreign suffixes.
649. Hietsch, Otto, "Moderne englische Wortbildungselemente," *Wiener
     Beiträge zur englischen Philologie* 66 (1958) 81–101. ¶ Prefixes: *auto-,
     tele-, para-,* etc., suffixes *-ese, -ism,* etc.
650. Hills, E. C., "Irradiation of Certain Suffixes," *AmSp.* 1 (1925–1926)
     38–39. ¶ *-eria, -torium, -ery.*
651. Hilmer, Hermann, *Schallnachahmung, Wortschöpfung und Bedeutungs-
     wandel auf Grundlage der Wahrnehmungen von Schlag, Fall, Bruch und
     derartigen Vorgängen dargestellt an einigen Lautwurzeln der deutschen und
     englischen Sprache*, Halle, 1914. [Eilert Ekwall, *Anglia Beibl.* 29 (1918)
     144–148.] ¶ See esp. pp. 12 ff. and pp. 116 ff.
[652. Hintner, [no initial], *Beiträge zur Tirolischen Dialektforschung*, Wien,
     1878.]
653. Hirt, Hermann, *Etymologie der neuhochdeutschen Sprache*, 2nd ed., Mu-
     nich, 1921.
654. ——, *Handbuch des Urgermanischen, Teil II: Stammbildungs- und Flexions-
     lehre*, Heidelberg, 1932.

655. ——, *Indogermanische Grammatik, Teil III: Das Nomen*, Heidelberg, 1927; Teil IV: *Doppelung, Zusammensetzung, Verbum*, Heidelberg, 1928. ¶ Part IV: chap. 1, Doppelung, Reduplikation; chap. 2, Zusammensetzung; chap. 5, Zusammengesetzte Verbalformen; chap. 6, Verbaladjektive und Partizipien im idg. Verbalsystem.

656. Hirt, Klaus, "Prinzipien sprachlicher Urschöpfung," *Orbis* 5 (1956) 421 ff.

657. ——, "Wortschöpfung, Schalldeutung, Wortumdeutung," *Orbis* 8 (1959) 130–142.

658. Hittle, Erla, *Zur Geschichte der altenglischen Präpositionen "mid" and "wið" mit Berücksichtigung ihrer beiderseitigen Beziehungen*, Heidelberg, 1901 (= *Anglistische Forschungen* 2).

659. Hittmair, A., *Die Partikel be in der mittel- und neuhochdeutschen Verbalcomposition*, Wien, 1882.

660. Hixson, J. C., "English Word-building," *Words* 4 (1938) 41–43. ¶ Vocabulary building.

661. Hoare, Edward N., *English Roots: and the Derivation of Words from the Ancient Anglo-Saxon*, Dublin, 1855. ¶ Two lectures.

662. Hodler, W., *Beiträge zur Wortbildung und Wortbedeutung im Berndeutschen*, diss., Bern, 1911 (= *Sprache und Dichtung* 16 [1915]).

663. Hoefer, A., "Zur Laut-, Wort- und Namenforschung: 4. Ungesühte und die Partikel un," *Germania* 14 (1869) 201 ff.; "5. Endig, Unende," 205 ff.; "Praepositionale Adverbien auf *-er*," 208 f.; "18. Das intensive *in*," *Germania* 15 (1870) 61–65; and "45. wan in Zusammensetzung," *Germania* 23 (1878) 5–8.

664. Höfler, Otto, "Altnordische Lehnwortstudien," *Arkiv* 48 (1932) 213–241. ¶ Feminines in OSw. *-ka*; *-eri-* group; masc. and fem. in *-e*.

665. Höge, Otto, *Die Deminutivbildungen im Mittelenglischen*, diss., Heidelberg, 1906.

666. Hoffmann, Ed., *Der mundartliche Vokalismus von Basel-Stadt, in seinen Grundzügen dargestellt*, Basel, 1890. ¶ Pp. 82 ff.: *-us, -enez, -ennes*.

667. Hoffmann, Erich, *Die althochdeutschen und mittelhochdeutschen Deverbativa mit ableitenden Suffixen*, diss., Breslau, 1921.

668. Hoffmann, Otto, *Reimformeln im Westgermanischen*, diss., Darmstadt, 1885.

669. Hoffmann-Krayer, E., "Ferndissimilation von *r* und *l* im Deutschen," in *Festschrift zur 49. Versammlung deutscher Philologen und Schulmänner*, Basel, 1907, 491–506. ¶ New forms of extant words.

670. ——, "Präterital-passivische Zusammensetzungen im Deutschen," in *Festschrift Friedrich Kluge zum 70. Geburtstage am 21. Juni 1926 dargebracht*, Tübingen, 1926, 57–61.

671. ——, "Suffix *-is, -s* in schweizerischen Mundarten," *ZfhdMaa.* 3 (1902) 26 ff. ¶ *-us*; *-inez, -enez*; *-en(n)es*; adverbs; misc.

41

672. ——, "Zu 'Lurjan,' " *ZfddtU* 7 (1893) 565. ¶ *-jan.*

673. Hofmann, Dietrich, *Die k-Diminutiva im Nordfriesischen und in verwandten Sprachen*, Köln, 1961 (= *Niederdeutsche Studien* 7).

674. ——, "Die niederdeutschen Diminutivsuffixe mit Berücksichtigung der friesischen," *NdKbl.* 63 (1956) 52 ff. ¶ Lecture.

675. Hofmann, Erich, "Ausdrucksverstärkung: Untersuchungen zur etymologischen Verstärkung und zum Gebrauch der Steigerungsadverbia im Balto-Slawischen und in anderen indogermanischen Sprachen," *Ergänzungsheft zur ZfvglSpr.* 9 (1930) 12 ff.

676. Hoge, John, *Die produktiven Abstraktsuffixe des Mittelniederdeutschen*, diss., Kahla (S.A.), 1912. ¶ OSaxon: *-iþa, -ida; -idi; -nussi, -nissi; -inga, -unga; -ie; -isli, -islo; -hêd; -skepi; -dôm; -dage.*

677. Hohenstein, Carl, *Das altengl. Präfix wið(er)- im Verlauf der engl. Sprachgeschichte mit Berücksichtigung der andern germ. Dialekte*, diss., Kiel, 1912. ¶ Verbs, nouns, adjectives, prepositions; excellent study; table of contents, pp. 122–123, gives synopsis.

678. Hol, A. R., "Het prefix in het verleden deelwoord," *Tijdschrift* 60 (1941) 249–293.

679. Hollander, L. M., *Prefixal s in Germanic together with the Etymologies of fratze, schraube, guter dinge*, Baltimore, 1905. [M. H. Jellinek, *AfdA* 31 (1908) 55.]

680. Holmberg, J., "Das Suffix *-tät*," *PBB* 61 (1937) 116–151.

681. Holthausen, Ferdinand, *Altsächsisches Elementarbuch*, 2nd ed., Heidelberg, 1921.

682. ——, *Vergleichendes und etymologisches Wörterbuch des Altwestnordischen*, Göttingen, 1948.

683. Holtzmann, Adolf, "Das Adjektiv in den Nibelungen," *Germania* 6 (1861) 1 ff.

684. Holz, Guido, "Die ISMEN," *Muttersprache* (1952) 79–85.

685. Hommen, B. H., "Oude verkleinwoorden," *Driemaandelijkse Bladen* 11 (1959) 54–63. ¶ Diminutives in the documents of Oldenzaal (Oversel) in the seventeenth and eighteenth centuries.

686. Hoops, Johannes, "Altenglisch *ealuscerwen, meoduscerwen*," *Engl.Stud.* 65 (1930–1931) 177–180.

687. ——, *Englische Sprachkunde*, Stuttgart, 1923. ¶ Pp. 98 ff., wf.

688. ——, *Über die altenglischen Pflanzennamen*, diss., Freiburg, 1889. ¶ Peripheral; mostly compounds.

689. Hopf, W., "Wörterbuch der Mundart von Habkern," *ZfdMaa.* (1906) 52 ff., 289 ff.

690. Horn, P., *Die deutsche Soldatensprache*, Giessen, 1905.

691. Horn, Wilhelm, "Die Wort und Konstruktionsmischungen im Englischen," *GRM* 9 (1921) 342 ff. ¶ Largely blends.

692. ——, "Einige Fälle von Dissimilation," *ZfhdMaa.* 1 (1900) 27–32.
693. ——, "Nhd. *arkelei* und die anderen Nebenformen von Artillerie," *PBB* 30 (1905), 208 ff.
694. ——, *Sprachkörper und Sprachfunktion*, 2nd ed., Berlin, 1923 (1st ed., Berlin, 1921 = *Palaestra* 135). ¶ Clipping. Introduction (pp. 1–21) clipping in compounds, derivatives; p. 74, adverbial suffix *-ly*.
695. ——, "Wahlspruchwörter und Imperativbildungen," *Herrigs Archiv* 179 (1949) 28–30. ¶ Such items as *Vergißmeinnicht, Dreadnought < I dread nought.*
696. ——, "Zur Lautlehre der französischen Lehn- und Fremdwörter im Deutschen," *ZffrzSpruLit.* 21 (1899) 69 ff. and 22 (1900) 56 ff.
[697. Hornbogen, Ingeborg, "Zur bevorzugten Verwendung des Suffixes *-ung* in der Sprache der Gegenwart," *Wissenschaftliche Zt. der Pädagogischen Hochschule Potsdam. Gesellschafts- und Sprachwissenschaftliche Reihe*, Sonderheft 1964, 59-62.]
698. Hortling, Ivar, "Zur altsächsischen Nominalbildung: *l*-Formation," *Mémoires de la Société néophilologique* 6 (1917) 127 ff.
699. ——, *Studien über die ō-Verba im Altsächsischen*, Helsinki, 1907. [T. E. Karsten, *Neuphil.Mitt.* 10 (1908) 37–39.]
700. Hotzenköcherle, Rudolf, *Die Mundart von Mutten*, Frauenfeld, 1934 (= *Beitr.z.Schweizerd. Grammatik* 19). ¶ Para. 82, prefixes.
701. Hovi, Nils, "Litt om adjektiv i Valdres-maalet," *Tidsskrift for Valdres historielag* 25 (1947) 50–60. ¶ Adjectives in *u-, -leg, -ande (-ende)*; groups in *-int (-in), -og* and *-ig, -ut*; compound adjective.
[702. Hubschmied, Ernst, *Über Praefixverben besonders im Berndeutschen: ein strukturlinguistischer Versuch*, diss., Winterthur, 1955.]
703. Hucko, Matthias, *Die Bildung der Substantiva durch Ableitung und Zusammensetzung im Altsächsischen*, diss., Strassburg, 1904. ¶ Suffixes and composition; substantivation.
[704. Hudler, Ingeborg, "Romanische Lehnwörter im Siebenbürgischen," diss., Innsbruck, 1964.]
705. Hulbert, J. P., "A Note on Compounds in *Beowulf*," *JEGP* 31 (1932) 504–508.
706. Hummelstedt, Eskil, "Nomina actionis i östsvenska dialekter, tre principer för bildande av saadana," *Svenska landsmaal och svenskt folkliv* 3. H., 219 fr. början (1936) 160–190. ¶ Verbal abstracts in *-as, -ase; -on; -in.*
707. ——, *Östsvenska verbstudier: morfologisk-semasiologisk undersökning*, Helsinki, 1939 (= *Folkmaalsstudier, Meddelanden fraan föreningen för nordisk filologi i Helsinfors* 6). ¶ Inchoative verbs in *-na* and verbs with suffix *k, l, r, s, t.*
708. Hungerland, Heinz, "Germ. *us-*," *NdKbl.* 36 (1917) 57–58.

709. Hunter, Edwin R., "Verb + Adverb=Nouns," *AmSp.* 22 (1947) 115–119.

710. Huth, Walter, *Die mit der gotischen Präposition "af" zusammenhängenden Adverbia und Präpositionen,* diss., Halle, 1903. ¶ *afta, aftana, afar, aftra.*

711. Hutson, Arthur E., "Gaelic Loan-Words in American," *AmSp.* 22 (1947) 18–23.

[712. Iarovici, Edith, "Conversiunea în engleza medie," *Revista de Filologie Romanică și Germanică* (Bucharest) 7 (1963) 305–314. ¶ Concerned with functional shift.]

713. Ideforss, Hjalmar, *De primära interjektionerna i nysvenskan,* Lund, 1928.

714. ——, "De primära lockorden i svenskan," *Arkiv* 47 (1931) 1–50. ¶ Formation of interjections.

715. Ivaškevič, L. V., "Složnye prilagatel'nye nemeckogo jazyka tipa *grauäugig, langlebig,*" *Učenye zapiski Leningradskogo ordena Lenina gosudarstvennogo Universitet im. A. A. Ždanova* 223 (1958) 139–151. ¶ Compound adjectives of the type *grauäugig,* etc.

716. Jaberg, Karl, "Spiel und Scherz in der Sprache," in *Festgabe für Samuel Singer,* Bern, 1930, 67–81. ¶ Compounds with doubling of syllables.

717. Jacob, Karl, "Wilhelminisch, nicht Wilhelmisch," *Historische Zt.* 162 (1940) 556–558.

718. Jacobi, F., "Schwäbische und schwäbisch-neuhochdeutsche Lehnwörter mit lateinischer und lateinisch-romanischer Grundlage," *Alemannia* 24 (1897) 252–261.

719. Jacobi, Hermann, *Kompositum und Nebensatz: Studien über die indogermanische Sprachentwicklung,* Bonn, 1897. ¶ Devoted in part to Gmc.; many non-IE items.

720. Jacobi, Theodor, *Untersuchungen über die Bildung der Nomina in den germanischen Sprachen,* 1. Heft, Breslau, 1848. ¶ *-a, -i, -ma, -þma, -na, -ana, -ina, -una, -la, -ila, -ala, -ula, -ra, -ara, -ura, -dara.*

721. Jäp, G., "Warum wendet sich die englische Sprache beim Entlehnen und Zusammensetzen neuer Worte vorzüglich an die klassischen Sprachen des Alterthums, statt den Wortschatz und die Plasticität des deutschen Sprachelementes in Anspruch zu nehmen?" *Herrigs Archiv* 9 (1851) 1–21. ¶ General.

722. Jaeschke, E., *Lateinisch-romanisches Fremdwörterbuch der schlesischen Mundart,* Breslau, 1908 (=*Wort and Brauch* 2).

723. Jaeschke, Kurt, *Beiträge zur Frage des Wortschwundes im Englischen,* Breslau, 1931.

724. Jakob, K. R., "Die Bildung des Eigenschaftswortes in der rheinfränkischen Mundart von Vergász," *Teuthonista* 3 (1926–1927) 172 ff. ¶ 1. simple "Adjektivierung"; 2. adj. in OHG, MHG *-în*; 3. adj. in *-iX,* OHG *-ag, -íg*; 4. adj. in *-liX*; 5. adj. suffix *-erig*; 6. adj. in *(ə)rliX*; 7. *-iš*; 8. *-sam, -haft, -bar, -fach.*

725. ——, "Die Bildung des Hauptwortes in der rheinfränkischen Mundart von Vergász," *Teuthonista* 3 (1926–1927) 11 ff. ¶ *-iŋ, -heit, -kheit, -tūm, -nis, -šaft, -t*; suffixless abstracts; verbal abstracts; *-ərei*; collective abstracts; *-əs*; substantivation; collectives; diminutives.

726. Jakob, Th[eodor], *Das Präfix* er- *in der transitiven mittel- und neuhochdeutschen Verbalkomposition*, Döbeln, 1900 (= *Wissenschaftliche Beilage zum 31. Jahresberichte des Königl. Realgymnasiums und der Höheren Landwirtschaftsschule zu Döbeln*, 1900).

727. Jakobsen, Alfred, "*Blaa-* og *rød-* som forsterkende forstavelser," *Maal og Minne* (1958 [1959]) 33–41. ¶ Reinforcing prefixes in the Scandinavian languages.

728. Jeitteles, Adalbert, *Neuhochdeutsche Wortbildung*, Troppau, 1858 (= *Programm der Kaiserlich-Königlichen Oberrealschule*).

729. ——, *Neuhochdeutsche Wortbildung*, Wien, 1865.

730. ——, "Über mit der Partikel 'miss' zusammengesetzte Zeitwörter," *ZfddtU* 13 (1899) 205–207.

731. Jellinek, M. H., *Geschichte der neuhochdeutschen Grammatik*, II, Heidelberg, 1914.

732. ——, "Das Suffix *-io-*," *PBB* 15 (1891), 287 ff. and *PBB* 16 (1892) 318 ff.

733. Jellinghaus, H., "*-dey*," *NdKbl.* 24 (1903) 12.

734. ——, "*-ing* in Westfalen," *NdKbl.* 32 (1911) 34–35.

735. Jensen, John, *Die 1. und 2. Ablautsreihe in der altenglischen Wortbildung*, diss., Kiel, 1913.

736. Jensen, P., "Wörter auf *-els*," *NdKbl.* 53 (1940) 12.

737. Jespersen, Otto, "The Ending '-ster,' " *MLR* 22 (1927) 129–136.

738. ——, "A Few Back-Formations," *Engl.Stud.* 70 (1935) 117–122.

739. ——, *Growth and Structure of the English Language*, 8th ed., Leipzig, 1935. [Arthur Langfors, *Neuphil.Mitt.* 36 (1936) 130–131; 1st ed., U. Lindelöf, *Neuphil.Mitt.* 8 (1906) 27–32.] ¶ See esp. chap. 7, pp. 154–179.

740. ——, "The History of a Suffix," *Acta Linguistica* 1 (1939) 48–56. ¶ Suffix *-en* to make verbs from adjectives, e.g., *sharpen*.

741. ——, "Monosyllabism in English," *Proc.Brit.Acad.* 14 (1928) 341–368. ¶ Development of Eng.

742. ——, *A Modern English Grammar on Historical Principles: Part VI Morphology*, Copenhagen, 1942. ¶ Predominantly wf.

743. ——, "Nature and Art in Language," *AmSp.* 5 (1929–1930) 89–103. ¶ Suffix, prefix blending, initials, etc.

744. ——, "Nogle *men*-ord," in *Studier tillägnade Esaias Tegnér*, Lund, 1918, 49 ff. ¶ Use of forms of *m* as a prefix with adversative value.

745. ——, "Om subtraktionsdannelser," in *Festskrift til Vilhelm Thomsen fra Disciple*, København, 1894, 1–30. ¶ Clipping and subtraction.

746. ——, *On the Development of English Verbs from Latin and French Past Participles*, Helsinki, 1934 (= *Societas Scientiarum Fennica, Commentationes Humanarum Litterarum* 6).

747. ——, "Origin of Grammatical Elements," in *Language*, London, 1922, 367–395.

748. ——, "A Supposed Feminine Ending," in *Linguistica: Selected Papers in English, French and German*, Copenhagen, 1933, 420–429. ¶ The suffix -*ster*.

749. ——, "Symbolic Value of the Vowel I," in *Linguistica: Selected Papers in English, French and German*, Copenhagen, 1933, 282–303. ¶ Sec. 5: diminutive suffixes, pp. 294–299.

750. ——, *Verb Doublets of Latin Origin in English*, Helsinki, 1936 (= *Societas Scientiarum Fennica, Commentationes Humanarum Litterarum* 8).

751. Jobst, Franz, "Über die Vorsilbe 'un,'" *Muttersprache* (1957) 408–412.

752. Jóhannesson, Alex., *Die Komposita im Isländischen*, Reykjavik, 1929. ¶ Nominal and verbal; compounds of uninflected words.

753. ——, *Die Suffixe im Isländischen*, Reykjavik, 1927.

[754. Johannisson, Ture, "Andöva: en studie i nordisk ordbildning och semantik," *Meijerbergs Arkiv för svensk ordforskning* 7 (1947) 117–149.]

755. ——, "Ett spraakets problembarn," *Svenska dagblade* 7/8 (1948). ¶ -*isk*, -*erisk*.

[756. ——, "Idrott: en studie över den germanska verbalpartikeln in- saasom ordbildningselement," *Meijerbergs Arkiv för svensk ordforskning* 5 (1943) 13–49.]

757. ——, "Isl. *orrusta* 'strid' och avledningarna paa -*usta*," *Göteborgs högskloas aarsskrift* 56 (1950) 179–198.

758. ——, "Om sammansätta verb i svenskan," *Nysvenska studier* 34 (1955) 162–181.

759. ——, "Tendenser i nutida svensk ordbildning," in *Nutidssvenska*, ed. Carl-Eric Thors, Stockholm, 1965, 7–22.

760. ——, "Über Rückbildung im heutigen Schwedisch," in *Erbe der Vergangenheit, Germanistische Beiträge: Festgabe für Karl Helm zum 80. Geburtstage 19. Mai 1951*, Tübingen, 1951, 257–263.

[761. ——, *Verbal och postverbal partikelkomposition i de germanska spruuken*, diss., Lindstedt, 1939. ¶ Ger. summary.]

762. ——, "Verbal och postverbal partikelkomposition i de germanska spraaken," *Neophilologus* 27 (1941–1942) 233 ff.

763. Johansson, Evald, *Die Deutschordenschronik des Nicolaus von Jeroschin: Eine sprachliche Untersuchung mit komparativer Analyse der Wortbildung. Ein Beitrag zur Erforschung der Ordenssprache und ihrer Rolle in der Entwicklung der nhd. Schriftsprache*, Lund and Copenhagen, 1964 (= *Lunder germ. Arbeiten* 36).

764. Johansson, K. F., "Nominalsammansättningar i Gotiskan," in *Nordiska Studier tillegnade Adolf Noreen paa hans 50-aarsdag den 13 mars 1904; af studiekamrater och lärjungar*, Uppsala, 1904, 455–485.

765. ——, "Über die idg. Verbindungen von *s(z)* + Guttural + *l, m, n* in den germanischen Sprachen," *PBB* 14 (1889) 289–368.

766. Johnson, Charles F., *English Words: An Elementary Study of Derivations*, New York, 1891.

767. Johnson, O. C., "Allusive Additions to the Vocabulary of English," *AmSp.* 4 (1928) 83 ff. ¶ Allusive derivation.

768. Johnson, W. G., "American Loanwords in American Swedish," in *Scandinavian Studies Presented to George T. Flom by Colleagues and Friends*, Urbana, Ill., 1942, 79–91 (= *Illinois Studies in Language and Literature 29*).

769. Jones, Daniel, "The Use of Syllabic and Non-Syllabic *l* and *n* in Derivatives of English Words Ending in Syllabic *l* and *n*," *Zt. für Phonetik und allgemeine Sprachwissenschaft* 12 (1959) 136–144.

770. Jones, Oscar F., "Icelandic Neologisms in *-ó*," *Word* 20 (1964) 18–27.

771. ——, "The Interrogative Particle *-u* in Germanic," *Word* 14 (1958) 213–223.

772. Jong, J. de Josselin de, "De verkleinwoorden in een noordbrabantsch dialect (Oirschot en omstreken)," *Tijdschrift* 21 (1902) 124 ff.

773. Jónsson, Finnur, *Det norsk-islandske skjaldesprog omtr. 800–1300*, Copenhagen, 1901. ¶ Listing of items according to Gmc. stems, classes, etc.; only occasional mention of wf, e.g., p. 14, nouns in *-angr, -ingr, -ungr*.

774. Jordan, Richard, *Die altenglischen Säugetiernamen*, diss., Heidelberg, 1902 (= *Anglistische Forschungen* 12 [1903]).

775. ——, *Eigentümlichkeiten des englischen Wortschatzes*, Heidelberg, 1906 (= *Anglistische Forschungen* 17). ¶ Chap. 3: Zur nominalen Stammbildung: *-nis, -ig, -welle, -ern, s-*stems, etc.

776. Jud, J., "Mots allemands d'origine romane," *Romania* 42 (1913) 581 ff.

777. Jungandreas, W., *Schlesische Zeitwortbildung: ein Beitrag zum schlesischen Wörterbuch*, Liegnitz, 1923.

778. Justi, Ferdinand, *Über die Zusammensetzung der nomina in den indogermanischen Sprachen*, Göttingen, 1861.

779. ——, *Die Zusammensetzung der Nomina in den indogermanischen Sprachen zunächst in Hinsicht ihrer Form*, diss., Marburg, 1861.

780. Juul-Hensen, H., "Om den lexikalske udnyttelse af efterleddet i sammensætninger," in *Studier tilegnede Verner Dahlerup paa Femog halvfjerdsaarsdagen d. 31. Oktober, 1934*, Aarhus, 1934, 8–24. ¶ Treats lexical "Ausnützung" of the second member in compounds.

781. Kärre, Karl, *Nomina agentis in Old English, Part I*, diss., Uppsala, 1915

(= *Uppsala universitets aarsskrift* 1). ¶ Suffixes -*l*- and -*end* as agent-forming elements with consideration of productivity.

782. Kaestner, W., "Die deutschen Lehnwörter des Polnischen," *NdKbl.* 50 (1937) 18 ff. ¶ Lecture.

783. ——, "Hauptwörter auf -*els*," *NdKbl.* 51 (1938) 34.

784. Kammradt, F., "Über die Bildung von Eigenschaftswörtern aus Orts- und Ländernamen," *Muttersprache* (1955) 270–273.

785. Karg-Gasterstädt, E., "Aus der Werkstatt des althochdeutschen Wör- terbuchs: ahd. *bilidi*," *PBB* 66 (1942) 291–308; "ahd. *thiu* und *thiorna*," 308–326.

786. Karsten, T. E., "Beiträge zur Geschichte der ē-Verba im Altgerma- nischen," *Mémoires de la Société Néophilologique* 2 (1897) 169–273.

787. ——, *Studier öfver de nordiska spraakens primära nominalbildning*, 2 vols., Helsinki, 1895 and 1900.

788. Karstien, C., "Nhd. Steinmetz, Metzger, got. mats," in *Beiträge zur germanischen Sprachwissenschaft: Festschrift für Otto Behaghel*, ed. Wil- helm Horn, Heidelberg, 1924, 289–323.

789. ——, *Die reduplizierten Perfekta des Nord- und Westgermanischen*, Gie- ßen, 1921 (= *Giessener Beiträge* 1).

[790. Kassel, [no initial], "Die Deminution der hanauischen Mundart," *Jahresbericht für Geschichte, Sprache und Litteratur Elsass-Lothringens* 15 (1899) 205–222.]

791. Kassel, A., *Die Diminutiva in der Hanauischen Mundart*, diss., Strassburg, 1899.

792. Kassewitz, Joseph, *Die französischen Wörter im Mittelhochdeutschen*, diss., Strassburg, 1890. [Albert Leitzmann, *ZffrzSpruLit.* 13 (1891) 211– 214; Theodor Maxeiner, *AfdA* 37 (1893) 44–52.]

793. Katara, Pekka, "Das Diminutivum bei Johannes Veghe," *AASF* B 84 (1954) 599–627.

794. ——, "Das Französische Lehngut in den mittelhochdeutschen Denk- mälern des 13. Jahrhunderts," *AASF* B (1942) 525 ff.

795. ——, *Die ursprünglich reduplizierenden Verba im Niederdeutschen*, Hel- sinki, 1939 (= *Mémoires de la Société Néophilologique* 27).

796. Kat Pzn. P., "Het voorzetsel," *Noord en zuid* 18 (1895) 65–70. ¶ Trans- fer of preposition to conjunction.

797. Kauffmann, F., *Geschichte der schwäbischen Mundart*, Strassburg, 1890.

798. ——, "Die innere Stammform der Adjectiva auf -*ko* im Germa- nischen," *PBB* 12 (1887) 201–210. ¶ -*agr*, -*ugr*.

799. Kaufmann, E., "Der Fragenkreis ums Fremdwort," *JEGP* 38 (1939) 42–63.

800. Kehrein, Joseph, *Grammatik der deutschen Sprache des 15. bis 17. Jahr- hunderts*, Vol. I, Part 2 *Wortbildungslehre*, 2nd ed., Leipzig, 1863.

801. Keiper, Philipp, "Imperativische Namen," *ZfddtU* 16 (1902) 149–171, 292–316, (Nachtrag) 478–492.
802. ——, "Nadlerstudien: 2. *Daawrian*," *ZfhdMaa.* 4 (1903) 220–235. ¶ Words in *-ian* (*-jan, -jann*).
803. ——, and Zink, Theodor, "Pfälzer Appellativnamen," *ZfdMaa.* (1910) 126–139.
804. Kelle, Johann, "Das Verbum und Nomen in Notkers Aristoteles," *ZfdPh.* 18 (1886) 342–369. ¶ Some discussion of wf in connection with "Flexion."
805. ——, "Das Verbum und Nomen in Notkers Boethius," *Sitzungsberichte der philosophisch-historischen Classe der Kaiserlichen Akademie der Wissenschaften Wien* 109 (1885) 229 ff. ¶ Some discussion of wf in connection with "Flexion."
806. ——, "Das Verbum und Nomen in Notkers De Syllogismis, De Partibus Logicae, De Rhetorica Arte, De Musica," *ZfdPh.* 20 (1888) 129–150. ¶ Some discussion of wf in connection with "Flexion."
807. ——, "Das Verbum und Nomen in Notkers Martianus Capella," *ZfdA* 30 (1886) 295–345. ¶ Some discussion of wf in connection with "Flexion."
808. Keller, May L., *The Anglo-Saxon Weapon Names*, Heidelberg, 1906 (= *Anglistische Forschungen* 15).
809. Kellner, Leon, "Englische Wortforschung," *GRM* 2 (1910) 27–35.
810. ——, "Das Suffix *-er* in passiver Bedeutung?" *Bausteine* 1 (1906) 327.
811. ——, "Die Wortkategorien im Englischen," *Bausteine* 1 (1906) 432–435. ¶ Transfer of words from one class to another, nouns as verbs, etc.
812. Kempen, W., *Die verkleinwoord in Afrikaans*, Kaapstad, 1940.
813. ——, *Woordvorming en funksiewisseling in Afrikaans*, Capetown, 1962. ¶ Wf and function change.
814. Kennedy, A. G., "Hyphenation of Compound Nouns," *Words* 4 (1938) 36–38. ¶ Deals with the question of when two words make a compound noun.
815. ——, *The Modern English Verb-Adverb Combination*, Stanford, Calif., 1920 (= *Stanford University Publications, University Series, Language and Literature* 1, 1).
816. ——, *On the Substantivation of Adjectives in Chaucer*, Lincoln, Neb., 1905 (= *The University Studies of the University of Nebraska* 5).
817. Keppler, Kurt, "Misleading German Compound Nouns," *GQ* 31 (1958) 287–297.
818. Kern, [no initial], "Eigennamen en Verkleinwoordjes," *Taal- en Letterbode* 2 (1871) 100 ff.
819. ——, "Verkleinwoorden op *-sa, -sia*," *Taal- en Letterbode* 5 (1874) 18 ff.

820. Kern, H., "huls, hulst," *Tijdschrift* 20 (1901) 37–43. ¶ Suffix *-el.*

821. Kern, J. H., "Zu einigen niederländischen Feminin-Suffixen," *PBB* 56 (1932), 361 ff. ¶ *-nede, -ster, -inne.*

822. Key, T. Hewitt, "On Diminutives: I. English," *Trans.Phil.Soc.* 9 (1856) 219–250.

823. ——, "On the German Prefix 'Ver' and Allied Forms," *Trans.Phil.Soc.* 19 (1867) 93–105.

824. ——, "Reconsideration of Substantives in *-let*," *Trans.Phil.Soc.* (1862–1863) 220–231.

825. ——, "Words Formed in Imitation of the South *kar*, as Heard in *scratching*," *Trans.Phil.Soc.* 19 (1867) 375–399.

826. Kieckers, E., *Handbuch der vergleichenden gotischen Grammatik*, Munich, 1928.

827. Kiefer, H., "Badener, doch Wiesbader," *Muttersprache* 54 (1939) 333–336.

828. Kilian, Dietlinde, "Homemade Words," *Die Neueren Sprachen* N.F. 8 (1959) 375–377. ¶ Blends, also involving suffixes, compounding.

[829. Kilian, Friedhelm, "Shakespeares Nominalkomposita, ein Beitrag zur Erforschung seiner Neuprägungen," diss., Münster, 1953.]

830. King, Arthur G., " 'Jeep' and 'peep,' 'pipable' and 'jeepable,' " *AmSp.* 37 (1962) 77–78.

831. Kip, Herbert Z., "Zur Geschichte der Steigerungsadverbien in der deutschen geistlichen Dichtung des 11. und 12. Jahrhunderts," *JEGP* 3 (1901) 143–237. ¶ *al-, aller-*, etc.

[832. Kirchhofer, Th., *Über die deutsche Partikel ge-*, Reval, 1875 (= *Revaler Gymnasialprogramm von 1875*).]

833. Kirchner, Gustav, "Amerikanisches in Wortschatz, Wortbildung und Syntax von Herman Melvilles 'Moby Dick,' " in Ferdinand Mossé, *Mélanges de linguistique et de philologie*, Paris, 1959, 208–217. ¶ *be-, -ment, -ness.*

834. ——, "Attributive Verwendung der mit Präfix '*a-*' gebildeten Adjektiva des Englischen 'An Unexpected Usage'?" *Die Neueren Sprachen* N.F. 11 (1962) 168–173.

835. ——, *Gradadverbien, Restriktiva und Verwandtes im heutigen Englisch*, Halle, 1955. ¶ Derivation and compounding.

836. ——, "Past Participles Prefixed by '*un-*,' " *English Studies* 32 (1951) 218–219.

837. ——, "Der Reimklang im Englischen," *Zt. für Angl. und Am.* 4 (1956) 389–447 and (Nachtrag) 7 (1959) 281–287. ¶ A. Reimwendungen, B. Reimkomposita.

838. ——, "Silbenverdoppelung ohne Vokaländerung," *Anglia* 65 (1941) 328–340. ¶ Reduplication.

[839. Kishimoto, Michio, "Remarque sur l'élément suffixal *-nt-* de l'indo-européen," *Kōbegai daironsō* 9 (1959) 123–134.]

840. Kissling, Gustav, "Lautmalende Wurzeln der indogermanischen Sprache," in *Festschrift der 45. Versammlung deutscher Philologen und Schulmänner*, Bremen, 1899, 291–357. ¶ IE roots, onomatopoetic wf, ablaut.

841. Kjelds, N. T., "Suffixal Word Derivation in New Danish," diss., Philadelphia, 1954.

842. Kjellman, Nils, *Die Verbalzusammensetzungen mit "durch,"* Lund, 1945.

843. Klapperich, J., "Die Steigerung des Adjektivs im Neuenglischen," *Engl.Stud.* 17 (1892) 225–229. ¶ Examples of formations "contrary to the rules," *beautifullest,* etc.

844. Klatt, I., *Das s- (z-) Suffix als Bildungssuffix*, Berlin, 1938 (= *Germanische Studien* 204).

845. Klein, Erich, *Die verdunkelten Wortzusammensetzungen im Neuenglischen*, diss., Königsberg, 1911.

846. Kleinpaul, R., *Das Fremdwort im Deutschen*, Leipzig, 1900. ¶ Chatty style, many etymologies, indirectly related to wf.

847. Kloeke, G. G., "Die Entstehung der niederländischen Diminutiven-dung *-tje*," *ZfdMaa.* (1923) 217–231.

848. ——, "Ostniederländische Diminutiva," *NdJb.* 55 (1929) 1–24.

849. Kluge, Friedrich, *Abriss der deutschen Wortbildungslehre*, 2nd ed., Halle, 1925. ¶ General.

850. ——, "Badener oder Badenser?" *ZfdW* 1 (1901) 60–63.

851. ——, *Deutsche Studentensprache*, Strassburg, 1895. ¶ Many topics; p. 35, for example, discusses the origin of the *s*-suffix.

852. ——, "Deutsche Suffixstudien," in *Festschrift zur 50-jährigen Doktor-jubelfeier Karl Weinholds am 14. January 1896*, Strassburg, 1896, 21–26. ¶ Gefässnamen in *-ín*; verbs in *-enzen*; bird names in *-itz*; diminutives in *-inklín*; *-er*.

853. ——, *Etymologisches Wörterbuch der deutschen Sprache*, 19th ed., W. Mitzka, Berlin, 1963. ¶ Individual articles.

854. ——, "Kater und Verwandtes," *PBB* 14 (1889) 585–587.

855. ——, "Nachlese zum Etymologischen Wörterbuch," *Neuphil.Mitt.* 24 (1923) 98–103.

856. ——, *Nominale Stammbildungslehre der altgermanischen Dialekte*, 3rd ed., L. Sütterlin and E. Ochs, Halle, 1926. [E. Schröder, *AfdA* 46 (1927) 70 ff.; Hugo Suolahti, *Neuphil.Mitt.* 28 (1927) 107.]

857. ——, "Seemannssprache," *ZfdW* 8 (1906–1907) 39–48. ¶ Some compounds.

858. ——, "Sprachhistorische Miscellen: 11. Urgermanische Lehnworte," *PBB* 10 (1885) 439.

859. ——, "Verbalpartikalen in der Zusammensetzung," *ZfvglSpr.* 26 (1883) 328.

860. ——, "Völkernamen als erste Glieder von Personennamen," *ZfdW* 8 (1906–1907) 141–142.

861. ——, *Vorgeschichte der altgermanischen Dialekte: Nominale Wortbildung*, 3rd ed., Strassburg, 1913 (= Hermann Paul, *Grundriss der germanischen Philologie*, Vol. II, chap. 9, 220–261). ¶ General.

862. ——, *Wortforschung und Wortgeschichte*, Leipzig, 1912. ¶ Essays on specific words with passing comments on compounding and derivation.

863. ——, "Der Worttypus *faulenzen*," *ZfdW* 6 (1904–1905) 40–46.

864. ——, "Zur Geschichte des Reimes im Altgermanischen," *PBB* 9 (1884) 422–450. ¶ "Reimformeln."

865. Klump, Wilhelm, *Die altenglischen Handwerkernamen sachlich und sprachlich erläutert*, Heidelberg, 1908 (= *Anglistische Forschungen* 24). ¶ Compounds.

866. Kluyver, A., "Tolpatsch," *PBB* 30 (1905) 211 f.

867. ——, "Trabant," *ZfdW* 4 (1903) 153 f.

868. Knapp, Arthur John, *Roots and Ramifications; or, Extracts from Various Books explanatory of the Derivation or Meaning of Divers Words*, London, 1857. ¶ Esp. chaps. 2, 3, and 8.

869. Koban, Charles, "Substantive Compounds in *Beowulf*," *DA* 24 (1965) 4175–4176.

870. Koch, C. Friedrich, *Historische Grammatik der englischen Sprache*, Vol. III *Wortbildung*, 2nd ed., R. Wülkur, Cassel, 1891. ¶ Verbal and nominal formations, compounding, onomatopoeia, foreign elements.

871. ——, *Linguistische Allotria: Laut-, Ablaut- und Reimbildungen der englischen Sprache*, ed. Eugen Wilhelm, 2nd ed., Eisenach, 1880.

872. ——, "Die vocalischen Ableitungen im Angelsächsischen und deren Verlauf: ein Beitrag zur englischen Wortbildungslehre," *Jahrbuch für romanische und englische Sprache und Literatur* 8 (1867) 217–227. ¶ Gmc. *-a, -i, -u, -ja*.

873. Koch, Edmund, "Die Wortbildungen aus der lebenden Rede in einer württembergischen Kleinstadt," diss., München, 1949. ¶ Sec. C.9, wf in nouns: without formant, prefixes, suffixes, compounding, miscellaneous; C.10, verbs: suffixes, prefixes, suffix *-ə*, compounds, miscellaneous; C.11, adjectives: without formant, prefixes, suffixes, compounding, miscellaneous; C.12, adverbs, pronouns, prepositions, conjunctions, interjections, sandhi.

874. Kock, Axel, "Altnordische Adjektive mit der Ableitungssilbe *-ug-*," excursus in *Altnordischer u-Umlaut in Ableitungs- und Beugungsendungen*, Lund, 1918, 26–30 (= *Lunds Universitets Aarsskrift* 14, 2, No. 28).

875. ——, "Ett par ordbildningsspörmal i fornnordisk sprak," *Arkiv* N.F. 21 (1905) 97–124. ¶ *-ligr, -la.*

876. ——, *Till fraagan om den östnordisk aveldningsändelsen* -else, Lund, 1902 (= *Filologiska föreningen i Lund, spraakliga uppsatser* 2).

877. Kögel, R., "Über einige germanische Dentalverbindungen," *PBB* 7 (1880) 171 ff.

878. Koekkoek, Byron J., "The English Loanword *Manager* in Present-day German," *GQ* 30 (1957) 162–166. ¶ Loanword and compounds.

879. ——, "Some German Trade Names with *-mat* and *-matic,*" *AmSp.* 34 (1959) 237–238.

880. Köhler, J. J., *Die altenglischen Fischnamen*, Heidelberg, 1906 (= *Anglistische Forschungen* 21).

881. Koenig, Karl F., "German Loan Words in America, 1930–1940," *GQ* 15 (1942) 163 ff.

882. Koeppel, Emil, "Analogiewirkungen zwischen wurzelverwandten Zeit-, Haupt- und Beiwörtern der englischen Sprache," *Herrigs Archiv* 106 (1901) 28–47. ¶ Compounding.

883. ——, "Tautological Compounds of the English Language," in *An English Miscellany Presented to Dr. Furnivall in Honour of his Seventy-fifth Birthday*, Oxford, 1901, 201–204.

884. ——, "Zur englischen Wortbildungslehre," *Herrigs Archiv* 104 (1900) 24 ff. and 279 ff. ¶ "Englische Neubildungen des Nominativs von den flektierten Formen aus."

885. Körting, G., "Die Entwickelung des Suffixes *-arius* im Französischen," *ZffrSpruLit.* 17 (1895) 188 ff. ¶ Related material; pertinent bibliography throughout.

886. Koning, Wilhelm, "Substantivierte infinite Verbformen mit verbaler Rektion," *Die Neueren Sprachen* 41 (1933) 90–98.

887. Koo, Zung-Fung Wei, "Old English Living Noun-Suffixes Exclusive of Personal and Place-Names," diss., Cambridge, Mass. (Radcliffe), 1946.

888. Kooiman, K., "Nogmaals het suffix *-heid,*" *Die Nieuwe Taalgids* 49 (1956) 112–113. ¶ Refers to Kostelijk, below.

889. ——, "Opmerkingen over de *h* en uitweidingen over het suffix *-heid,*" *Taal en Tongval* 8 (1956) 150–161.

890. Kopperstad, Knut, "Sammensetning og betoning i Sunmørs-maalet," *Maal og Minne* (1932) 29–98. ¶ Stress (accentuation) in compounds.

891. Koppmann, K., "Zur Assonanz im Niederdeutschen," *NdKbl.* 21 (1899–1900) 35–47.

892. Kostelijk, C., "Het suffix *-heid* in het Noordhollands," *De Nieuwe Taalgids* 48 (1955) 337–338 and 49 (1956) 198–199, 249.

[893. Kostomarov, V. G., "Zametiki po anglijskomo slovoobrazovaniju: suffiksy suščestvitel'nych *ee* i *ful,*" in *Problemy obščego i častnogo jazy-*

koznanija, Moscow, 1960, 117–140. ¶ Eng. noun suffixes *-ee* and *-ful*.]

894. Koziol, Herbert, "Blends," *Die Neueren Sprachen* N.F. 3 (1954) 25.

895. ——, "Förderung und Hemmung analoger Wortbildungen im Englischen," *Wiener Beiträge zur englischen Philologie* 62 (1955) 101–110 (= *Festschrift zum 70. Geburtstag von Professor Dr. Leo Hibler-Lebmannsport*). ¶ Deals with (mostly feminine) suffixes and competition between them: *-ese, -en, -ster, -trix, -ess*, etc.

896. ——, *Handbuch der englischen Wortbildungslehre*, Heidelberg, 1937.

897. ——, "Kontaminationen lautähnlicher Wörter und Verwandtes im Englischen," in *Mnemes charin: Gedenkschrift für Paul Kretschmer*, Wien, 1956, Vol. I, 181 ff.

898. ——, "Rhyming Slang," *Die Sprache* 2 (1950) 77–84.

899. ——, "Schalldeutungen und Schalldeutungswörter," *Orbis* 6 (1957) 185–191.

900. ——, "Shakespeare's Komposita in deutschen Übersetzungen," *Die Neueren Sprachen* N.F. 6 (1957) 457–463.

901. ——, "Die Silbenverdopplung im Englischen," *Engl.Stud.* 75 (1942) 67–73. ¶ Deals with stress of reduplicated compounds.

902. ——, "Untersuchung zur englischen Wortbildung," *Forschungen und Fortschritte* 33, 12 (1959) 378–380. ¶ Summarizes different types.

903. ——, "Zu Neubildungen und Lehnwörtern im amerikanischen Englisch," *Orbis* 10 (1961) 169–174. ¶ *Up-and-down; -age; -ee, -ette; -rama*; Wortmischung.

904. ——, "Zur Aufnahme von Wortneubildungen im Englischen," *Orbis* 4 (1955) 452–458. ¶ Prefix *de-*; suffix *-ee*.

905. ——, "Zur Wortbildung im amerikanischen Englisch," *Wiener Beiträge zur englischen Philologie* 66 (1958) 127–138. ¶ Words formed from word groups and sentences; suffixes, as in *do-nothingness, go-getter*; reduplication, *hubbub*, etc.

906. ——, "Zur Wortbildung im Englischen," *Anglia* 65 (1941) 51–63. ¶ Doublets.

907. Krackow, Otto, *Die Nominalcomposita als Kunstmittel im altenglischen Epos*, diss., Weimar, 1903.

908. Krahe, Hans, *Germanische Sprachwissenschaft*, Vol. II *Formenlehre*, Berlin, 1948.

909. ——, "Über einige Gewässernamen mit *st*-Suffix," *Beiträge zur Namenforschung* 10 (1959) 1–17.

910. ——, "Über *st*-Bildungen in den germanischen und indogermanischen Sprachen," *PBB* 71 (1949) 225–250. ¶ *henigst*, etc.

911. ——, "Zum westgerm. Abstraktsuffix *-unni̯ō-*," *IF* 50 (1932) 280–281.

912. Kramer, Günter, "Zur Abgrenzung von Zusammensetzung und Ablei-

tung: Ein Beitrag zur inhaltsbezogenen Wortbildungslehre," *PBB* (Halle) 84 (1962) 406–438.

913. Krapp, G. P., *The English Language in America*, 2 vols., New York, 1925. ¶ Wf: Vol. I, pp. 68–168.

914. Krause, K. E. H., "Imperativische Thier- und Pflanzennamen," *NdKbl.* 6 (1881) 18.

915. Krauss, Paul G., "The Increasing Use of English Words in German," *GQ* 31 (1958) 272–286.

916. Kremble, John M., "On a Peculiar Use of the Anglo-Saxon Patronymical Termination -*ing*," *Proc.Phil.Soc.* 4 (1848) 1–10.

917. Kremer, Julian, "Behandlung der ersten Compositionsglieder im germanischen Nominalcompositum," *PBB* 8 (1882) 371–460. ¶ Influence of stress.

918. Krenn, Ernst, *Föroyische Sprachlehre*, Heidelberg, 1940. ¶ Contains a section on wf.

919. Kretschmer, Paul, "Kontamination lautähnlicher Wörter," *Die Sprache* 2 (1951) 150–155.

[920. ——, "Die Wortschöpfer," in *Germanistische Forschungen (Festschrift anlässlich des 60semestrigen Stiftungsfestes des Wiener Akademischen Germanistenvereins)*, Wien, 1925, 227 ff.]

921. Kristensen, Marius, "De danske Folkemal III," *Danske Folkemaal* 4 (1930) 65–71. ¶ Expressions for milk, including compounds.

922. ——, *Fremmedordene i det ældste danske Skriftsprog*, diss., København, 1906. ¶ Mostly a compilation of loanwords from Lat., Eng., etc., but with remarks on derivation.

923. ——, "Modbemærkinger til Prof. Erik Arups Artikel 'Danmarks Historie,'" *Højskolebladet* No. 47 (1925). ¶ Compounds in -*bót*.

924. Kroesch, Samuel, "Change of Meaning by Analogy," in *Studies in Honor of Hermann Collitz*, Baltimore, 1930, 176–189. ¶ Note on Ger. compounds as translations from Lat.

925. ——, "The Form of Compound Words in Gothic," *Mod.Phil.* 5 (1907–1908) 377–382. ¶ Syllable quantity.

926. ——, "Semantic Borrowing in Old English," in *Studies in English Philology, A Miscellany in Honor of Frederick Klaeber*, Minneapolis, 1929, 50 ff.

927. Krogmann, Willy, "Hoch- und tiefstufige Doubletten in Zusammensetzungen," *PBB* 59 (1935) 313 ff.

928. ——, "Die Sippen germ. **lit-* und **leut-* 'klein,'" *IF* 53 (1935) 44–48. ¶ Words formed from these roots.

929. Krüger, Gustav, *Schwierigkeiten des Englischen, III Teil Syntax, nebst Beiträgen zur Stilistik, Wortkunde und Wortbildung*, Dresden and Leipzig, 1904. ¶ Noun wf: paras. 138–149, compounding and deriva-

tion; 2060–2063, negative prefixes, formations from Lat., French; 2064–2077, formations based on "Spieltrieb: Töne und Geräusche."

930. Kruisinga, Etsko, "Diminutieve en affektieve suffixen in de Germaanse talen," *Mededeelingen van der Nederlandse Akademie van Wetenschappen, Afdeling Letterkunde*, N.R. 5 (1942) 443–504.

931. ——, *A Handbook of Present-Day English*, Part II. *Accidence and Syntax*, 5th ed., Groningen, 1932. ¶ Derivation, pp. 36–71; composition, pp. 72–79; conversion, pp. 80–123; other methods of wf, pp. 124–131.

932. ——, "The Verbal *-ing* in Living English," *English Studies* 12 (1932) 24–31, 58–66.

933. ——, "Woordvorming door Abstrahering," *Taal en Leven* 5 (1942) 184–188. ¶ Term "Abstrahering" for process of back-formation; Eng. examples.

934. Ksoll, Anton, *Die französischen Lehn- und Fremdwörter in der englischen Sprache der Restaurationszeit*, Breslau, 1933.

935. Kühlewein, Wilhelm, "Präfixstudien zu Goethe," *ZfdW* 6 (1904–1905) 1–36.

936. Kühner, Gertrud, *Die Intensiv-Adverbien des Frühneuenglischen*, diss., Heidelberg, 1934.

937. Künzel, Georg, *Das zusammengesetzte Substantiv und Adjektiv in der englischen Sprache*, diss., Borna-Leipzig, 1910.

938. Kuhn, Hans, *Das Füllwort of—um im Altwestnordischen: eine Untersuchung zur Geschichte der germanischen Präfixe; ein Beitrag zur altgermanischen Metrik*, Göttingen, 1929 (= *Ergänzungsheft zur ZfvglSpr.* 8).

939. ——, "Stamm- und Genitivzusammensetzung in den germanischen Ortsnamen," *Beiträge zur Namenforschung* 4 (1953) 159–175.

940. ——, *Verbale l- und r-Bildungen im Schweizerdeutschen*, Frauenfeld, 1961 (= *Beitr.z.Schweizerd. Grammatik* 11).

941. Kuntze, F., "Das *verbum substantivum* im Germanischen," *ZfddtU* 10 (1896) 314–331.

942. Kuntzemüller, Albert, *Zur Geschichte des substantivierten Infinitivs im Neuhochdeutschen*, diss., Strassburg, 1902; also *ZfdW* 4 (1903) 58–94.

943. Kurth, Richard, "Bildung und Gebrauch der Wörter auf *-ung*," *PBB* (Halle) 78 (1956) 307–316.

944. ——, "Das Fragen, das Gefrage, die Fragerei, die Befragung," *Muttersprache* (1957) 188–192. ¶ Wf.

945. ——, "Über den Gebrauch der Bildungen auf *-ei*, *-erei* und *-elei*," *PBB* 75 (1953) 442–451.

946. ——, "Zum Gebrauch der sogenannten *ge*-Abstrakta," *PBB* 75 (1953) 314 ff.

[947. Laaftman, E., *Studier i ordbildning: en keps: hur vi benämna engelska ting*,

Boraas, 1940 (= *Redogörelse f. högre allmänna läroverket i Boraas 1939–40, Bilaga*).]

948. Laan, K. ter, "Groninger woorden met *-el-*," *Driemaandelijkse Bladen* 14 (1962) 64.

949. Lachmann, Karl, "Alliteration," *Kleinere Schriften zur deutschen Philologie*, ed. Karl Müllenhoff, Berlin, 1876, 137–139. ¶ Encyclopedia-type article, dealing with Reimformeln.

950. Lagman, Edvin, "Om nominala samansättningar i fornsvenskan och i nutida svenska dialekter," *Arkiv* 79 (1964) 172–194.

951. Landau, A., "Das Deminutivum der galizisch-jüdischen Mundart," *Deutsche Mundarten* 1 (1895) 46–58. ¶ *-l, -dl, -ali*, etc.; wealth of material.

952. Lange, W., "Zahlen und Zahlenkompositionen in der Edda," *PBB* 77 (1955) 306 ff.

953. Langenfelt, Gösta, "Hurly-Burly, Hallaloo, Hullabaloo," *Neuphil.Mitt.* 51 (1950) 1–18.

954. ——, "The Hypocoristic English Suffix *-s*," *SN* 14 (1939–1942) 197–213.

955. ——, *Select Studies in Colloquial English of the Late Middle-Ages*, Lund, 1933. ¶ Esp. pp. 70 ff.

956. ——, "*y* in Billy, etc.," *Studier i modern Spraakvetenskap* 15 (1943) 67–92.

957. Langenhove, George C. van, *On the Origin of the Gerund in English*, Ghent, Paris, 1925 (= *Recueil de Travaux Publiés par la Faculté de Philosophie et Lettres de l'Université de Gand* [Ghent], 56th fascicle).

958. Larsson, Carl, "Naagra kontruktioner i svenskt skriftspraak," *Modersmaalslärarnas förenings aarsskrift* (1936) 59–86. ¶ Verbal substantives, *-ande (-ende)*.

959. Larsson, Ludvig, "Folk Fölbitare," *Svenska Dagbladet* 14 (April 1928). ¶ *-er* formation from *bita*.

960. Lasch, A., "Zu den Nomina agentis auf *-ster*," *NdKbl.* 39 (1924) 19 f.

961. ——, "Zur Deminutivbildung in der mecklenburgisch-vorpommerschen Mundart," *NdJb.* 38 (1912) 81 ff., 104 ff.

962. Last, W., *Das Bahuvrîhi-Compositum im Altenglischen, Mittelenglischen, und Neuenglischen*, diss., Greifswald, 1925.

963. Latendorf, Friedrich, "Collectivische und generalisierende Zusammensetzungen mit wark, warks," *NdKbl.* 4 (1879) 5–7.

964. ——, "Die Deminutiva der niederdeutschen Ausgabe von Agricola's Sprichwörtern," *NdJb.* 3 (1877) 101–103.

965. ——, "*-else*," *NdKbl.* 5 (1880) 4.

966. ——, "Das füllende *-el* in Kindelbier und ähnlichen Wortbildungen," *NdKbl.* 16 (1892) 70.

967. Laur, W., "Die germanischen Frauennamen auf -*gard*/*gerðr* und ihr Ursprung aus dem Bereich des Kultischen," *PBB* 78 (1951) 321 ff.

968. Lawson, Richard H., "The Prefix *gi*- as a Perfectivizing Future Significant in OHG *Tatian*," *JEGP* 64 (1965) 90–97.

969. Lee, Donald Woodward, *Function Change in Early English*, diss., Menasha, Wis., 1948. ¶ Essentially foreign borrowings in different centuries, with lists, comments on derivation, etc.

970. Leeb-Lundberg, W., *Word-formation in Kipling: A Stylistic-Philological Study*, diss., Lund, 1909. ¶ Pp. 49–106, compounding, derivation, blendings, etc., of nouns, adjectives, verbs, and adverbs.

971. Lees, Robert B., *The Grammar of English Nominalizations*, Bloomington, Ind., 1960.

972. Legner, Wolfram K., "The Compound Nouns in the Works of Andreas Gryphius," *JEGP* 44 (1945) 36–55. ¶ Lists, classified by types of components.

973. Lehmann, August, *Forschungen über Lessings Sprache*, Braunschweig, 1875. ¶ Sections in Part V deal with adjectives in -*weise*, nouns in -*er*, -*ung*, -*in*, -*e*, etc., and adjectives in -*lich*, *un*-, *miß*-.

974. Lehmann, Wilhelm, *Das Präfix uz- besonders im Altenglischen mit einem Anhang über das präfigierte westgerm. *ō- (*ā-): ein Beitrag zur germanischen Wortbildungslehre*, Kiel, 1906 (= *Kieler Studien zur englischen Philologie*, N.F. 3). ¶ Nominal composition, pp. 1–57; verbal composition, pp. 58–150.

975. Leidig, Paul, *Französische Lehnwörter und Lehnbedeutungen im Englischen des 18. Jahrhunderts: Ein Spiegelbild französischer Kultureinwirkung*, Bochum-Langendreer, 1941 (= *Beiträge zur englischen Philologie* 37). [W. Horn, *Herrigs Archiv* 185 (1948) 150; G. Rohlfs, *Herrigs Archiv* 184 (1944) 67.]

976. Leinen, Rudolf, *Über Wesen und Entstehung der trennbaren Zusammensetzung des deutschen Zeitwortes*, diss., Strassburg, 1891. ¶ Emphasis on Go. and OHG.

977. Leisi, E., *Das heutige Englisch*, 2nd ed., Heidelberg, 1960. ¶ Part III: Wortform und -bedeutung (16. substantival wf; 17. conversion).

978. Leithaeuser, Julius, *Bergische Ortsnamen*, Elberfeld, 1901. ¶ Not directly applicable; deals with the components of place names, e.g., the meanings of the components and examples of compounding; three categories: das Gelände, das Gewässer, and die Gewächse.

979. ——, *Gallicismen in niederrheinischen Mundarten*, Barmen, 1894 (= *Programm des Realgymnasiums zu Barmen*).

980. ——, "Rheinische Ortsnamen auf -*ich*, -*ig*, -*ick*," *ZfhdMaa.* 5 (1904) 367–369.

981. Lekebusch, Julius, *Die Londoner Urkundensprache von 1430–1500: ein Bei-*

trag zur Entstehung der neuenglischen Schriftsprache, diss., Halle, 1906. ¶ Part II: vowel quality in unstressed word and sentence position, prefixes, pp. 83–84, suffixes (Ger. and French), pp. 85–87.

982. Lenz, Philipp, "Auslautendes *-ig, -ich* und verwandte Wortausgänge im Deutschen," *ZfhdMaa.* 4 (1903) 195 ff. ¶ Thirty-five sources discussed.

983. ——, *Der syntactische Gebrauch der Partikel* ge- *in den Werken Alfred des Großen*, Darmstadt, 1886.

984. ——, "Zur Statistik der Fremdwörter im Deutschen," *ZfhdMaa.* 1 (1900) 136–138.

985. Lenze, Josef, *Das Praefix* bi- *in der ae. Nominal- und Verbalkomposition mit gelegentlicher Berücksichtigung der anderen germanischen Dialekte*, diss., Kiel, 1909.

986. Leo, H., "Die Intensiven der deutschen Sprache," *ZfdPh.* 2 (1870) 167–172. ¶ List of 28 items plus comments.

987. Leopold, Max, *Die Entwicklung des Präfixes* ver- *im Germanischen*, diss., Breslau, 1905 (also = *Germanistische Abhandlungen* 27 [1907]).

[988. ——, *Zur Behandlung des Artikels* ver- *im Deutschen Wörterbuch*, Breslau, 1910.]

989. Lerch, Eugen, "Deutsch *-isieren*, französisch *-iser*, englisch *-ize (ise)*," *Sprachkunde* 2 (1938) 4–9.

990. ——, "Hyperkorrekte Sprachformen," *Archiv für die gesamte Psychologie* 105 (1940) 432–477. [Emil Öhnmann, *Neuphil.Mitt.* 43 (1942) 199–201.]

[991. Lessen, Jacoba H. van, "Over het Germaansche praefix *â-*," in R. Verdeyen, *Album*, The Hague, 1943, 359–370.]

992. ——, "Over possessieve samenstellingen met *af-, on-, ge-* en *aan-* en daarvan gevormde substantiva," *Tijdschrift* 59 (1940) 53–70.

993. ——, *Samengestelde Naamwoorden in het Nederlandsch*, diss., Groningen, 1928. ¶ 1. compound of two substantives, 2. compound of adjective + substantive, 3. compounding of verbal stem + substantive, 4. compounding of substantive + adjective, 5. compound derivations.

994. Lessiak, P., "Die Mundart von Pernegg in Kärnten," *PBB* 28 (1903) 1 ff. ¶ Comments on wf contained in the vocalism.

995. Leumann, E., "Einiges über Composita," *IF* 8 (1898) 297–301. ¶ Appositional compounds.

996. Levin, Samuel R., "Some Minor Compound Types in Germanic," *General Linguistics* 3 (1958) 55–61.

[997. Levitienė, L. G., "K voprosu o sočetaemosti glagolov s *mit* v sovremennom nemeckom jazyke," *Kalbotyra: Lietuvos TRS Ankštųjų Mokyklų Mokslo Darbai* (Vilnius. With Russian summaries) 9 (1963) 152–161. ¶ Verbs that can be combined with *mit* in NHG.]

[998. Levkovskaja, K. A., "Über die Wortbildung und ihr Verhältnis zur Grammatik," *Vierteljahreszeitschrift der Gesellschaft zum Studium der Kultur der Sowjetunion, gesellschaftswissenschaftliche Abteilung* (1954) 578–607 (= trans. of "O slovoobrazovaniji i jego otnošeniji k grammatike," in *Voprosy teoriji i istoriji jazyka v svete trudov I. V. Stalina po jazykoznaniju*, Moscow, 1952, 153–181).]

999. Lévy, Ernest, "Vermeintliche Streckformen," *ZfdW* 10 (1908–1909) 45–47. ¶ Refers to H. Schröder.

1000. L[ewis], G. C., "On English Diminutives," *The Philological Museum* 1 (1832) 679–686.

[1001. Lichošerst, N., "O produktivnosti konversii v sovremennom anglijskom jazyke," *Naučnye zapiski Kievskogo pedagogičeskogo instituta inostrannych jazykov* (1962) 43–50. ¶ Productivity of conversion in Eng.]

1002. Liedtke, Ernst, *Die numerale Auffassung der Kollektiva im Verlaufe der englischen Sprachgeschichte*, diss., Königsberg, 1910.

1003. Lienhart, H., *Laut- und Flexionslehre der Mundart des mittleren Zornthales im Elsaß*, diss., Strassburg, 1886.

1004. Lienhart, Maria, *Aufkommen der zusammengesetzten Epitheta in der englischen Literatur*, diss., Freiburg, 1927.

1005. Lincke, O., *Über die Wortzusammensetzung in Carlyles 'Sartor Resartus,'* diss., Berlin, 1904.

1006. Lindelöf, U., "English Agent-nouns with a Suffixed Adverb, *Neuphil. Mitt.* 36 (1935) 257–282.

1007. ——, *English Verb-Adverb Groups Converted into Nouns*, Helsinki 1937 (= *Societas Scientiarum Fennica, Commentationes Humanarum Litterarum* 60, 5). ¶ "A runaway, a stand-still."

1008. ——, *Some Observations on the English Adjective Formations in -ative and -atory*, Helsinki, 1943 (= *Societas Scientiarum Fennica, Commentationes Humanarum Litterarum* 13, 4).

1009. Lindemann, John W. R., "Ge as a Preverb in Late Old English Prose: Its Meaning and Functions as Suggested by a Collation of West-Saxon, Mercian, and Northumberland Versions of *The Gospel According to Saint Matthew*," *DA* 17 (1957) 2004–2005.

1010. ——, "Old English Preverbal ge-: A Re-Examination of Some Current Doctrines," *JEGP* 64 (1965) 65–83.

1011. Lindemans, J. ,"Het diminutiefsuffix -cin in het Nederlands," in *Album Edgard Blancquaert: De gehuldigde aangeboden gelegenheid van zijn ermeritaat door kollega's, vakgenoten en oud-leerlingen*, Tongeren, 1958, 437–440. ¶ Concerned with personal names.

1012. Lindén, Bror, "Västnordisch och svensk särskilt dalsk, ord- och namnbildning paa -ald och -älde," *Arkiv* 70 (1955) 196–209.

1013. Lindgren, Kaj B., *Die Apokope des mhd. -e in seinen verschiedenen Funktionen*, Helsinki, 1953 (= *AASF* B 78, 2).

1014. Lindheim, B. von, "Die weiblichben Genussuffixe im Altenglischen," *Anglia* 76 (1958) 479–504.

1015. Lindner, Felix, *Über das Präfix a im Englischen*, Habilitationsschrift, Jena, 1871, Rostock, 1873.

1016. Lindqvist, Axel, "Probleme der deutschen Wortbildung," *SN* 12 (1939–1940) 191–204.

1017. ——, "Studien über Wortbildung und Wortwahl im Althochdeutschen mit besonderer Rücksicht auf die nomina actionis," *PBB* 60 (1936) 1–132.

1018. ——, *Urg. daẓan-, daẓa- in Wörtern des Typus ahd. siohtago, mnd. ríkedage, an. skildagi, bzw. mhd. irretac*, Lund, 1918 (= *Lunds universitets aarsskrift* n.f. avd. 1, 14, 25). [F. Holthausen, *AfdA* 43 (1924) 147.]

1019. Lindroth, Hjalmar, "En egendomlig halländsk ordbildningstyp," *Halländsk Bygdekultur* (1925) 68 ff. ¶ Adjectival and verbal abstracts in *-eke*.

1020. ——, "Folke Filbyter—en replik," *Svenska Dagbladet* (April 21, 1928). ¶ Against Ludvig Larsson, above, as *-er* formations from strong verbs do not exist.

1021. ——, *Om adjektivering af particip, en studie inom nusvensk betydelselära*, Lund, 1906.

1022. Linnig, Franz, *Bilder zur Geschichte der deutschen Sprache*, Paderborn, 1881. ¶ Para. 26: Umdeutschung fremder Wörter.

[1023. Linskij, S. S., "Neologizmy s obščim značeniem 'dejstvujuščeog lica' (nomina agentis) v slovarnom sostave anglijskogo jazyka 16 veka," *Učenye zapiski Dal'nevostočnogo universiteta. Serija filologičeskaja* 5 (1962) 57–68. ¶ Agent nouns in sixteenth-century Eng.]

[1024. Littmann, E., *Morgenländische Wörter im Deutschen*, 2nd ed., Tübingen, 1924. ¶ Contains an appendix concerning American words.]

1025. Livant, William Paul, "Productive Grammatical Operations [in English]. 1. The Noun Compounding of 5-Year-Olds," *Language Learning* 12 (1962) 15–26.

1026. Ljunggren, Karl Gustav, *Adjektivering av substantiv i svenskan: undersökningar i svensk ordbildnings- och betydelselära*, Lund, 1939 (= *Lunds universitets aarsskrift* n.f. avd. 1, 35, 3).

1027. ——, "Ytterligare om termerna avledning och retrograd avledning," *Arkiv* 71 (1956) 69–70. ¶ Terms for derivation and back-formations; see Aakermalm, no. 4, above.

1028. Llewellyn, E. C., *The Influence of Low Dutch on the English Vocabulary*, Oxford, 1936.

1029. Llewellyn, Robert Hall, "Adjective Suffixes in Old Norse, A Study in Word-Formation," diss., Cambridge, Mass., 1946.

1030. Lockard, E. N., "Fertile Virgins and Fissle Breeders: Nuclear Neologisms," *AmSp.* 25 (1950) 23–27.

1031. Löfstedt, Ernst, "Zur Diminutivbildung in der Mundart von Amrum und Föhr," *SN* 30 (1958) 78–94.

1032. Löfstedt, Inga, "Zum Sekundärumlaut von germ. *a* in bairischen Adjektiven auf mhd. *-ic, -ec* und *-isch*," *SN* 20 (1947–1948) 225–257.

1033. Löfström, S. A., *Über die Zusammensetzungen im Plattdeutschen*, diss., Lund, 1875.

1034. Löhner, Rudolf, "Trennbare und untrennbare Verbalkomposition mit *durch, hinter, über, um, unter, wider (wieder)*," *ZfddtU* 3 (1889) 117–127.

1035. Loewe, Richard, "Die Anfügung von *-t* im Deutschen und das *ē* von ahd. *einēst*," *ZfvglSpr.* 47 (1916) 141–146.

1036. ——, "Die germanischen Iterativzahlen," *ZfvglSpr.* 47 (1915–1916) 95 ff.

1037. Loewenthal, John, "Etymologica," *PBB* 53 (1929) 303, 462–463; 54 (1930) 156–157, 316–318. ¶ Masc. *-ungr*.

1038. ——, "Zur germanischen Wortkunde," *Arkiv* 32 (1916) 270–301; 33 (1917) 97–131. ¶ Masc. *-urr, -ill, -ann*.

1039. Loey, A. van, "Middelnederlandse werkwoorden op *-rzen*," *Verslagen en Mededelingen van de Koninklijke Vlaamse Academie voor Taal- en Letterkunde* (1958) 647–651.

1040. Logeman, H., "Det saakaldte passive nutidsparticip i norsk og beslægtede sprog," *Arkiv* 30 (1913–1914) 17–42. ¶ Eng. gerund from infinitive.

1041. ——, *Rule of St. Benet*, London, 1888 (= *SPE* Tract 90). ¶ Pp. 119–121 deal with the origin of the Eng. gerund from infinitive.

1042. Lohmeyer, Ed., "*-else*," *NdKbl.* 5 (1880) 4.

1043. Loman, Bengt, *Fornsvenska verbalsubstantiv paa* -an, -ning och -else, diss., Stockholm, 1961 (= *Stockholm Studies in Scandinavian Philology* 4).

1044. ——, "Verbalsubstantiv paa *-ning* och *-ande* i nusvenskt riksspraak," *Meijerbergs arkiv för svensk ordforskning* 11 (1962) 1–30.

1045. Lombard, Alf, "Sydsvenska och uppsvenska: bidrag till en jämförelse mellan tvaa former av svenskt riksspraak," *Arkiv* 60 (1945) 1–72. ¶ Wf, pp. 21 ff.

1046. Lommel, Hermann, *Studien über indogermanische Femininbildungen*, Göttingen, 1912.

1047. Lorch, Hermann, *Arteigene Sprachlehre; Wortbildung und Wortbedeutung als deutsches Bildungsgut*, 2nd ed., Leipzig, 1941 (= *Völkisches Lehrgut* 1).

1048. Lotz, J., "The Suffix '-rama,'" *AmSp.* 29 (1954) 156–158.

1049. Loubser, Jacques Emil, *Die saamgestelde verbale vorm, van Nederlands na Afrikaans*, diss., Groningen, 1961. ¶ Compound verb.

1050. Loy, Karl, "Zusammengesetzte Stammortsnamen," *Beiträge zur Namenforschung* 6 (1955) 96–98.

1051. Ludovicy, E., "Remarques sur les diminutifs," *Bulletin linguistique et ethnologique de l'Institut Grand-ducal, Section de linguistique, de folklore et de toponymie* 2 (1954) 21–25. ¶ German.

1052. Ludwig, A., "Über den vocalischen Ausgang der Bildungssuffixe," *ZfvglSpr.* 15 (1866) 443–447.

1053. Lübben, A., "Mit *âl* zusammengesetzte Wörter," *ZfdPh.* 6 (1875) 454–566.

1054. ——, *Mittelniederdeutsche Grammatik*, Leipzig, 1882. ¶ Wf in adverbs, pp. 123 ff.

1055. Lüngen, Werner, *Das Praefix "on(d)-" in der altenglischen Verbalkomposition mit einem Anhang über das Praefix "oð- (ūð),"* diss., Kiel, 1911.

1056. Luft, Wilhelm, "Die lateinischen Diminutiva auf *-ell-* und *-ill-* im Deutschen," *ZfdA* 41 (1896) 241–242.

1057. Luginbühl, Emil, *Studien zu Notkers Übersetzungskunst*, diss., Zürich, 1933. ¶ Concerned with the translation of Lat. into OHG with some reference to derivation and compounding.

1058. Luick, Karl, "Die fremden Bestandteile im englischen und im deutschen Wortschatz," *Wissenschaftliche Beihefte zur ZdallgdSprv.* Vols. 12/13 (1896) 70–82.

1059. ——, "Über Vokalverkürzung in abgeleiteten und zusammengesetzten Wörtern," *Engl.Stud.* 54 (1920) 177–186.

1060. ——, "Zu den lateinischen Lehnwörtern im Altenglischen," *Herrigs Archiv* 126 (1911) 35–39.

1061. ——, "Zu den mit *Beau-* (*Bel-*) gebildeten Eigennamen," *Anglia Beibl.* 17 (1906) 232–233.

1062. Lutstorf, Heinz Theo, *The Stressing of Compounds in Modern English*, Bern, 1960.

1063. Lyman, John, " 'Jockey' Compounds," *AmSp.* 37 (1962) 72.

1064. McAtee, W. L., "Irradiations of the Suffixes '-ee' and '-eer,'" *AmSp.* 20 (1945) 75–76.

1065. MacGillivray, H. S., *The Influence of Christianity on the Vocabulary of Old English*, diss., Halle, 1902 (= *Studien zur englischen Philologie* 8).

1066. McKnight, George H., *English Words and Their Background*, New York, 1923.

1067. Mackensen, Lutz, "Adjektivbildungen mit den Nachsilben '-los' und '-frei,'" *Muttersprache* 72 (1962) 54.

1068. ——, "Sprachmischung als Wortbildungsprinzip," *ZfdPh.* 51 (1926) 406–412.

[1069. Made, Georg, *Das Verbum substantivum im Englischen*, diss., Giessen, 1910.]

1070. Mätzner, Eduard, *Englische Grammatik, 1. Teil Die Lehre vom Worte*, 3rd ed., Berlin, 1880. ¶ Derivation and compounding, pp. 479–564.

1071. Magoun, Francis P., Jr., "Recurring First Elements in Different Nominal Compounds in *Beowulf* and in the *Elder Edda*," in *Studies in English Philology: A Miscellany in Honor of Frederick Klaeber*, ed. Kemp Malone and Martin B. Ruud, Minneapolis, 1929, 73–78.

1072. ——, "Word Formation," in N. H. Turk, *An Anglo-Saxon Reader*, rev. ed., New York, 1930, 48a–48m.

1073. Maier, Gustav, *Das ge-Partizip im Neuhochdeutschen*, diss., Strassburg, 1901.

1074. Makey, Herman O., "Compound Words," *English Journal* 40 (1951) 567–569.

1075. Makovskij, M. M., "K probleme vida v gotskom jazyke," *Učebnye zpiski* 19 (1959) 41–98. ¶ *ga-* prefix in Go.

1076. Malherbe, D., *Das Fremdwort im Reformationszeitalter*, diss., Freiburg, 1906. ¶ General; also *-tion*; *-tz*, *-z*; *-ntz-*, *-ntie-*, *-tz-*; *-ieren*.

1077. Malkiel, Yakov, "Three Old French Sources of the English *arriv-al, withdraw-al* Type," *JEGP* 43 (1944) 80–87.

1078. Mankel, W., *Laut- und Flexionslehre der Mundart des Münsterthales im Elsaß*, Strassburg, 1886.

1079. Marache, Maurice, *Le composé verbal en ge- et ses fonctions grammaticales en moyen haut allemand: Étude fondée sur l'Iwein de Hartmann von Aue et sur les Sermons de Berthold von Regensburg*, Paris, 1960 (= *Germanica* 1).

1080. ——, "Die gotischen verbalen *ga*-Komposita im Lichte einer neuen Kategorie der Aktionsart," *ZfdA* 90 (1960) 1–35.

1081. Marchand, Hans, "Die Ableitung desubstantivischer Verben mit Nullmorphem im Englischen, Französischen und Deutschen," *Die Neueren Sprachen* 13 (1964) 105–118.

1082. ——, "Das amerikanische Element in der englischen Wortbildung," in *Sprache und Literatur Englands und Amerikas: Lehrgangsvorträge der Akademie Comburg*, Vol. III *Die wissenschaftliche Erschliessung der Prosa*, ed. Gerhard Müller-Schwefe, Tübingen, 1959, 155–166. ¶ Excellent summary of modern trends; *-ade*, *-teria*, *-torium*, *-thon*, *-rama*, *-fest*, *-ive*, *-iveness*; compounds such as *he-man, cigarette-fiend*.

1083. ——, *The Categories and Types of Present-day English Word-Formation: A Synchronic-diachronic Approach*, Wiesbaden, 1960.

1084. ——, "Compound and Pseudo-compound Verbs in Present-Day English," *AmSp.* 32 (1957) 83–94.

1085. ——, "Compounds with Locative Particles as First Elements in Present-day English, *Word* 12 (1956) 319–398.

1086. ——, "Esquisse d'une description des principales alternances derivativs dans le français d'aujourd'hui," *Studia Linguistica* 5 (1951) 95–112. ¶ Pp. 95–98 deal with wf resulting from alternation; general application though refers specifically to French.

1087. ——, "Die Länge englischer Komposita und die entsprechenden Verhältnisse im Deutschen," *Anglia* 78 (1960) 411–416.

1088. ——, "The Negative Verbal Prefixes in English," in *Mélanges de linguistique et de philologie Ferdinand Mossé in memoriam*, Paris, 1959 267–276. ¶ *un-, dis-, de-.*

1089. ——, "Notes on English Prefixation," *Neuphil.Mitt.* 55 (1954) 297–300.

1090. ——, "Notes on English Suffixation," *Neuphil.Mitt.* 54 (1953) 246–272.

1091. ——, "Notes on Nominal Compounds in Present-day English," *Word* 11 (1955) 216–227.

1092. ——, "Phonetic Symbolism in English Word-formation," *IF* 64 (1958–1959) 146–168, 256–277.

1093. ——, "Phonology, Morphology, and Word Formation," *Neuphil. Mitt.* 52 (1951) 87–95.

1094. ——, "A Set of Criteria for the Establishing of Derivational Relationship between Words Unmarked by Derivational Morphemes," *IF* 69 (1964) 10–19.

[1095. ——, "Synchronic Analysis and Word-formation," *Cahiers Ferdinand de Saussure* (publiés par la Société Genevoise de Linguistique) 13 (1955) 7–18.]

1096. ——, "Über zwei Prinzipien der Wortableitung in ihrer Anwendung auf das Französische und Englische," *Herrigs Archiv* 190 (1954) 217–221.

1097. ——, "Der Wortbildungstypus *anti-aircraft* (*battery*) und Verwandtes," in *Festschrift zum 75. Geburtstag von Theodor Spira*, ed. H. Viebrock and W. Erzgräber, Heidelberg, 1961, 335–342.

1098. Marckwardt, Albert H., *American English*, New York, 1958. ¶ Compounding, blends, derivation, loans, prefixes, suffixation, portmanteau words, word invention.

1099. ——, "The Verbal Suffix *-ettan* in Old English," *Language* 18 (1942) 275–281.

1100. Marcus, Hans, "Sprachliche Neubildungen in der anglo-amerikanischen Gegenwartsliteratur," *Neuphilol.Zt.* 3 (1951) 44–48.

1101. ——, "Sprachliche Neubildungen in der englischen Gegenwartsliteratur," *Neuphil.Monatsschrift* 11 (1940) 29–37. ¶ New compounds, nouns > adjectives with *-ly*, onomatopoeia, slang.

1102. Mark, Yudel, "Presumable, Dubitable, and Useful Germanism," *Yidishe Shprakh* 24 (1964) 1–19.

1103. Marquardsen, Ida, "Der Einfluss des Mnd. auf das Dänische im 15. Jahrhundert," *PBB* 33 (1908) 405–458. ¶ I. loanwords, II. MLGer. prefixes and suffixes.

1104. Martens, Heinrich, "Die verba perfecta in der Nibelungendichtung," *ZfvglSpr.* 12 (1863) 31–41, 321–335. ¶ List.

1105. Martin, Friedrich, *Die produktiven Abstraktsuffixe des Mittelenglischen,* diss., Strassburg, 1906.

1106. Martin, W., and Lienhart, H., *Wörterbuch der elsässischen Mundarten,* 2 vols., Strassburg 1899, 1907.

1107. Martinet, A., *La gémination consonantique d'origine expressive dans les langues germaniques,* Copenhagen and Paris, 1937. ¶ Diminutives, pp. 158 ff.

1108. Marzell, H., *Wörterbuch der deutschen Pflanzennamen,* 1 ff., Leipzig, 1937 ff.

1109. Maslov, Ju. C., "Kategorija predel'nosti/nepredel'nosti glagol'nogo dejstvija v gotskom jazyke," *Voprosy jazykoznanija* 5 (1959) 69–80. ¶ Go. *ga-*.

1110. Massey, B. W. A., *The Compound Epithets of Shelley and Keats,* Poznán, 1923.

1111. Massmann, H. F., "Ableitung und Verdeutschung: 3. -rid," *Germania, Neues Jahrbuch der Berlinischen Gesellschaft für deutsche Sprache und Alterthumskunde* 10 (1953) 197–198.

1112. Matra, Chr., "Um endingina -*laga* i føroyskum staðarhjáorðum," in *Festskrift til Finnur Jónsson (29/5 1928),* Copenhagen, 1928, 407–410. ¶ Adverbial -*laga* from -*la.*

1113. Matthews, Brander, "The Art of Making New Words," *Unpopular Review* 9 (1918) 58–69.

1114. ——, *The Englishing of French Words,* Oxford, 1921 (= *SPE* Tract 5). ¶ Borrowings.

1115. Matthews, Cecily C., *A Dictionary of Abbreviations,* London, 1947. ¶ Type *radar,* etc.

1116. Maurer, Friedrich, "Über Arten der deutschen Wortbildung besonders Wortkreuzung," *ZfdPh.* 53 (1928) 167–183.

1117. ——, *Volkssprache: Abhandlungen über Mundarten und Volkskunde, zugleich eine Einführung in die neueren Forschungsweisen,* Erlangen, 1933 (= *Fränkische Forschungen* 1). [Emil Öhmann, *Neuphil.Mitt.* 36 (1935) 137–139.] ¶ Chap. 7, "Über Arten der deutschen Wortbildung, besonders Wortkreuzung," pp. 95–114.

1118. Mautner, Franz H., "Word Formation by Shortening and Affixation: The 'Sudetens' and the 'Yugos,' " *AmSp.* 18 (1943) 200–207.

1119. Mawson, C. O. Sylvester, *Dictionary of Foreign Terms Found in English and American Writings of Yesterday and Today*, New York, 1934.

1120. Maxeiner, Theodor, *Beiträge zur Geschichte der französischen Wörter im Mittelhochdeutschen*, diss., Marburg, 1897. ¶ Good work on suffixes; some etymologies.

1121. ———, *Die mhd. Substantive mit dem Suffix -ier*, Braunschweig, 1903; also *Herrigs Archiv* 110 (1903) 312–346 and 111 (1903) 404.

1122. Maxwell, W. Cary, *Reimwortuntersuchungen im Deutschen*, diss., Heidelberg, 1932.

1123. Mead, Leon, *Word-Coinage, Being an Inquiry into Recent Neologisms, Also a Brief Study of Literary Style, Slang, and Provincialisms*, New York, 1902. ¶ Eng.; pp. 11–14, prefixes, suffixes; chatty, of marginal scholarly value.

1124. Meer, M. M. van der, *Historische Grammatik der niederländischen Sprache*, Vol. I *Einleitung und Lautlehre*, Heidelberg, 1927. ¶ Reference to wf intermixed in the sections on foreign words and sounds in Du.

[1125. Mehring, Marga, "Die Lehnprägungen in Notkers Übersetzung der 'Nuptiae Philologiae et Mercurii' des Martianus Capella," diss., Bonn, 1958.]

1126. Meisinger, Othmar, "Die hebr. Fremdwörter der Rappenauer Mundart," *ZfhdMaa.* 1 (1900) 172–177, 2 (1901) 73–75. ¶ Dictionary.

1127. ———, "Die Rappenauer Mundart," *ZfhdMaa.* 2 (1901) 97–137. ¶ Sec. 140, suffixes, pp. 134–135; sec. 142 f., prefixes, p. 135; sec. 24, *-i* in nouns; sec. 26, diminutives.

1128. ———, "Die weiblichen Appellativnamen in den hochdeutschen Mundarten," *ZfhdMaa.* 6 (1905) 84.

1129. ———, "Zur Bildung des Beiworts in der Rappenauer Mundart," *Teuthonista* 4 (1927–1928) 57–60. ¶ Compounds; intensive formations; MHG *-în*, OHG *-isc*, MHG *-îg*, *-eht*, *-oht*, *-loht*, *-leht*, *-lîch*, *-bære*, *-haft*, *-sam*.

1130. Meissner, R., "Sunufatarungo, ein Beitrag zur Geschichte des *ng*-Suffixes," *ZfdA* 70 (1933) 25 ff.

1131. Mel'cer, E. M., "K voprosu o processach slovoobrazovanija sovremennogo anglijskogo jazyka," *Inostrannye jazyki v škole* 4 (1957) 17–27. ¶ Processes of wf in present-day Eng.

1132. Mencken, H. L., *The American Language, An Inquiry into the Development of English in the United States*, 3rd ed., New York, 1923; *Supplement I*, New York, 1945; *Supplement II*, New York, 1948; 4th ed. and the two supplements, abridged with annotations and new material by Raven I. McDavid, Jr., New York, 1963.

1133. ———, "The Current Suffixes," *AmSp.* 21 (1946) 67–69. ¶ *-ability*, *-burger*, *-cide*, *-ee*, *-eria*, etc.

1134. ——, "New Verbs," *Words* 1 (1934) 5. ¶ Nouns made into verbs, e.g., *to profit*; back-formations, e.g., *to plumb* from *plumber*.

1135. Mendt, A., "'s als Substantivendung," *NdKbl.* 4 (1879) 10.

[1136. Menges, Heinrich, "Das Suffix *-i* in der Mundart von Rufach," *Jahresbericht für Geschichte, Sprache und Litteratur Elsass-Lothringens* 13 (1897) 184–202.]

1137. Mensel, Ernst H., "Zu den langen Flexions- und Ableitungssilben im Althochdeutschen," *JEGP* 4 (1902) 25–46. ¶ Particularly pp. 42 ff., Ableitungssilben.

1138. Mensing, Otto, "Hauptwörter auf *-els*," *NdKbl.* 51 (1938) 35.

1139. ——, "Präfix *to* = hochd. *zer*," *NdKbl.* 32 (1911) 11–14.

1140. Meredith, Mamie J., "Be a Cabette," *AmSp.* 27 (1952) 74–76. ¶ Suffix *-ette* in names of female professions.

1141. ——, "'Doctresses,' 'Authoresses,' and Others," *AmSp.* 5 (1929–1930) 476–481.

1142. ——, "Irradiation of the Suffix *-cillin*," *AmSp.* 23 (1948) 222.

1143. ——, "More 'Cafeteria' Progeny," *AmSp.* 3 (1927–1928) 37.

1144. Merwe, H. J. J. M. van der, "Die tweeklanke en verkleinwoorde by Van Riebeeck," *Tydskrif vir Wetenskap en Kuns*, nuwe reeks 20 (1960) 9–26. ¶ Afrikaans.

1145. Messing, E. J. J., "Das Suffix *-schaft* (eng. *-ship*, nl. *-schap*) nach Ursprung und Entwicklung," *Neophilologus* 2 (1916–1917) 185 ff., 272 ff.

1146. Mettig, R., *Die französischen Elemente im Alt- und Mittelenglischen (800–1258)*, diss., Marburg, 1910.

1147. Meulen, R. van der, "De etymologie van het woord schobbejak," *Mededeelingen der Nederlandsche Akademie van Wetenschappen*, nieuwe reeks, deel 7, afdeeling letterkunde (1944) 121–130.

1148. Meyer, Heinrich, *Die Sprache der Buren*, Göttingen, 1901. ¶ Pp. 48 f. deal with *-ie*, *-je* (Du.) diminutive suffix in South Africa; derivation, compounding, doubling.

1149. Meyer, Kurt, *Die Adjektivableitung im Schweizerdeutschen: Suffixformen*, Frauenfeld, 1960 (= *Beiträge zur schweizerdeutschen Mundartforschung* 10).

1150. Meyer, Leo, "Die deutsche Abstractbildung auf *-ung-*," *Bezzenberger Beiträge* 3 (1879) 151–152.

1151. ——, *Die gotische Sprache*, Berlin, 1869. ¶ Suffixes and prefixes are treated under their main sound in the Lautlehre, i.e., *iska* under *k*, *dupi* under *d*, etc.

1152. ——, "Das Suffix *ka* im Gothischen," *ZfvglSpr.* 6 (1857) 1–14.

1153. Meyer, Richard M., "Copulative Eigennamen," *ZfdA* 43 (1899) 158–169. ¶ Various suffixes.

1154. ——, "Erstarrte Infinitiva," *ZfdW* 8 (1906–1907) 153–161.

1155. ——, "Klassensuffixe," *PBB* 22 (1897) 548.

1156. ——, "Nietzsches Wortbildungen," *ZfdW* 15 (1914) 98–146.

1157. ——, "Die Umbildung fertiger Worte," *ZfdW* 2 (1901) 36–42. ¶ Sets up three parts of wf: Übersicht der deutschen Wurzeln, Lehre von den Suffixen und Präfixen, and Umbildung fertiger Worte.

1158. Meynell, Alice, "An Article on Particles," *Living Age* 303 (1919) 787–788. ¶ Chiefly about the affixes *un-* and *-less*.

1159. Mezger, Fritz, "Der germanische Kult und die ae. Feminina auf *-icge* and *-estre*," *Herrigs Archiv* 168 (1935) 177–184.

1160. ——, "Some Formations in *-ti-* and *-tr(i)-*," *Language* 24 (1948) 152–159. ¶ Nouns based on ancient adverbs or adverbial locatives.

1161. ——, "Zu den ablautend-reduplizierenden Verben im Germanischen," *Herrigs Archiv* 171 (1937) 66–68.

1162. ——, "Zu einigen idg. *g-* und *l-* Bildungen," *ZfvglSpr.* 72 (1954) 97–118. ¶ 2. Gmc. *-k*, *-l* formations; 5. *l-* formations.

1163. Michel, K., *Die mit -i̯- abgeleiteten denominativen Verba im Altgermanischen*, diss., Giessen, 1912.

1164. Michels, L. C. "Nog een woordgeworden affix," *De Nieuwe Taalgids* 55 (1962) 342. ¶ *cel(lo) < violoncel(lo)*.

1165. ——, "Woordvorming van affixen," *De Nieuwe Taalgids* 50 (1957) 79–82. ¶ Formation of affixes from independent words.

1166. Michels, V., *Mittelhochdeutsches Elementarbuch*, 3rd and 4th eds., Heidelberg, 1921.

1167. Mieck, [no initial], "Über Gemination und Reduplikation in den Volksmundarten und in der Kindersprache," *Herrigs Archiv* 46 (1870) 293–302.

1168. Mielck, W. H., "*-end* im substantivierten Infinitiv," *NdKbl.* 16 (1892), 77.

1169. ——, "Imperativische Thier- und Pflanzennamen," *NdKbl.* 6 (1881) 18.

1170. ——, "Das Substantiv des Verbums im Niederdeutschen," *NdKbl.* 8 (1883) 49–63. ¶ Infinitive $+ t$ yields verbal noun.

1171. ——, "Substantiva auf *-ert*, Adjectiva auf *-ern*," *NdKbl.* 16 (1892) 78.

1172. ——, "Substantiva auf *-ing*, *-ung*," *NdKbl.* 16 (1892) 76.

1173. ——, "Verba mit *af* zusammengesetzt," *NdKbl.* 1 (1876) 24, 64.

1174. ——, "Verkleinerungsformen des Hauptworts im Niederdeutschen," *NdKbl.* 4 (1879) 62–64. ¶ b. Die Deminutivendung *-ken* nach *k*.

1175. ——, "Die Vorsilbe *er-* vor Verben," *NdKbl.* 16 (1892) 69. ¶ Not originally LowGer.

1176. Miettinen, Erkki, "Beiträge zur deutschen Volksetymologie: Assoziative Umbildungen und Umdeutungen romanischer und lateinischer Entlehnungen," *Neuphil.Mitt.* 66 (1965) 28–91.

1177. ——, *Zum mundartlichen Fortleben mhd.-mnd. Lehnwortguts romanischer Herkunft*, Helsinki, 1962 (= *AASF* B, 126). ¶ Of significance insofar as further derivatives and compounds are built from the loans.

[1178. Miklaševskaja, G. A., "Naibolee produktivnye sposoby obrazovanija neologizmov za period s 1946 po 1957 god," *Naučnye zapiski Kievskogo pedagogičeskogo instituta inostrannych jazykov* 5 (1962) 61–77. ¶ Most productive means of forming neologisms in the period from 1946 to 1957.]

1179. Mitzka, W., *Deutsche Mundarten*, Heidelberg, 1943.

1180. Mjačina, A. V., "K voprosu ob obratnom obrazovanii glagolov ot ischodnych slov s koneňym ělementom -*ing* v anglijskom jazyke," *Vestnik Leningradskogo gosudarstvennogo Universiteta* 17 (1962) 131–136. ¶ Verbal back-formation from acronyms + *ing*.

1181. Mjöberg, J., "Spraakbruk och spraaknorm," *Modersmaalslärarnas Förenings Aarsskrift* (1929) 16–40. ¶ Loanwords, new formations in respect to how standard language can modify usage.

1182. Mladenov, Stefan, "Zu den vermeintlichen finnischen Lehnwörtern im Altgermanischen," *Wörter und Sachen* 12 (1929) 58–62.

1183. Modéer, Ivar, *Fornvästnordiska verbstudier*, 2 parts, Uppsala, 1941, 1943 (= *Uppsala universitets aarsskrift* [1941] 10, [1943] 8).

1184. ——, "Om de germanska *i*-verben," *Arkiv* 61 (1946) 271–284.

1185. Møller, Kristen, "Diminutiver i moderne dansk," *APhS* 17 (1943–1945) 1–126.

1186. ——, "Jyske Adjektiver paa -*eret*," *Sprog og Kultur* 3 (1934) 1–32.

1187. ——, *Træk af de romanske sprogs indflydelse paa nygermansk*, Vol. I *Studier over lyd, form og nydannelse*, Copenhagen, 1926. ¶ Paras. 70–114, suffixes; 128–131, Greek-Romance suffixes.

1188. ——, *Zur Methodik der Fremdwortkunde*, Copenhagen, 1933 (= *Acta Jutlandica* 5, 1). ¶ General methodology, pp. 53–54; Neubildungen.

1189. Möller, P., *Fremdwörter aus dem Lateinischen im späteren Mittelhochdeutschen und Mittelniederdeutschen*, diss., Giessen, 1915.

1190. Moerkerken, P. H. van, "Over den uitgang 'ing,'" *Taalstudie* 2 (1880) 37–42.

[1191. Moers, J., *Die Form- und Begriffsveranderung der französischen Fremdwörter im Deutschen*, Bonn, 1884 (= *Programmbeilage der Höheren Bürgerschule in Bonn 1884*).]

1192. Molde, Bertil, "Avledningar paa -*lek* i svenskan och danskan," *Sprog og Kultur* 16 (1948) 107–116.

1193. ——, "Naagra danska abstraktbildningar paa -*else*," in *Runer og rids, Festskrift til Lis Jacobsen 29. januar 1952*, Copenhagen, 1952, 65–72.

1194. Moller, Adolf, *Die reduplicirenden Verba im Deutschen als abgeleitete Verba, eine etymologische Untersuchung*, Potsdam, 1866.

1195. Monsterberg, S. V., "Der Infinitiv nach *wellen* und den Verba Prae-terito-praesentia in den Epen Hartmanns von Aue (Schluß): das Präfix *ge-* beim Infinitiv in den Epen Hartmanns von Aue," *ZfdPh.* 18 (1886) 301–320.

1196. Morciniec, Norbert, "Die nominalen Wortzusammensetzungen in den Schriften Notkers des Deutschen," *PBB* (Halle) 81 (1959) 263–294.

1197. ——, "Wort, Wortzusammensetzungen und Wortgruppe: ein Bei-trag zur Strukturerkenntnis der westgermanischen Sprachen," *Ze-szyty naukowe Uniwersytetu Wrocławskiego im. B. Bieruta* 24 (1960) 115–145 (= *Germanica Wratislaviensia* 4).

[1198. ——, "Wortbedeutung und Wortzusammensetzung," *Germanica Wratislaviensia* (Wrocław) 9 (1964) 127–168.]

1199. ——, "Z badań nad wysokoniemieckimi złożeniami nominalnymi," *Kwartalnik Neofilologiczny* 5 (1958) 211–225. ¶ Problems of nom-inal compounding in HighGer.; Ger. summary.

[1200. ——, "Złożenia egzocentryczne języka holenderskiego," *Kwartalnik Neofilologiczny* 9 (1962) 269–278. ¶ Exocentric compounds in Du.]

1201. ——, "Złożenia nominalne języków zachodniogermanskich," *Annales de lettres* 11 (1962) 47–62. ¶ Nominal compounds in West Gmc.

1202. Morgenroth, K., "Sprachpsychologische Bemerkungen zur Wort-bildung," *GRM* 6 (1914) 615–632.

1203. Morris, Richard, *Historical Outlines of English Accidence, Comprising Chapters on the History and Development of the Language, and on Word-Formation*, rev. by L. Kellner with Henry Bradley, London, 1895. ¶ Chap. 19, derivation; chap. 20, composition.

1204. ——, "On the Words *groveling* and *grovelling*, and the Connection of the Syllable *-ling* in *groveling* and the *-long* in *headlong, sidelong*, etc.," *Trans.Phil.Soc.* (1862–1863) 85–113.

1205. Mossé, Fernand, *Esquisse d'une histoire de la langue anglaise*, Lyon, 1947. ¶ Pertinent parts: chap. 1, parts 5 and 6; chap. 2, part 3; chap. 5, part 3 (derivation, compounding, borrowing, etc.).

1206. Motsch, Wolfgang, *Das System der Adjektivableitungsmorpheme in der deutschen Sprache der Gegenwart*, diss., Berlin, 1960.

1207. ——, *Zur Stellung der "Wortbildung" in einem formalen Sprachmodell*, Berlin, 1962 (= *Studia Grammatica* 1).

1208. Mühlefeld, Karl, *Einführung in die deutsche Wortbildungslehre mit Hilfe des Systems der Bedeutungsformen*, Halle, 1908.

1209. Müller, Alfons Fridolin, *Die Pejoration von Personenbezeichnungen durch Suffixe im Neuhochdeutschen*, Altdorf, 1953. [W. Fleischhauer, *AfdA* 70 (1957–1958) 141.] ¶ (Swiss emphasis); pejoration with suffixes, prefixes, compounding: -er, -ling, -ler, -el, -(e)rich, -bold, -hart, -ert, -ian, -jan, -ianus; foreign suffixes: -aster, -aille, -ist, -ant, -eur, -ax, -us, -icus, -inski, -anski.

1210. Müller, Carl, "Materialien zur nhd. Wortbildung: I Wörter auf -ling," *ZfdW* 2 (1902) 186–201.

1211. ——, "Obersächsische Feminina auf che (ke)," *ZfdMaa.* (1907) 29–34.

1212. Müller, Ewald, *Vornamen als appellative Personenbezeichnungen: onomatologische Studien zur Wortkonkurrenz im Deutschen,* Helsinki, 1929 (= *Societas Scientiarum Fennica, Commentationes Humanarum Litterarum* 3, 1). ¶ Compounding, derivation.

1213. Müller, Gertraud, "Die ahd. Partikelkomposita," *PBB* 70 (1948) 332–350.

1214. Müller, Josef, "Die Prägnanz der Ausdrücke des Tadels und Unwillens in den rheinischen Mundarten," *Zeitschrift des Vereins für rheinische und westfälische Volkskunde* 1 (1904) 113 ff.

1215. Müller, Leo, "Neuenglische Kurzformbildungen," *Giessener Beiträge zur Erforschung der Sprache und Kultur Englands und Nordamerikas* 1 (1923) 33–76. ¶ *Hand* for *handwriting,* *newsboy* for *newspaperboy,* etc.

1216. Müller, Max., *Die Reim- und Ablautkomposita des Englischen,* diss., Strassburg, 1909.

1217. Müller, Wolfgang and Editha, "Wortbildung—Ausdruck der Zeit," *Muttersprache* 71 (1961) 65–78.

1218. Müller-Schotte, Hans, "Das Blending und sein Ergebnis, das portmanteau-word," *Die Neueren Sprachen* N.F. 2 (1953) 449–454.

1219. ——, "Zur typisch-englischen Kürze und Bündigkeit des Ausdrucks," *Die Neueren Sprachen* N.F. 6 (1957) 219–228. ¶ *un-; -er, -ee;* contrast formations; metonymies, etc.

1220. Münch, F., *Grammatik der ripuarisch-fränkischen Mundart,* Bonn, 1904.

1221. Münz, P. J., "Taufnamen als Gattungsnamen in sprichwörtlichen Redensarten Nassaus," *Annalen des Vereins für Nassauische Alterthumskunde und Geschichtsforschung* 10 (1870) 89–112.

1222. Muller, H. C., *Beiträge zur Lehre der Wortzusammensetzung im Griechischen, mit Excursen über Wortzusammenstellung im Indogermanischen, und in verschiedenen anderen Sprachfamilien,* Leiden, 1896. ¶ Chap. 6, Gmc. languages.

1223. Muller, J. W., "Over ware en schijnbare Gallicismen in het Middelnederlandsch," *De Nieuwe Taalgids* 14 (1920) 1–19, 65–78.

1224. ——, "Sprokkelingen: 3. De afleidingsuitgangen -ioen (-joen) en -ilioen (-eljoen) in het nederlandsch," *Tijdschrift* 63 (1944) 100–103.

1225. Munsa, Franz, *Eine Untersuchung der deutschen Wortfamilien auf germ. -pp,* diss., Wien, 1933.

1226. Munske, Horst H., *Das Suffix *inga /unga in den germanischen Sprachen*, diss., Marburg, 1964 (= *Marburger Beiträge zur Germanistik* 6).

1227. Murray, J. A. H., "Old English Verbs in *-cgan* and their Subsequent History," *Trans.Phil.Soc.* (1882–1884) 249–250.

[1228. Mushacke, E., *Über Pleonasmus und Tautologie in der deutschen Wortzusammensetzung*, Hannover, 1883 (= *Programm* 1883).]

1229. Naert, Pierre, "Utvecklingen av suffixet i fvn. *norrønn, suðrønn* osv. . . ; nyisl. *hafrœnn* m. fl.," *Arkiv* 57 (1944) 161–177.

1230. Nagasawa, Yoshijiro, "Some Gallicisms in English," in *Essays in English and American Literature in Commemoration of Prof. Takejiro Nakayama's 61st Birthday*, Tokyo, 1961.

1231. Nagl, J. W., "Wie werden in unserer Mundart die Verkleinerungswörter gebildet?" *Feuilleton der Deutschen Zeitung* (Wien), June 20 (1900).

1232. Neck, M. G. van, "On Derivation and Composition," *Taalstudie* 9 (1888) 282–292.

1233. Neckel, G., "Exozentrische Composition," *IF* 19 (1906) 249–254. ¶ Based on OIcel.

[1234. Nestle, E., "Die schwäbischen Familiennamen auf *-lin*," *ZfddtU* 9 (1895) 557–558.]

1235. ——, "Vom 'ge-' des Perfekts," *ZfddtU* 18 (1904) 667–668.

1236. Neubauer, Joh., "Die Fremdwörter im Egerländer Dialecte," *Verein für Geschichte der Deutschen in Böhmen, Mitteilungen* 27 (1889) 171–185.

1237. Neubauer, Walter, "Deformation isolierter Bezeichnungen *wiederkäuen* in deutscher Wortgeographie," *Beiträge zur deutschen Philologie* 19–23 (1958) 297–521.

1238. Neumann, J. H., "A Nineteenth Century 'poetic' Prefix," *MLN* 58 (1943) 278 ff. ¶ *a-* in *afoot*, etc.

1239. Neumann, Werner, "Die Bildungsweise der Verbalabstrakta zu präfixkomponierten Verben im Frühalthochdeutschen," *Wissenschaftliche Zeitschrift der Humboldt-Universität, Berlin; Gesellschafts- und sprachwissenschaftliche Reihe* 10 (1916) 121–122. ¶ Diss. abstract.

1240. Newman, Stanley S., "English Suffixation, A Descriptive Approach," *Word* 4 (1948) 24–36. ¶ General theory.

1241. Nicholson, G. A., *English Words with Native Roots and with Greek, Latin or Romance Suffixes*, diss., Chicago, 1916.

1242. Nichtenhauser, Dora, *Rückbildungen im Neuhochdeutschen*, diss., Freiburg, 1920.

1243. Nicolai, Otto, *Die Bildung des Adverbs im Altenglischen*, diss., Kiel, 1907. ¶ Affixes, compounds.

1244. Niekerken, Walther, "Zur niederdeutschen Wortbildung," in *Album*

73 1262. Oehl

Edgard Blancquaert: De gehuldigde anngeboden gelegenheid van zijn emeritaat door kollega's, vakgenoten en oud-leerlingen, Tongeren, 1958, 301–310. ¶ 1. adverbs and pronouns; 2. verbs.

1245. Nodnagel, A., "Zur Lehre von der Zusammensetzung der Wörter im Deutschen," *Herrigs Archiv* 4 (1848) 279–290. ¶ Pedagogical.

1246. Nörrenberg, E., "Das westfälische Diminutivum und verwandte Erscheinungen mit besonderer Berücksichtigung der Mundarten des Kreises Iserlohn," *NdJb.* 49 (1923) 1 ff. ¶ Diss.

1247. Nolte, A., "Zu Gottfrieds Tristan," *ZfdA* 52 (1910–1911) 61–83. ¶ Pp. 78 f. deal with adjectives in *-bære* in Hartmann von Aue's work.

1248. Nolte, E., "The *-thon* Suffix," *AmSp.* 29 (1954) 229.

1249. Nordfelt, A., "Fransk-svenska laanord av typen *grenadjär* m. fl.," *Nysvenska studier* 12 (1932) 56–76. ¶ *-jär* or *-iär*.

1250. ——, "Om franska laanord i svenskan: III. Reformationstidens fransk-svenska laanord, omkr. 1520-omkr. 1611," *Studier i modern spraakvetenskap* 10 (1928) 79–111. ¶ Suffixes *-era*, *-i* (*-eri*), *-ion*, *-ism*, *-ist*, *-ant*, *-ent*.

1251. Nordin, Per Gunnar, *Die Zusammensetzung von Adjektiv oder Adverb mit Adjektiv oder Partizip im Spätmittelhochdeutschen*, diss., Lund, 1945 (= *Lunder Germanistische Forschungen* 18).

1252. Nordling, Arnold, "Norr. *vandblœss, vandgœfr, vinnr*," Helsinki, 1930 (= *Studier i nordisk filologi* 20). ¶ Agent noun, compounds of *vinnr*.

1253. Noreen, Adolf, *Altisländische Grammatik*, Halle, 1923.

1254. ——, "Suffixablaut im Altnordischen," *IF* 14 (1903) 396–402.

1255. Nyquist, Alvar, "Stress, Intonation, Accent, Prominence in Disyllabic Double-stress Compounds in Educated Southern English," *Proceedings of the Fourth International Congress of Phonetic Sciences* 4 (1961) 710–713.

1256. Oberdörffer, Wilhelm, *Das Aussterben altenglischer Adjektive und ihr Ersatz im Verlaufe der englischen Sprachgeschichte*, diss., Kiel, 1908. ¶ Among the various categories: "ungebräuchliche Suffixe" (*-ol*, *-en*).

1257. Ochs, Ernst, "Ahd. *Taguwizzi*, ahd. *Murken*," *Neuphil.Mitt.* 60 (1959) 403–404.

1258. ——, "Klammerformen," *ZfdMaa.* (1920) 175.

1259. ——, "Südwestdeutsche *urig*," *Neuphil.Mitt.* 60 (1959) 126–128.

1260. Odell, Ruth, "More and More '*-burgers*,'" *AmSp.* 25 (1950) 315–316.

1261. Odermatt, Esther, *Die Deminution in der Nidwaldner Mundart*, diss., Zürich, 1903 (also: *Abhandlung*, hg. von der Gesellschaft für deutsche Sprache in Zürich, 1904).

1262. Oehl, W., "Elementare Wortschöpfung," *Anthropos* 12 (1917) 575–624, 13 (1918) 1047–1068. ¶ Theoretical; starts with onomatopoeia.

1263. ——, "Das Lallwort in der Sprachschöpfung," Freiburg (Switzerland), 1933. ¶ Speech presented on Nov. 15, 1932.

1264. Öhmann, Emil, "Beobachtungen im Umkreis der Homonymie: das deutsche Verbalpräfix 'ver-,' " in *Festgabe für Ulrich Pretzel zum 65. Geburtstag dargebracht von Freunden und Schülern*, ed. Werner Simon, Wolfgang Bachofer, and Wolfgang Dittmann, Berlin, 1963, 327–337.

1265. ——, "Die deutschen Ländernamen auf *-ien*," *Mémoires de la Société Néophilologique* 8 (1929) 319–325.

1266. ——, "Die Diminutiva im Mittelhochdeutschen," *Neuphil.Mitt.* 47 (1946) 115–125.

1267. ——, "Der französische Einfluß auf die deutsche Sprache im Mittelalter," *Neuphil.Mitt.* 32 (1939) 195 ff.

1268. ——, "Die französischen Wörter im Altnordischen," *Neuphil.Mitt.* 25 (1924) 135–151.

1269. ——, "Hyperhochdeutsche Formen in mitteldeutschen Mundarten," *Neuphil.Mitt.* 29 (1928) 64–73.

1270. ——, "Kleine Beiträge zum deutschen Wörterbuch," *Neuphil.Mitt.* 54 (1953) 149–159.

1271. ——, *Die mittelhochdeutsche Lehnprägung nach altfranzösischem Vorbild*, Helsinki, 1951 (= *AASF* B 63, 3). ¶ 1. Lehnübersetzung; 2. Lehnsyntax, Lehnwendung, und Stilistisches; 3. Lehnbedeutung.

1272. ——, "Das mittelhochdeutsche stoffnamenbildende Suffix *-ât*," *PBB* 53 (1929) 42 ff.

1273. ——, "Die mittelniederländischen Verba auf *ont-*," *Neuphil.Mitt.* 53 (1952) 213–224.

1274. ——, "Nachkommen der mitteldeutschen Kollektiva auf *ge- — -(e)ze* in heutigen deutschen Mundarten," in *Studia Germanica, Festschrift Ernst Albin Kock*, Lund, 1934, 429–432.

1275. ——, "Niederländische Lehnprägungen nach französischem Vorbild," *Neuphil.Mitt.* 54 (1953) 144–149.

1276. ——, "Nochmals über die mittelhochdeutschen Wörter auf *-ier*, *-ierære* und *-ierre*," *Neuphil.Mitt.* 55 (1954) 271–275.

1277. ——, "Romanische Randwörter der mittelhochdeutschen Zeit im Kontinentalgermanischen," *ZfMdaf.* 20 (1951–1952) 93–101.

1278. ——, "Die romanischen Bestandteile im mittelhochdeutschen Wortschatz," *PBB* 73 (1951) 273 ff.

1279. ——, *Der s-Plural im Deutschen*, Helsinki, 1924 (= *AASF* B 18, 1). [Hugo Suolahti, *Neuphil.Mitt.* 26 (1925) 250–251.] ¶ Deals incidentally with many loanwords and loan derivative elements.

1280. ——, *Studien über die französischen Worte im Mittelhochdeutschen im 12. und 13. Jahrhundert*, diss., Helsinki, 1918.

1281. ——, "Das Suffix -tät im Deutschen," *Neuphil.Mitt.* 24 (1923) 157–164.

1282. ——, "Über den italienischen Einfluß auf das Niederländische," *Verslagen en Mededelingen van de Koningklijke Vlaamse Academie voor Taalen Letterkunde* (1955) 131-152.

1283. ——, *Über den italienischen Einfluß auf die deutsche Sprache bis zum Ausgang des Mittelalters*, 2 vols., Helsinki, 1942, 1944 (= *AASF* B 51, 53).

1284. ——, "Über die Pluralbildung von abstrakten Substantiven im Deutschen," *PBB* 65 (1941) 134 ff.

1285. ——, "Über die Verbreitung der Adjektivabstrakta auf -*ida* > -(*e*)*de* im Deutschen," *Neuphil.Mitt.* 21 (1920), 65–72.

1286. ——, *Über Homonymie und Homonyme im Deutschen*, Helsinki, 1934 (= *AASF* B 32, 1).

1287. ——, "Zu den finnisch-germanischen Lehnbeziehungen," *Neuphil. Mitt.* 26 (1925) 237–239.

1288. ——, "Zum spanischen Einfluß auf die deutsche Sprache," *Neuphil. Mitt.* 41 (1940) 35 ff. and 144.

1289. ——, "Zum sprachlichen Einfluß Italiens auf Deutschland, I. Das deutsche Wort *Ketzer*," *Neuphil.Mitt.* 40 (1939) 213–221; "II. Über einige mhd. Ausdrücke der Seefahrt," *Neuphil.Mitt.* 41 (1940) 145 f.; "III. Über einige Ausdrücke des süddeutschen Weinbaus," *Neuphil.Mitt.* 42 (1941) 15–34; "IV. Über einige mhd. Ausdrücke des Kriegswesens," *Neuphil.Mitt.* 42 (1941) 79–87; "V. Über einige mhd. Benennungen von Hausgeräten und dgl.," *Neuphil.Mitt.* 42 (1941) 103–117; "VI. Über einige mhd. Benennungen von Massen," *Neuphil.Mitt.* 42 (1941) 145–149; "VII. Über einige mhd. Ausdrücke der Landwirtschaft," *Neuphil.Mitt.* 42 (1941) 149–152; "VIII. Über einige mhd. Ausdrücke der Flora und Fauna," *Neuphil.Mitt.* 43 (1942) 20–26; "IX. Über einige mhd. Ausdrücke der Baukunst," *Neuphil.Mitt.* 43 (1942) 27–28; "X. Über einige mhd. Benennungen von Teilen der Kleidung," *Neuphil.Mitt.* 43 (1942) 28–30; "XI. Wortgeographische Streifzüge," *Neuphil.Mitt.* 43 (1942) 1–22; "XIII. Administrative Ausdrücke," *Neuphil.Mitt.* 54 (1953) 226–237; "XIV. Italienisches bei Heinrich von Neustadt," *Neuphil.Mitt.* 55 (1954) 134–143; "XV. Nachlese," *Neuphil.Mitt.* 57 (1956) 103–117; *Neuphil.Mitt.* 57 (1956) 103–117.

1290. ——, "Zur Chronologie zweier Lehnsuffixe im Deutschen (-*erie*, -*ant*)," *Neuphil.Mitt.* 34 (1933) 125 ff.

1291. ——, *Zur Geschichte der Adjektivabstrakta auf -ida, -î, und -heit im Deutschen*, Helsinki, 1921 (= *AASF* B 15, 4).

1292. ——, "Die Zusammensetzungen mit *rück* und *zurück* im Deutschen," *Neuphil.Mitt.* 45 (1944) 104–105.

1293. ——, Seppänen, Lauri V., and Valtasaari, Kullervo, "Zur Geschichte des deutschen Suffixes *-ieren*," *Neuphil.Mitt.* 54 (1953) 159–176.

1294. Öhmann, Suzanne, *Wortinhalt und Weltbild: vergleichende und methodologische Studien zur Bedeutungslehre und Wortfeldtheorie*, Stockholm, 1951. ¶ Chap. 3; Lehnwörter und Lehnbedeutungen.

1295. Östberg, H. O., *Personal Names in Appellative Use in English*, Uppsala, 1905.

1296. Offe, Johannes R. W., *Das Aussterben alter Verba im Englischen*, diss., Kiel, 1908. ¶ Various reasons for this are given, among them further compounding and derivation.

1297. Ojansuu, Heikki, "Über den Einfluß des Estnischen auf das Deutsche der Ostseeprovinzen," *Neuphil.Mitt.* 8 (1906) 87–98.

1298. Olson, Emil, *De appellativa substantivens bildning i fornsvenskan*, Lund, 1916. ¶ Point of departure is Gmc. suffixes: I. personal designations (masc., fem., collective), "djurnamn"; II. concrete nouns; III. abstract nouns.

1299. Olsson, Yngve, "Implications and Complications of the Stressed Suffix *-el*," *English Studies* 45 (1964), suppl., 40–43.

1300. Onions, C. T., *The Fate of French -é in English*, Oxford, 1943 (= *SPE* Tract 61).

1301. Osthoff, H., "Praefix *py* im Griechischen; *py-*, *bhy-* im Germanischen," *PBB* 18 (1894) 243.

1302. ——, "Die Suffixform *-sla-*, vornehmlich im Germanischen," *PBB* 3 (1876) 335 ff. ¶ The equivalent of MHG, NHG *-sal*.

1303. ——, "Über das eingedrungene *s* in der nominalen Suffixform *-stra-* und vor dental anlautenden Personalendungen des deutschen, griechischen und altbaktrischen Verbums," *ZfvglSpr.* 23 (1887) 313–333.

1304. ——, *Das Verbum in der Nominalkomposition*, Jena, 1878. ¶ I. Die deutschen Nominalcomposita mit verbalem ersten Gliede (Go., OHG, MHG, NHG, OS, OE, ON); Adjectivbildende Primärsuffixe aus zweiten Compositions-Gliedern; Imperativnamen.

1305. ——, "Zur Frage des Ursprungs der germanischen *n*-Deklination," *PBB* 3 (1876) 1 ff.

1306. ——, *Zur Geschichte des schwachen deutschen Adjektivums*, Jena, 1876 (= *Forschungen im Gebiete der indogerm. nominalen Stammbildung* 2).

1307. Oudkerk Pool, Th., "Nog eens *-ette*," *De Nieuwe Taalgids* 54 (1961) 198–201; 53 (1960) 159–164.

1308. Overdiep, G. S., "De samenstelling als korte taalvorm in de krant," *Onze Taaltuin* 1 (1932–1933) 363–367. ¶ Compounds originating from a desire for conciseness, e.g., *treinbotsing* from *botsing van tween personentreinen*.

1309. ——, "Werkwoorden op *-tsen*," *Onze Taaltuin* 2 (1933–1934) 274–380.

1310. Oyler, John Edward, "The Compound Noun in Harsdörffer's *Frauen-zimmer-Gesprächspiele*," *DA* 17 (1957) 3022.

1311. ——, "Harsdörffer and the Compound Noun," *CMLR* 19 (1963) 17–18.

1312. Padelford, F. M., and Maxwell, W. C., "The Compound Words in Spenser's Poetry," *JEGP* 25 (1926) 498–516. ¶ Essentially a list.

1313. Palander (Suolahti), Hugo, *Die althochdeutschen Tiernamen: 1. Die Namen der Säugetiere*, Darmstadt, 1899. [T. E. Karsten, *Neuphil.Mitt.* 1 (1899) 13.]

1314. ——, *Der französische Einfluß auf die deutsche Sprache im 12. Jahrhundert*, Helsinki, 1902 (= *Mémoires de la Société Néophilologique* 3).

1315. ——, "Ein deutscher Tiername," *Mémoires de la Société Néophilologique* 2 (1897) 99–100. ¶ Suffix *-s* in *Dachs, Lachs, Fuchs*, etc.

1316. ——, "Volksetymologische Umbildungen im Englischen," *Neuphil. Mitt.* 7 (1905) 125–127.

1317. Palm, H., "Her und hin zugleich als Praefixe und Suffixe," *Fromanns Deutsche Mundarten* 6 (1859) 348–350.

1318. Palmér, Johna, "Betydelseutvecklingen i isl. *heiðr*," *APhS* 5 (1930–1931) 289–304. ¶ Part 2: *heið-* as first part of compounds, pp. 293–297.

1319. ——, *Spraakutveckling och spraakvaard*, Lund, 1945. ¶ Chapter on wf.

1320. Palmer, Philip Motley, *Der Einfluß der neuen Welt auf den deutschen Wortschatz, 1492–1800*, Heidelberg, 1933.

1321. ——, *The Influence of English on the German Vocabulary to 1700*, Berkeley, 1950.

1322. ——, *The Influence of English on the German Vocabulary to 1800. A Supplement*, Berkeley and Los Angeles, 1960 (= *University of California Publications in Linguistics* 7, 2).

1323. ——, *Neuweltwörter im Deutschen*, Heidelberg, 1933.

1324. Palmgren, Carl, *English Gradation-Nouns in their Relation to Strong Verbs*, diss., Uppsala, 1904. ¶ *Tale /tell, blood /bleed*, etc., from various parts of the verb.

1325. ——, "De N.E. *en-*verben i historisk belysning," *Nordisk tidskrift*, 3rd ser., 19 (1910–1911) 27–51.

1326. Paludan, Hans Aage, *Filologiske Smuler: Studier over franske laaneords betydningselasticitet i Dansk*, Copenhagen, 1939 (= *Studier fra sprog-og oldtidsforskning* 181). ¶ Loans with different meanings; projection words.

1327. Palzer, Alois, *Zur Geschichte von englisch -ize; Gebrauch und Vorkommen der Endung im englischen Schrifttum von der Renaissance bis zum 18. Jahrhundert*, diss., Mainz, 1954.

1328. Partridge, Eric, *A Dictionary of Abbreviations*, London, 1942. ¶ Type *radar, waac*, etc.

1329. Paul, Hermann, *Deutsche Grammatik,* V. *Wortbildungslehre,* 4th ed., Halle, 1959.

1330. ——, *Mittelhochdeutsche Grammatik,* 18th ed., rev. W. Mitzka, Tübingen, 1960.

1331. ——, *Prinzipien der Sprachgeschichte,* 4th ed., Halle, 1920.

1332. ——, "Über die Aufgaben der Wortbildungslehre," *Sitzungsberichte der phil.-hist. Klasse der königlichen bayrischen Akademie der Wissenschaften* (1896) 692–713.

1333. ——, "Die Vocale der Flexions- und Ableitungssilben in den ältesten germanischen Dialecten," *PBB* 4 (1877) 315 ff.

1334. ——, "Das Wesen der Wortzusammensetzung," *IF* 14 (1903) 251–255.

1335. ——, "Zur Geschichte des germanischen Vocalismus," *PBB* 6 (1879) 1 ff.

[1336. Pauwels, J. L., "Kempens of Kempisch?" *Dietsche Warande en Belfort* (1962) 500–503. ¶ Concerning the adjective derived from the noun.]

[1337. Pavlov, V. M., "K voprosu ob otnošenii slovosloženija k sintaksisu nemeckogo jazyka," in *Voprosy teorii nemeckogo jazyka. I. Materialy mežvuzovskogo naučnogo soveščanija po voprosam sintaksisa nemeckogo jazyka,* Irkutsk, 1959 (1960), 137–157. ¶ Relation of word compounding to syntax in Ger.]

1338. Pedersen, Holger, "Zur Lehre von den Aktionarten," *ZfvglSpr.* 37 (1900) 219–250.

1339. Pée, Willem, *Dialectgeographie der Nederlandsche diminutiva,* Tongeven, 1936 (= *Verslagen en Mededelingen van de Koninklijke Vlaamsche Academie voor Taalen Letterkunke,* Ser. 6, 58). ¶ Definitive work on the diminutive in Du. and Flemish.

1340. Peltola, Niilo, *The Compound Epithet and its Use in American Poetry,* Helsinki, 1956 (= *AASF* B 105).

1341. Person, Henry A., "'Ware the Escapee," *Word Study* 34 (1958) 6–8. ¶ Words in *-ee.*

1342. Persson, P., *Beiträge zur indogermanischen Wortforschung,* 2 vols., Uppsala, 1912. ¶ Individual roots (words) and derivatives and compounds.

1343. ——, *Studien zur Lehre von der Wurzelerweiterung und Wurzelvariation,* Uppsala, 1891 (= *Uppsala Universitets Aarsskrift* 1891). ¶ IE.

1344. Petersen, W., "Der Ursprung der Exozentrika," *IF* 34 (1914–1915) 254–285. ¶ Bahuvrîhi formations derive from the principle of name-giving; see family names such as *Liebe, Spott, Mercy, Joy.*

1345. ——, "The Origin of the Indo-European Nominal Stem-Suffixes," *AJPh.* 38 (1916) 173–193, 255–281.

1346. Peterson, P. N., "Naagot om verb och smaaord i Valldamaalet," in *Västsvenska hembygdsstudier tillägnade Hjalmar Lindroth*, Göteborg, 1928, 71–78. ¶ Compounding of particles with verbs and verbal abstracts in -*ane*, -*ene*, -*ing*.

1347. Pfaff, Friedrich, "Zur Handschuhsheimer Mundart," *PBB* 15 (1891) 178–194. ¶ Diminutives; -*ət*, -*əs*, etc.

1348. Pfeifer, [no initial], *Über deutsche Deminutivbildung im 17. Jahrhundert*, Meiningen, 1898.

1349. Pfennig, Heinrich, "Das Deminutivum bei Schiller und seinen Zeitgenossen," *ZfdW* 6 (1904–1905) 1–40.

1350. Phoenix, Walter, *Die Substantivierung des Adjektivs, Partizips und Zahlwortes im Angelsächsischen*, diss., Berlin, 1918.

1351. Pietsch, P., "Einige Bemerkungen über *ge*- bei Verben," *PBB* 13 (1888) 516 ff.

1352. ——, "Nochmals *ge*- beim Mittelwort der Vergangenheit," *ZdallgSprv.* (1906) 357–361.

1353. Pilch, Herbert, "Das ae. Präverb *ge*-," *Anglia* 71 (1952–1953) 129–139.

1354. ——, "Me. *I*- beim Participium präteriti," *Anglia* 73 (1955–1956) 279–291.

1355. ——, *Der Untergang das Präverbs* ge- *im Englischen*, Kiel, 1951.

1356. ——. "Der Untergang des Präverbs *ge*- im Englischen," *Anglia* 73 (1955–1956) 37–64.

1357. Piltz, Günter, *Die Bedeutungsentwicklung der Substantiva auf* -heit, -schaft *und* -tum, diss., Hamburg, 1951.

1358. Piltz, Oskar, "Zur englischen Wortbildungslehre: 1. Über die Vorsilbe *be*-," *Herrigs Archiv* 6 (1849) 371–389; 8 (1851) 36–40; "2. Über die Vorsilbe *a*-," *Herrigs Archiv* 8 (1851) 40–58; "3. Über *like* und die Bildungssilbe *ly*," *Herrigs Archiv* 10 (1852) 361–380; 11 (1852) 192–208, 365–382; 12 (1853) 295–312; 13 (1853) 292–309; and 14 (1853) 342–378.

[1359. Pisani, V., "Latino provincia, il suffisso -*enq*- e la formazioni germaniche in -*ingo*- -*ungo*-," *Rendiconti dell'Istituto Lombardo di Scienze e Lettere* 74 (1940–1941) 148–170.]

1360. Plate, Rudolf, *Englische Wortkunde auf sprach- und kulturgeschichtlicher Grundlage*, Munich, 1934. ¶ Doublets, blends, clippings, suffixes, hybrids, etc.

1361. Platt, J., "Angelsächsisches: 7. ags. fem. Bildung -*icze*," *Anglia* 6 (1883) 177.

1362. Pogatscher, A., "Über den Ursprung des westgermanischen Deminutivsuffixes -*inkil*," *Anglia Beibl.* 15 (1904) 238–247.

1363. ——, "Das westgermanische Deminutivsuffix -*inkil*," *Anglia* 23 (1901) 310–315.

1364. ——, *Zur Lautlehre der griechischen, lateinischen und romanischen Lehnworte im Altenglischen*, Strassburg, 1888 (= *Quellen und Forschungen*
64).

1365. Polack, Fritz, "Über die Wörter auf *-ese* und *-eser*," *Muttersprache*
(1939) 279–282. ¶ *Japaner/Japanese.*

1366. Poldauf, Ivan, "Die Bildung der englischen Adjektiva auf *-ble*: ein
Beitrag zur Theorie der synchronen Wortbildungslehre," *Zt. für
Angl. und Am.* 7 (1959) 229–245.

1367. Pollard, Eric A., *Über die -ôn und -jan Verba in den altgermanischen
Sprachen (Das Vordrängen der -ôn Verben im Althochdeutschen)*, diss.,
Hamburg, 1935. ¶ Iterative, intensive, instrumental, adverbial *ôn*-
verbs; *ôn*-verbs from personal designations; more recent suffixes
-alôn, -ilôn, -arôn, -îrôn, -isôn, -inôn; compounds.

1368. Polzin, Albert, *Geschlechtswandel der Substantiva im Deutschen (mit Ein-
schluß der Lehn- und Fremdworte)*, Hildesheim, 1903. ¶ Peripheral;
Reimassoziation: *die Backe/Backen, die Lade/Laden.*

1369. ——, *Studien zur Geschichte des Deminutivums im Deutschen*, Strassburg,
1901 (= *Quellen und Forschungen* 88). [M. H. Jellinek, *ZfdPh.* 35
(1903) 140–141.]

[1370. Popov, O. K., "Imennoe slovosloěnie v sovremennom švedskom
jazyke," *Vestnik Moskovskogo Universiteta. Serija 7, filologija, žurna-
listika* 18, 2 (1963) 70–76. ¶ Nominal word compounding in modern Sw.]

1371. Porzig, Walter, "Die Leistung der Abstrakta in der deutschen
Sprache," *Blätter für deutsche Philosophie* 4 (1930) 66–77.

1372. Poston, Lawrence III, " 'Happy,' 'merry,' and 'jolly' as Nouns,"
AmSp. 37 (1962) 289.

1373. Postma, G., "Wirdfoarming," *Forjit my net* (1901) 49–50. ¶ *wan* in
compounds.

1374. Pott, August Friedrich, *Doppelung (Reduplikation, Gemination) als eines
der wichtigsten Bildungsmittel der Sprache beleuchtet aus aller Welttheile*,
Lemgo and Detmold, 1862.

1375. ——, *Etymologische Forschungen auf dem Gebiete der indo-germanischen
Sprachen insbesondere des Sanskrit, Griechischen, Lateinischen, Littau-
ischen und Gothischen*, Vol. II: *Grammatischer Lautwechsel und Wortbildung*, Vol. III, Abschnitt: *Wortlehre*, Lemgo, 1836.

1376. ——, "Verschiedene Bezeichnung des Perfects in einigen Sprachen,
und Lautsymbolik," *Zt. für Völkerpsychologie und Sprachwissenschaft*
15 (1884) 287–337. ¶ Wortableitung, pp. 336–337.

1377. Potter, S., "Trends in Current English," *Moderna spraak* 50 (1956)
255–267. ¶ General.

1378. Pound, Louise, *Blends. Their Relation to English Word Formation*, Heidelberg, 1914 (= *Anglistische Forschungen* 42).

1379. ——, "Extensions of Usage of a Pronoun," in *Curme Volume of Linguistic Studies*, ed. H. Hatfield, James Taft, Werner Leopold, and A. J. F. Zieglschmid, Baltimore, 1930, 118–119 (= *Language Monograph* 7). ¶ *it. . . ; itfulness*, etc.

1380. ——, "Odd Formations: (a) Domestication of the Suffix *-fest*," *Dialect Notes* 4 (1913–1917) 353–354.

1381. ——, "On Indefinite Composites and Word-coinage," *The University Studies of the University of Nebraska* 13 (1913) 407 ff.

1382. ——, "Then and Now," *PMLA* 71 (1956) 1–13. ¶ Acronyms, blends.

1383. ——, "Vogue Affixes in Present-day Word Coinage," *Dialect Notes* 5 (1918–1927) 1–14. ¶ Suffixes: *-ee, -ite, -ist, -ster, -er, -ette, -dom, -ism, -itis, -ese, -ology, -craft, -ment, -ization*, etc.; prefix *super-*.

1384. ——, "Walt Whitman's Neologisms," *American Mercury* 4 (1925) 199–201. ¶ *-ess*, etc.

1385. ——, "Word-coinage and Modern Trade-Names," *Dialect Notes* 4 (1913–1917) 29–41. ¶ General.

1386. Praz, Mario, "The Italian Element in English," *Essays and Studies* 15 (1929) 20–66. ¶ Primarily loans, except at the beginning there is some treatment of suffixes.

1387. Prenner, Manuel, "The Current Tendency toward Denominative Verbs," *AmSp.* 13 (1938) 193–196. ¶ *We service, hostessing,* etc.

1388. ——, "More Notes on Neo-Suffixes," *AmSp.* 18 (1943) 71. ¶ *-roo*.

[1389. Preusler, Walther, "Deutsch von heute: II. Wortbildung," *Taal en Leven* 7 (1943–1944) 52–56.]

[1390. ——, "Diminutive und Koseformen im heutigen Hochdeutsch," *Taal en Leven* 6 (1942–1943) 145–149.]

1391. Preuss, Fritz, "Ableger des 'Sputnik,'" *Sprachforum* 3 (1959–1960) 318–320. ¶ New words in *-nik* in Eng. and Ger.

1392. ——, "-mobile," *Die Neueren Sprachen* N.F. 8 (1959) 480–482. ¶ New words in *-mobile*.

1393. ——, "near-," *Die Neueren Sprachen* N.F. 7 (1958) 539–542.

1394. Priebsch, R., and Collinson, W. E., *The German Language*, New York, 1938. ¶ Part III: wf; Part IV: loanwords and foreign words.

1395. Priess, Max, *Die Bedeutungen des abstracten substantivierten Adjektivs und des entsprechenden abstrakten Substantivs bei Shakespeare*, Halle, 1906 (= *Studien zur englischen Philologie* 28).

1396. Prokosch, E., *A Comparative Germanic Grammar*, Philadelphia, 1939.

[1397. Pudić, I., *Prefiks ga- u gotskom jeziku. Prilog učenju o glagolskom vidu*, Sarajevo, 1956 (= *Djela Naučnog društva NR Bosne i Hercegovine* 7 [*Odjeljenje istorisko-filoloških nauka* 6]).]

1398. Purtscher, Fridalin, *Die untrennbaren Partikeln im ahd. Tatian*, diss., Chur, 1902.

1399. Pyles, T., *Words and Ways of American English*, New York, 1952.

1400. Quartararo, I., *Il suffisso -ling nella lingua tedesca; sua formazione ed evoluzione*, Catania, 1942.

1401. Raabe, Paul, "Zum Suffix *-ler* in der Gegenwartssprache," *PBB* 78 (1956) 45–56.

1402. Radlof, J. G., "Merkwürdiger Entschluß der teutschen Gelehrten im Betreffe der Endsilbe *-tum*," *Der Verkündiger* (1808) 95.

[1403. ——, "Rheinpfälzische Mundart," *Teutschkundliche Forschungen* 1 (1825) 216–256.]

1404. Raith, Arnim, "Die Berufsnamen im Deutschen, Ableitungen mit dem Suffix *-er*," *Deutschunterricht für Ausländer* 9 (1959) 164–171.

1405. Raith, Joseph, *Die englischen Nasalverben*, Leipzig, 1931 (= *Beiträge zur englischen Philologie* 17).

1406. Rakers, Arnold, "Die Bentheimer Verkleinerungssilben," *NdJb.* 55 (1929) 147–154.

1407. Ramler, Karl Wilhelm, *Über die Bildung der deutschen Nennwörter*, Berlin, 1796 (*Beiträge zur deutschen Sprachkunde* 2).

1408. Ranke, Friedrick, "Mhd. *vrîbære* 'frei im Entschluß, freiwillig,' " *ZfdA* 79 (1942) 178–179. ¶ Suffix *-bære*.

1409. Rattke, Robert, *Die Abstraktbildungen auf -heit bei Meister Eckart und seinen Jüngern*, diss., Berlin, 1906.

1410. Rau, Marie Luise, "Das *-ette-* Suffix im Englischen," *Die Neueren Sprachen* 13 (1964) 501–512.

1411. Rausch, H., "Die Bildungssilbe *-rich*," *Muttersprache* 55 (1940) 54–57.

1412. Raven, Frithjof, *Die schwachen Verben des Althochdeutschen*, Band I: *Lang-, mehr- und kurzsilbige jan-Verba*, University, Ala., 1964.

1413. Recha, Carl, *Zur Frage über den Ursprung der perfektivierenden Funktion der Verbalpräfixe, nebst Einleitung über das Zusammenwirken des syntaktischen und phonetischen Factors*, Dorpat, 1893.

1414. Regel, C., *De syllabae a ad formanda adverbia substantivis vel adjectivis in lingua Anglica praefixae origine ac natura*, Gotha, 1855 (= *Programm des gymnasii illustris zu Gotha*, 1855).

1415. Regel, Karl, *Die Ruhlaer Mundart*, Weimar, 1868. ¶ Laut- und Wortbildung, Wortvorrat, Textproben.

1416. Rehling, Erik, *Det danske sprog. Fremstilling for lærere og seminarier*, Copenhagen, 1932. ¶ Includes sections on word classes and wf.

1417. Reichling, Anton J. B. N., *Het Woord*, diss., Utrecht, 1935. ¶ General semantics, wf, etc.

1418. Reifferscheid, Alex., "Lexicalisch-syntactische Untersuchungen über die Partikel *ge-*," *ZfdPh. Ergänzungsband* 2 (1874) 319–446. ¶ Collection of examples.

1419. Rein, Kurt, "Die Bedeutung von Tierzucht und Affekt für die Haustierbenennung," *Beiträge zur deutschen Philologie* 19–23 (1958), 191–295.

1420. Reinius, Josef, *On Transferred Appellations of Human Beings, Chiefly in English and German*, diss., Göteborg, 1903 (= *Göteborgs kungl. Vetenskaps- och vitterhetssamhälles Handlingar* 5, 1). ¶ Deals mostly with semantic change, with some treatment of derivation and compounding.

1421. ——, *Onomatopoetische Bezeichnungen für menschliche Wesen, besonders im Deutschen und Englischen*, Stockholm and Uppsala, 1908 (= *Studier i modern sprakvetenskap* 4).

1422. Reismüller, G., *Romanische Lehnwörter (Erstbelege) bei Lydgate. Ein Beitrag zur Lexicographie des Englischen im XV. Jahrhundert*, Munich, 1911 (= *Münchener Beiträge* 48).

1423. Remus, Hans, *Die kirchlichen und speziell-wissenschaftlichen romanischen Lehnworte Chaucers*, Halle, 1906 (= *Studien zur englischen Philologie* 14). ¶ Essentially a list of words by semantic categories with notes on formation.

1424. Renicke, Horst, "Fragen zur Kompositionslehre," *ZfdPh.* 84 (1965) 409–419.

[1425. Renský, Miroslav, "Nominal Tendencies in English," *Philologica Pragensia* 7 (1964) 135–150.]

1426. Reuter, Ole, *On the Development of English Verbs from Latin and French Past Participles*, Helsinki, 1934 (= *Societas Scientiarum Fennica, Commentationes Humanarum Litterarum* 6, 6).

1427. Rey, J., *Die Wortbildung im Neuhochdeutschen*, Aarau, 1893.

1428. Rice, Allan L., *Gothic Prepositional Compounds in their Relations to their Greek Originals*, diss., Philadelphia, 1934 (= *Language Dissertation* 16).

1429. Richter, Elise, *Fremdwortkunde*, Leipzig, 1919. ¶ II, 3: Wie wird aufgenommen? (Germanizing), and III. Die internationalen Bildungen und die Wanderwörter.

1430. Richter, Gerlinde, *Die Althochdeutschen missa-Bildungen und ihre Entwicklung zum Neuhochdeutschen*, diss., Leipzig, 1961.

1431. ——, "Zur Bedeutungsgeschichte der althochdeutschen *missa*-Bildungen," *PBB* (Halle) 85 (1963) 313–334.

1432. Riegel, Hermann, " 'Grobian, Dummrian' usw.," *ZdallgdSprv.* 5 (1890) 36–37.

1433. Riemer, Guido C. L., *Die Adjektiva bei Wolfram von Eschenbach stilistisch betrachtet. Der Wort- und Begriffsschatz*, diss., Leipzig, 1906. ¶ List of adjectives and their formation included.

1434. Ries, John, *Was ist Syntax?* 2nd ed., Prag, 1927. ¶ Specific chapters on syntax and wf.

[1435. Riess, Ludwig, "Die Endsilbe -schaft," in *Historik*, Berlin and Leipzig, 1912, 373–384.]

1436. Roberts, Willa, " 'Cafeteria' Again," *AmSp.* 3 (1927–1928) 344. ¶ -*eria*: Sp. suffix.

1437. Rockwell, Leo L., "Older German Loan-words in American English," *AmSp.* 20 (1945) 247–257.

1438. Roedder, E., *Volkssprache und Wortschatz des badischen Frankenlandes dargestellt auf Grund der Mundart von Oberschefflenz*, New York, 1936. [Hugo Suolahti, *Neuphil.Mitt.* 39 (1938) 269.]

1439. Roedder, Edwin Carl, "Wortlehre des Adjectivs im Altsächsischen," *Bulletin of the University of Wisconsin No. 50, Philology and Literature Series* 1, 4 (1901) 337–415. ¶ Derivation, pp. 344–360; composition, pp. 361–371; substantivation of adjectives, pp. 374–379.

1440. Röhling, Martin, *Das Präfix ofer- in der altenglischen Verbal- und Nominal-Komposition mit Berücksichtigung der übringen germanischen Dialekte*, diss., Heidelberg, 1914.

1441. Roelandts, K., "Expressieve naam- en woordvorming. Een teorie en een program," *Mededelingen van de Vereniging voor Naamkunde te Leuven en de Commissie voor Naamkunde te Amsterdam* 34 (1958) 75–95.

1442. ——, "Regressieve en secundaire woordvorming," *Medelingen von de Vereniging voor Naamkunde te Leuven en de Commissie voor Naamkunde te Amsterdam* 36 (1960) 89–124. ¶ Regressive derivation and analogical formation.

1443. Rösener, Fr., *Die französischen Lehnwörter im Frühneuenglischen*, diss., Marburg, 1907.

1444. Rössing, Hans, "Wortzusammensetzung und Wortbedeutung. Untersuchungen im Anschluß an die germanischen Bezeichnungen für Skarabäiden," *Beiträge zur deutschen Philologie* 19–23 (1958) 523–635.

1445. Rogge, Christian, "Die Analogie im Sprachleben, was sie ist und wie sie wirkt. Das Grundkapitel in der Psychologie der Sprache," *Archiv für die gesamte Psychologie* 52 (1925) 441–468.

1446. ——, "Der psychologische Ablauf der Wortzusammensetzung," *Archiv für die gesamte Psychologie* 53 (1925) 485–500.

1447. ——, "Sprachforschung und Dialekt auf Grund der Analogiewirkung," *Teuthonista* 3 (1926–1927) 64 ff. ¶ Explanation of several words as blend compounds: *Pferd = Perd + Fohlen*, *Füllen*, etc.

1448. ——, "Der tote Punkt in der etymologischen Forschung," *ZfdPh.* 51 (1926) 1–12. ¶ Force of analogy; blends and contaminations.

1449. Rohde, E., "Abkürzungen durch Anfangsbuchstaben," *Moderna spraak* 1 (1907) 53–59.

1450. Roitinger, Franz, "Zur Partizipialbildung in den *eo*-Mundarten Oberösterreichs," *ZfMaa.* 20 (1951–1952) 114–117.

1451. Rolffs, Friedrich Wilhelm, *Gotisch dis- und du-*, diss., Breslau, 1908.

1452. Roos, Karl, *Die Fremdwörter in den elsässischen Mundarten. Ein Beitrag zur elsässischen Dialektforschung*, diss., Strassburg, 1903. ¶ Chap. 4, wf; chap. 5, "Wortumbildungen."

1453. Rooth, Erik, "Das Verb *eratmen* bei Goethe und seine Stellung im System der Verben mit *er*-Präfix," in *Mélanges de philologie offerts à M. Johan Melander*, Uppsala, 1943, 161–197.

1454. ——, "Zur Geschichte der englischen Partizip-Präsens-Form auf *-ing*," *SN* 14 (1941–1942) 71–85.

1455. Rosell, Erland, *Prefixet o- i nordiska spraak. En betydelsehistorisk studie*, Uppsala, 1942 (= *Fornnordiska. Uppsala universitets aarsskrift* 7).

1456. Rosen, Harold, *Old High German Prepositional Compounds in Relation to their Latin Originals*, diss., Philadelphia, 1934 (= *Language Dissertation* 16).

1457. Rosenfeld, Hans Friedrich, "Zu den alem. nordgerm. Wortgleichungen," *Neuphil.Mitt.* 51 (1950) 61–109.

1458. Rosenfeld, Hellmut, "Die Kosenamen und Lockrufe unserer Haustiere und die Leitrufe unserer Zugtiere," *Rheinisches Jahrbuch für Volkskunde (Meizen)* 6 (1955) 50–51.

1459. ——, "Die *n*-Stämme in der Namen- und Wort-Komposition und die *ing*-Namen," *Beiträge zur Namenforschung* 9 (1958) 190–201.

1460. Rosenqvist, Arvid, *Der französische Einfluß auf die mittelhochdeutsche Sprache in der 1. Hälfte des 14. Jahrhunderts*, diss., Helsinki, 1932 (= *Mémoires de la Société Néophilologique* 9). [Emil Öhmann, *Neuphil.Mitt.* 33 (1932) 227–241.]

1461. ——, *Der französische Einfluß auf die mittelhochdeutsche Sprache in der 2. Hälfte des 14. Jahrhunderts*, Helsinki, 1943 (= *Mémoires de la Société Néophilologique* 14). [Hugo Suolahti, *Neuphil.Mitt.* 43 (1942) 217–224.]

1462. ——, "Über die mittelhochdeutschen Wörter auf *-ier, -ieræere, -ierre*," *Neuphil.Mitt.* 55 (1954) 81–134.

1463. ——, "Über Wanderungen romanischer Fremdwörter im Deutschen," *AASF* B 50 (1942) 249 ff.

1464. ——, "Das Verbalsuffix *-(i)eren*," *AASF* B 30 (1934) 587 ff.

1465. Rossberg, K., *Deutsche Lehnwörter*, Leipzig, 1881.

1466. Rother, Karl, "Das Worttypus *faulenzen*," *ZfdW* 14 (1912–1913) 219–220.

[1467. Rotomskiené, T., "K probleme substantivacii prilagatel'nych v sovremennom anglijskom jazyke," *Vilniaus Pedagoginio Instituto Mokslo darbai* 9 (1960) 133–175. ¶ Substantivation of adjectives in present-day Eng.]

1468. Rotzoll, Eva, *Das Aussterben alt- und mittelenglischer Deminutivbildungen im Neuenglischen*, diss., Heidelberg, 1909.

1469. ——, *Die Deminutivbildungen im Neuenglischen*, Heidelberg, 1910 (= *Anglistische Forschungen* 31).

1470. Royen, O. F. M. G., "Bij -lik en -loos," *Taal en Leven* 5 (1941–1942) 49–62. ¶ Substitution of a voiceless for a voiced consonant before the suffix *-lij* (*-lik*) (e.g., *vergeven*: *vergefelij*) but not before *-loos*.

1471. ——, "Van naïveteit tot naïviteit," *De Nieuwe Taalgids* 42 (1949) 280–289. ¶ Formation of words in *-iteit*.

1472. Rozwadowski, Jan van, *Wortbildung und Wortbedeutung. Eine Untersuchung ihrer Grundgesetze*, Heidelberg, 1904. ¶ Theoretical.

1473. Rudnyćkyj, J. B., " 'Sputnik' and Its Derivatives in North American English," *Proceedings of the Linguistic Circle of Manitoba and North Dakota* 1 (1959) 27–28.

1474. ——, "*Sputnik* and *-nik* Derivatives in the Present Language of North America," *Études slaves et est-européennes* 4 (1959–1960) 142–150.

1475. Rudolphi, R., *Über die Erweiterung der Wurzelsilbe deutscher Wörter durch die Nasale* m *und* n, Erfurt, 1864.

1476. Rüdel, K., "Die Partikel *ge-* vor dem Particip des Präteritums in der Nürnberger Volkssprache," *Fromanns Deutsche Mundarten* 1 (1854) 226–228.

1477. Ruppel, H., *Rückbildung deutscher Substantiva aus Adjektiven*, diss., Freiburg, 1911.

1478. Russell, I. Willis, "The Suffix *-manship*," *South Atlantic Bulletin* 31 (1966) 3. ¶ Abstract of a paper.

1479. ——, and Boyett, Woodrow W., "Among the New Words," *AmSp.* 32 (1957) 292–296. ¶ New words in *-ism*.

1480. Ryan, William M., "A Plethorama," *AmSp.* 36 (1961) 230–233. ¶ New words in *-rama*.

1481. Ryder, F. G., "Verb-Adverb Compounds in Gothic and Old High German: A Study in Comparative Syntax," diss., Ann Arbor, 1950.

1482. Rytkönen, Ahti, "Avledning paa *-is* i svenskt och finskt slangspraak," *Hufvudstadsbladet* (Helsinki) No. 190 (1953).

1483. Sachs, Emmy, "On *steinalt*, *stockstill*, and Similar Formations," *JEGP* 52 (1963) 581–596.

1484. Sadilek, Exha Akins, "American Intensives in *ka-*, *ke-* and *ker-*," *AmSp.* 7 (1931–1932) 142.

1485. Salus, Peter H., "The Compound Noun in Indo-European—A Survey," *DA* 24 (1964) 3741–3742.

1486. ——, "More about *mannskratti*," *Íslenzk Tunge* 4 (1963) 109–111.

1487. ——, "Syntactic Compounds in Modern English," *English Studies* 45 (1964) 462–464.

1488. Salverda de Grave, J. J., "Bijdragen tot de kennis der uit het Fransch overgenomen woorden in het Nederlandsch IV: Over afgeleide werkwoorden," *Tijdschrift* 21 (1902) 297–315.

1489. ——, "Eenige woordaflcidingen," *Tijdschrift* 19 (1900) 85–102. ¶ Individual etymologies with discussion of various suffixes.

1490. ——, *De franse woorden in het Nederlands*, Amsterdam, 1906 (= *Verhandlingen der Koninklijke Akademie van Wetenschappen te Amsterdam: Afdeeling Letterkunde*, nieuwe reeks, deel 7).

1491. ——, *L'influence de la langue française en Hollande d'après les mots d'empruntés*, Paris, 1913. ¶ Esp. "Nouveaux mots néerlandais formés au moyen d'éléments français," pp. 98 ff.

1492. ——, "Les mots dialectaux du français en néerlandais," *Romania* 30 (1901) 65–112. ¶ Principally sound correspondences.

1493. Samuels, M., "The *ge-* Prefix in the Old English Gloss to the Lindisfarne Gospels," *Trans.Phil.Soc.* (1949) 62–116.

1494. Samuelsson, K. J., "Naagra ord om sammansättningar med *-lös* och *-fri*," in *Svenska Studier tillägnade Gustaf Cederschiöld*, Lund, 1914, 394–405.

1495. Sandahl, Bertin, *Middle English Sea Terms*, 2 vols., Uppsala, 1951 and 1958 (= *Essays and Studies* 8 and 20). ¶ Individual etymologies with reference to compounding and derivation.

1496. Sanders, Daniel, "Die Endsilbe '-bar,' " *Zt. für deutsche Sprache* 8 (1895) 53 ff.

1497. ——, "Scheinbar zusammengesetzte Zeitwörter," *Zt. für deutsche Sprache* 4 (1890) 262–264.

1498. ——, "Die Verkleinerungssilbe '-chen,' " *Zt. für deutsche Sprache* 6 (1893) 422–427, 447–450; 7 (1894) 93–100, 130–132.

1499. Sandmann, M., "On Neuter Adjectives Determining Verbs, with Special Reference to French and Spanish," *MLR* 41 (1946) 24–34.

1500. Sarrazin, O., "Neuere Lehnwörter," *ZdallgdSprv.* 14 (1899) 133–137.

1501. Sass, [no initial], "Hauptwörter auf *-els*," *NdKbl.* 51 (1938) 39.

1502. Schach, Paul, "The Formation of Hybrid Derivatives in Pennsylvania German," *Symposium* 3 (1949) 114–129. ¶ Based on nouns, adjectives, and verbs.

1503. ——, "Hybrid Compounds in Pennsylvania German," *AmSp.* 23 (1948) 120–134.

1504. ——, "Die Lehnprägungen der pennsylvania-deutschen Mundart," *ZfMdaf.* 22 (1954) 215–222.

[1505. Schaedel, Karl, *Das altenglische Element in den neuenglischen Dialekten*, diss., Frankfurt, 1911.]

[1506. Schagerström, August, *Om sv. bär- och fruktnamn paa -on*, Uppsala, 1884 (= *Redogörelse för Uppsala h. a. l.* 1883–1884.)]

1507. Schatz, J., "*Pilger—Piligrim* und verwandte Bildungen,' *PBB* 49 (1925) 125 ff.

1508. Scheel, Willy, *Neuhochdeutsche Sprachlehre* 1. *Laut- und Wortbildungslehre*, Heidelberg, 1908. ¶ Chap. 4, wf.

1509. Scheffler, K., "Einiges über Zusammensetzungen," *ZdallgdSprv.* 6 (1896) 104–108.

1510. Scheinert, Moritz, *Die Adjectiva im Beowulfepos als Darstellungsmittel,* diss., Halle, 1905.

1511. Scherer, Anton, *Gestirnnamen bei den indogermanischen Völkern,* Heidelberg, 1953 (= *Indogermanische Bibliothek,* 3. Reihe; also *Forschungen zum Wortschatz der indogermanischen Sprachen* 1). ¶ Pp. 244–245 are an index list of suffixes with page and language references.

1512. Scherer, Philip, "Aspect in Gothic," *Language* 30 (1954) 211–223.

1513. ——, "Aspect in the Old English of the Corpus Christi MS," *Language* 34 (1958) 245–251.

1514. ——, "Aspect in the Old High German of Tatian," *Language* 32 (1956) 423–434.

1515. ——, "The Theory of the Function of the Gothic Preverb *ga-*," *Word* 20 (1964) 221–245.

1516. ——, "The Theory of the Function of the Preverb GA," in *Proceedings of the Ninth International Congress of Linguists, Cambridge, Mass. August 27–31, 1962,* ed. Horace G. Lunt, The Hague, 1964, 859–861.

1517. Scherzberg, Johanna, "Vielgliedrige Zusammensetzungen," *Wissenschaftliche Zeitschrift der Pädagogischen Hochschule Potsdam. Gesellschafts- und sprachwissenschaftliche Reihe* (Sonderheft 1964) 43–45.

1518. Schiepek, Josef, *Satzbau der Egerländer Mundart,* 2 parts, Prague, 1899 and 1908. ¶ In both parts there is a section called Wortklassen with occasional comments on wf.

1519. Schirmer, Alfred, "Über mehrgliedrige Zusammensetzungen," *Muttersprache* (1949) 128–132.

1520. Schirokauer, A., "Die Geschichte des *t*-Suffixes in *Axt*," *MLQ* 4 (1943) 21–25.

1521. ——, "Die Wortbildung *Zirlin-mirlin*. Aufkommen, Verbreitung und Bedeutungsspielraum eines Modeworts," *JEGP* 47 (1948) 398–402.

1522. Schlaug, Wilhelm, *Die altsächsischen Personennamen vor dem Jahre 1000,* Lund, 1962 (= *Lunder germanistische Forschungen* 34). ¶ Chap. 4 is a survey of the formation of Kurznamen.

1523. Schleicher, August, *Die Unterscheidung von Nomen und Verbum in der lautlichen Form,* Leipzig, 1865 (= *Abhandlungen der philologisch-historischen Classe der königlich-sächsischen Gesellschaft der Wissenschaften* 4, 5). ¶ Comparative; partly IE, large number of non-IE languages.

1524. Schlepper, Erich, *Die Neubildung von Substantiven in den Übersetzungen König Alfreds mit einem Ausblick auf Chaucer,* diss., Gütersloh, 1936. ¶ Suffixes, compounding, etc.

[1525. Schlothauer, Günter, "Der reine Verbalstamm als Substantiv bei Shakespeare," diss., Jena, 1951.]

1526. Schlüter, Wolfgang, *Die mit dem Suffix ja gebildeten deutschen Nomina*, Göttingen, 1875.

1527. Schmeding, Otto, *Über Wortbildung bei Carlyle*, Halle, 1900 (= *Studien zur englischen Philologie* 5).

1528. Schmeller, A. J., *Bayerisches Wörterbuch*, 2 vols., Stuttgart, Tübingen, 1827–1837.

1529. Schmid, P., "Über die Herkunft und Bedeutung der germanischen Bildungssilben *ag*, *ig* und *lik*," *ZfdA* 49 (1908) 485 ff.

1530. Schmidt, August F., "Gonis," *Danske studier* (1939) 79–80. ¶ *-is* as a diminutive-pejorative suffix.

1531. Schmidt, B., *Die Siegerländer Mundart*, Halle, 1894. ¶ Compounds, pp. 109–112; affixes, pp. 119–136.

1532. ——, *Der Vokalismus der Siegerländer Mundart*, diss., Halle, 1849.

1533. Schmidt, Immanuel, *Grammatik der englischen Sprache*, Berlin, 1867. ¶ Paras. 151, 159, participles that have become adjectives.

1534. Schmidt, Johannes, "Das Suffix des Participium perfecti activi," *ZfvglSpr.* 26 (1883) 329–377.

1535. Schmidt, Karl H., *Präfixwandlungen im Mittelenglischen und Neuenglischen bei Verben, Substantiven und Adjektiven*, diss., Sobernheim, 1909. ¶ Heimische Präfixe, pp. 1–6; fremde Präfixe, pp. 7–69.

1536. Schmitt, A., "Über Wortbildungen besonders der neueren Sprachen," *Herrigs Archiv* 3 (1847) 136–149.

1537. Schmittbetz, K., "Das Adjektiv in 'Sir Gawayn and the Grene Knyȝt,' " *Anglia* 32 (1909) 1–60, 163–189, 359–383.

1538. Schneider, J., "Über skandinavische Lehnwörter im Deutschen," *Neuphil.Mitt.* 56 (1955) 284–296.

1539. Schöfer, Erasmus, "Die Wortbildung in den Schriften Martin Heideggers," *Wirkendes Wort* 14 (1964) 219–233.

1540. Schön, Eduard, *Die Bildung des Adjektivs im Altenglischen*, Kiel, 1905 (= *Kieler Studien zur englischen Philologie*, N.F. 2). ¶ Derivation, compounding, and formation without suffix.

1541. Schönfeld, M., *Historiese Grammatica van het Nederlands*, 5th ed., ed. A. van Loey, Zutphen, 1954.

1542. Schönfelder, Karl-Heinz, "Deutsche Wortbildungselemente im amerikanischen Englisch. Ein Beitrag zu Stalins Theorie über die Sprachmischung," *Wissenschaftliche Zeitschrift der Universität Leipzig, gesellschafts- und sprachwissenschaftliche Reihe* 5 (1951–1952) 8–18. ¶ Compounds in *-bund*, *-burger*, *-fest*, *-heimer*, etc.

1543. ——, *Deutsches Lehngut im amerikanischen Englisch. Ein Beitrag zur Problem der Völker- und Sprachmischung*, Halle, 1957. ¶ Esp. Part III: "Deutsche Einflüsse auf die Wortbildung im amerikanischen Englisch," dealing with *-fest*, *-furter*, *-burger*, *-heimer*, etc.

1544. Schönoff, H., "Französische Lehnworte in den niedersächsischen Mundarten," *GRM* 1 (1909) 356 ff.

1545. Schoof, W., "Beiträge zur Kenntnis der Schwälmer Mundart," *Zfd-Maa.* (1906) 74 ff., 199 ff., 354 ff.

1546. Schook, H. W. J. A., "De causatieven en hun voorwerpen," *Noord en zuid* 18 (1895) 31–38. ¶ Substitutes for causative verbs.

1547. Schoppe, Georg, "Beiträge zur deutschen Wortgeschichte," *Neuphil. Mitt.* 28 (1927) 1–16. ¶ Silesian compounds and derivatives.

1548. Schrader, Wilhelm, For- *und* fore- *Verbalcomposita im Verlaufe der englischen Sprachgeschichte*, diss., Greifswald, 1914.

1549. ——, "Wortbildungs-Trieb und -Kraft der deutschen Sprache," *Zeitschrift für deutsche Sprache* 6 (1893) 1–9.

1550. Schröder, Edward, "Bunte Lese III: 9. Altmitteldeutsches *-ěren*," *ZfdA* 63 (1926) 175 f.

1551. ——, "Exkurs über die gotischen Adjektiva auf *-ahs*," *ZfdA* 35 (1891) 367–379.

1552. ——, "Kleinigkeiten zum König Rother," *ZfdA* 48 (1906) 363–364. ¶ Adj. in *-lĭch*.

1553. ——, "*Lâr* und *-lar*," *ZfdA* 65 (1928) 131.

1554. ——, "Die mittelhochdeutschen Kollektiv-Abstrakta auf *-ie, -eie*," *ZfdA* 75 (1938) 193–195.

1555. ——, "Die Nomina agentis auf *-ster*," *NdJb.* 48 (1922) 1–8.

1556. ——, "Pfennig," *ZfdA* 37 (1893) 124–127. ¶ Suffix *-ig/-ing*.

1557. ——, "Steigerung und Häufung der Alliteration in der westgermanischen Dichtung," *ZfdA* 43 (1899) 361–385. ¶ Use of alliterating nominal compounds.

1558. Schröder, Heinrich, "Schüttelformen," *ZfdPh.* 37 (1905) 256–260. ¶ *morantisch* for *romantisch*, etc.

1559. ——, "Streckformen," *PBB* 29 (1903–1904) 346–354.

1560. ——, *Streckformen. Ein Beitrag zur Lehre von der Wortentstehung und der germanischen Wortbetonung*, Heidelberg, 1906. ¶ Streckform: a wf produced by the wilful insertion of a vowel (and consonant) between the initial consonant and the stem vowel.

1561. Schröder, Marianne, "Die frühmittelhochdeutschen *-lich*-Bildungen," *PBB* (Halle) 83 (1961) 151–194.

1562. Schudt, H., *Wortbildung der Mundart von Wetterfeld* (Oberhessen), Giessen, 1927 (= *Giessener Beiträge* 20)

1563. Schütte, Gudm., "Ingtypens udvikling i geografiske navne og slægtsnavne," *Fortid og nutid* (1925) 103–136. ¶ *-ing, -heim*.

1564. Schütte, Otto, "Bildungen auf *-rich* bei Wilhelm Raabe," *ZfdW* 11 (1909) 308–309.

1565. ——, "Substantive auf *-ling* bei Raabe," *ZfdW* 12 (1910–1911) 269 f.

1566. Schütz, Karl, *Die Lehnprägungen der Reichenauer Glossare Rb, Rc, Rd, Re und Rf*, diss., Bonn, 1958. ¶ "Wortbildung des nicht-religiösen Wortschatzes," pp. 236 ff.; "Die Wortbildung des religiösen Lehngutes," pp. 246 ff.

1567. Schuldt, Claus, *Die Bildung der schwachen Verba im Altenglischen*, Kiel, 1905 (= *Kieler Studien zur englischen Philologie* N.F. 1). ¶ Chap. 1, sec. 2: weak verbs formed by suffixes; chap. 2: loanwords.

1568. Schulte, Werner, "Die Verkleinerungssilben -tien, -tsien, -tier, -tsier um Drolshagen und Olpe im südlichen Sauerlande," *ZfMdaf.* 17 (1941) 158–164.

1569. Schultink, H., "De bouw van nieuwvormingen met *her-*," *Tijdschrift* 80 (1964) 150–184.

1570. Schults, H., "Imperativische thier- und Pflanzennamen," *NdKbl.* 6 (1881) 18.

1571. Schulze, C., "Imperativisch gebildete Substantiva," *Herrigs Archiv* 43 (1868) 13–40. ¶ Ger., French, Italian, etc.

1572. Schulze, Gustav, "Die Wortbildung in der Technik," *Muttersprache* (1952) 148–157.

1573. Schulze, Wilhelm, "Zur Kurznamenbildung," *ZfvglSpr.* 33 (1895) 401–402.

1574. Schwagmeyer, Friedrich, "Die wortbildende Kraft des westfälischen *Kraft*," *Muttersprache* (1929) 371–376.

1575. Schwarz, Ernst, "Das Alter der genetivischen Zusammensetzungen bei den germanischen Ortsnamen," *Beiträge zur Namenforschung* 2 (1950–1951) 40–55.

1576. Schwarz, Hermann, *Das Suffix -lich(t) beim Adjektiv im Neuhochdeutschen*, diss., Freiburg, 1905.

[1577. Schwarz, H. O., "Die Lehnbildungen der Notkerschen Psalmenübersetzung," diss., Bonn, 1957.]

1578. Schwarz, W., *Studien über die aus dem Lateinischen entlehnten Zeitwörter der englischen Sprache*, diss., Strassburg, 1903.

1579. Schwend, Adolf, "Lautlehre der Mundart von Oberschopfheim," *ZfhdMaa.* 1 (1900) 305–345. ¶ Paras. 81, *ge-*; 82, diminutives; 83, *-ung, -ing*.

1580. Schwentner, Ernst, "Das altfriesische Abstraktsuffix -nisse, -nesse (-ense) mit besonderer Berücksichtigung des Altsächsischen und Altniederfränkischen," *NdJb.* 74 (1951) 1–10.

1581. ——, "Zum altfriesischen Abstraktsuffix -nisse, -nesse, -ense," *NdKbl.* 60 (1953) 12 ff.

1582. Scott, Charles P. G., "English Words Which Have Gained or Lost an Initial Consonant by Attraction," *Trans.Amer.Phil.Assn.* 23 (1892) 179–305.

1583. Seelig, Fritz, *Die Komparation der Adjektiva und Adverbien im Altenglischen*, Heidelberg, 1930 (= *Anglistische Forschungen* 70). ¶ *-ra, -ost, -est, -m, -or,* etc.

1584. Seelmann, Wilhelm, "Mittelnd. und neund. Infinitive mit *ge-* Präfix," *NdKbl.* 41 (1927) 35–37.

1585. ——, "Niederdeutsche Diminutive auf *-el,*" *NdJb.* 45 (1919) 18 ff.

1586. ——, "Suffix *-ster,*" *NdJb.* 47 (1921) 42–44.

1587. ——, "Zur *e*-Apokope," *NdKbl.* 51 (1938) 4.

1588. Seibicke, Wilfried, "Wörter auf '-mässig.' Sprachkritik und Sprachbetrachtung," *Muttersprache* (1963) 33 ff., 73 ff.

1589. Seidel, Eugen, and Seidel-Slotty, Ingeborg, *Sprachwandel im Dritten Reich*, Halle (Saale), 1961. ¶ Derivation, pp. 27 ff.; compounding, pp. 33 ff.

1590. Seidenadel, Emil, *Frauenzimmer. Eine wortgeschichtliche Untersuchung*, diss., Strassburg, 1903. ¶ The compound.

1591. Seifert, Lester W., "The Diminutives of Pennsylvania German," *Monatshefte* 34 (1947) 285–293.

1592. Seiler, Friedrich, *Die Entwicklung der deutschen Kultur im Spiegel des deutschen Lehnworts*: III. *Das Lehnwort der neueren Zeit*, 1. and 2. Abschnitt, Halle, 1924; VI–VIII. *Das deutsche Lehnsprichwort*, 2.–4. Teil, Halle, 1923–1924.

1593. Seip, D. A., "Om bøiningen av adjektiver paa *-lig* og *-ig,*" *Norsk tidsskrift for sprogvidenskap* 5 (1932) 151–166. ¶ Primarily inflection, some derivation.

1594. ——, "Om suffikset *-else* i nordisk," in *Festskrift til professor Olaf Broch paa hans 80-aarsdag fra venner og elever*, Oslo, 1947, 209–242 (= *Avhandlingar utg. av Det norske videnskaps-akademi i Oslo. II. Hist.-filos. kl.* 1947).

1595. Seip, Elsbeth, *Die gotischen Verba mit dem Präfix and-*, Giessen, 1923 (= *Giessener Beiträge zur deutschen Philologie* 10).

1596. Senn, Alfred, *Germanische Lehnwortstudien*, diss., Heidelberg, 1925.

1597. ——, "Verbal Aspects in Germanic, Slavic, and Baltic," *Language* 25 (1949) 402–409.

1598. Serjeantson, Mary, *A History of Foreign Words in English*, London, 1935.

1599. Seymour, Richard K., "Nominal Word Formation by Suffixes in the Swabian Dialect," diss., Philadelphia, 1956.

1600. ——, "Old High German *-âta, -ât* in Middle High German and in Present-day German Dialects," *Language* 39 (1963) 235–241.

1601. ——, "Schwäbisches *Aberär,*" *ZfdW* 17 (1961) 185–186.

1602. ——, "Zu den schwäbischen nominibus agentis auf *-äre,*" *ZfMdaf.* 25 (1957) 216–221.

1603. Shankle, George Earlie, *Current Abbreviations*, New York, 1945. ¶ Dictionary; type "radar," etc.

1604. Sheldon, Esther K., "A Very Nice-Type Girl," *AmSp.* 23 (1948) 251–256. ¶ *-type* as a semi-suffix.

1605. Shetter, William Z., "The Dutch Diminutive," *JEGP* 58 (1959) 75–90.

1606. Shook, L. K., "A Technical Construction in Old English, Translation Loans in *-lic*," *Mediaeval Studies* 2 (1940) 253–257.

1607. Shuman, R. Baird, and Hutchings, H. Charles, "The *un*-Prefix. A Means of Germanic Irony in *Beowulf*," *Mod.Phil.* 58 (1960) 217–222.

1608. Sieber, Siegfried, "Nachtrag zu den Wörtern auf *-ling*," *ZfdW* 14 (1912–1913) 221 f.

1609. ——, "Die Wörter auf *-ling*," *Muttersprache* (1927) 133–139.

1610. Sieberer, Anton, "Das Wesen des Deminutivs," *Die Sprache* 2 (1950) 85–121.

1611. Siemerling, Otto, *Das Präfix "for(e)-" in der altenglischen Verbal- und Nominalkomposition*, diss., Kiel, 1909.

1612. Sievers, Eduard, *Altenglische Grammatik*, ed. K. Brunner, Halle, 1942.

1613. ——, "Kleine Beiträge zur deutschen Grammatik," *PBB* 5 (1878) 519 ff. ¶ The nominal suffix *tra* in Gmc.; the *r*- and *l*- forms.

1614. ——, "Über germanische Nominalbildungen auf *aja-*, *-ēja-*," *Ber. der Kgl. Sächs. Ges. der Wsch. zu Leipzig, phil.-hist. Klasse* (1894) 129–152.

1615. ——, "Zur Accent und Lautlehre der germanischen Sprachen," *PBB* 4 (1877) 522–539; 5 (1878) 137 ff. ¶ Deals in part with accent on suffixes.

1616. Sigl, Joh., "Unsere 'ing'-Namen," *Monatsschrift für die ostbairischen Grenzmarken* 10 (1921) 134–136.

1617. Simon, Max, "Mit Vorsilben, namentlich mit der Vorsilbe 'um' echt oder unecht zusammengesetzte Zeitwörter," *Zt. für deutsche Sprache* 4 (1891) 117–123, 148–152.

1618. Sjöros, Bruno, "Beiträge zur Kenntnis des Suffixes *-ung*, *-ing* in den germanischen Sprachen," *Neuphil.Mitt.* 18 (1917) 24–33.

1619. Skautrup, Peter, *Det danske sprogs historie. I. Fra guldhornene til Jyske Lov*, Copenhagen, 1944. ¶ Sections on wf.

1620. Skeat, W. W., "English Words Borrowed from French before the Conquest," *The Academy* 48, No. 1221 (1895) 252.

1621. ——, *An Etymological Dictionary of the English Language*, 4th ed., Oxford, 1924.

1622. ——, "On the Prefix *a-* in English," *Journal of Philology* 5 (1874) 32–43.

1623. ——, *Principles of English Etymology*, 1st ser.: *The Native Element*, Oxford, 1887 (rev. 1892), and 2nd ser.: *The Foreign Element*, Oxford, 1891.

1624. Skorochodova, G. I., "K voprosu o suffikse *-mässig* v prilagatel'nych sovremennogo švedskogo jazyka," *Skandinavskij sbornik* 4 (1959) 169–176. ¶ Suffix *-mässig* in modern Sw.

1625. ——, "K voprosu o zaimstvovannych slovoobrazovatel'nych suffiksach (Na materiale prilagatel'nych švedskogo jazyka, obrazovannych s suffiksom *-aktig*)," *Učenye zapiski Leningradskogo ordena Lenina gosudarstvennogo Universiteta im. A. A. Ždanova*. 260 (Filol. nauk 49) (1958) 31–43. ¶ On loan suffixes, esp. Sw. adjectives in *-aktig*.

1626. Slater, Joseph, "A Renewed Meaning for the Suffix *-ly*," *AmSp.* 38 (1963) 301.

1627. Slettengren, Emrik, *Contributions to the Study of Aphaeretic Words in English*, diss., Lund, 1912.

1628. Smith, C. A., "A Note on the Concord of Collectives and Indefinites in English," *Anglia Beibl.* 23 (1900–1901) 242–248.

1629. Smith, G. C. Moore, "Superlative Adjectives Formed from Substantives," *Review of English Studies* 5 (1929) 203 ff.

1630. Smock, John C., *The Greek Element in English Words*, ed. Percy W. Long, New York, 1931. ¶ Part I gives Eng. words and combining forms as derived and formed from Greek; Part II gives Greek terminal elements frequently represented in Eng. and then Greek words and combining forms as they appear in Eng.

1631. Smuts, J., "Proef van 'n statistiese ontleding van woordvorming in Afrikaans," *Tydskrif vir Volkskunde en Volkstaal* 18 (1962) 16–18. ¶ Tentative statistical analysis of wf in Afrikaans.

[1632. Soboleva, P. A., "Komponentnyj analiz značenij glagola na osnove slovoobrazovateil'nogo priznaka," in *Problemy strukturnoj lingvistiki. Sbornik statej*, Moscow, 1962, 175–189. ¶ Componental analysis of verbal meanings on the basis of word-building properties; with Eng. summary.]

1633. Söderbergh, Ragnhild, *Suffixet -mässig i svenskan: En historisk-semantisk ordbildningsstudie*, Stockholm, 1964 (= *Stockholm Studies in Scandinavian Philology*, N.S. 5).

1634. Söhns, Franz, "Niederdeutsche Thiernamen," *Natur* 29 (1890) 402–403. ¶ Compounding and derivation of specific names.

1635. Solta, Georg Renatus, *Gedanken über das nt-Suffix*, Vienna, 1958 (= *Sitzungsberichte der philosophisch-historischen Klasse der Königlichen Akademie der Wissenschaften Wien* 232, 1).

[1636. Sorensen, J. K., *Danske bebyggelsesnavne pa -sted*, Copenhagen, 1958.]

1637. Spalding, Keith, "Lichtenberg's Use of *heim*-Compounds," *MLR* 51 (1956) 570–572.

1638. Specht, Franz, "Zur ahd. Stammbildung," in *Altdeutsches Wort und Wortkunstwerk: Goerg Baesecke zum 65. Geburtstage 13. Januar 1941*, Halle, 1941, 109–123. ¶ Derivatives; IE *is*, *us* stems.

1639. ——, "Zur Bildung der adjektivischen *u*-Stämme," *ZfvglSpr.* 65 (1938) 193–207.

1640. Spector, Robert Donald, "Compound Words in Baseball," *AmSp.* 30 (1955) 153.

1641. Sperlbaum, Margret, *Tiernamen mit k-Suffix in diachronischer und synchronischer Sicht*, Giessen, 1957 (= *Beiträge zur deutschen Philologie* 16). ¶ *k, sk > sch; -erich*; with maps.

1642. Speyer, J. S., "Enige opmerkingen omtrent de nederlandsche substantiva gevormd met het suffix *-ling*," *Tijdschrift* 32 (1913) 35–46.

1643. Spies, H., "Alliteration und Reimklang im modern-englischen Kulturleben," *Engl.Stud.* 54 (1920) 149–158.

1644. Spiess, B., *Die fränkische-hennebergische Mundart*, Vienna, 1873.

1645. Spitzbardt, Harry, "Präfigierte Verstärkungselemente im Englischen," *Wissenschaftliche Zeitschrift der Freidrich-Schiller-Universität, Jena. Gesellschafts- und sprachwissenschaftliche Reihe* 11 (1962) 135–143.

1646. Spitzer, Leo, "Confusion schmooshum," *JEGP* 51 (1952) 226–233. ¶ Use of Yiddish prefix *schm-* for jocular repetition.

1647. ——, "Warum ersetzt frz. *-erie* (dtsch. *-erei*) das alte *-ie* (*-ei*)?" *ZfrPh.* 51 (1931) 70–75.

1648. ——, *Die Wortbildung als stilistisches Mittel, exemplifiziert an Rabelais. Nebst einem Anhang: Über die Wortbildung bei Balzac in seinen "Contes drôlatiques,"* Halle, 1910 (= *Beihefte zur ZfrPh.* 29). ¶ Pp. 1–26, introduction; general discussion on Augenblicksbildungen as opposed to those for enrichment of the language; discussion pertinent to this aspect of wf in general although directly applicable only to French.

1649. Sprenger, R., "*Kaland-*," *NdKbl.* 24 (1903) 41.

1650. ——, "*-kêk(e)*," *NdKbl.* 24 (1903) 60, 70, 92.

1651. ——, "Zusammensetzungen mit *-angel*," *NdKbl.* 24 (1903) 13.

1652. Springer, Otto, "New High German *-el-* in Nominal Compounds," *Language* 25 (1949) 410–415. ¶ Adjectives in *-in*; new examples of *n-l* dissimilation.

1653. Spruch, Christine, "Die Verwendung der Mundart bei Rudyard Kipling," *Giessener Beiträge zur Erforschung der Sprache Englands und Nordamerikas* 6 (1930) 64 ff. ¶ Wf, pp. 169–170.

1654. Spycher, Peter C., "Die Struktur der Adjektive auf *-ig* und *-lich* in der deutschen Schriftsprache der Gegenwart, Erster Teil: Allgemeines," *Orbis* 4 (1955) 74–90; "Zweiter Teil, I: Die Bedeutungs- und Wortbildungskategorien der Suffixtypen *-ig* und *-lich*," *Orbis* 5 (1956) 435–452; "Zweiter Teil, II," *Orbis* 6 (1957) 410–426.

1655. Staaff, Erik, *Le suffixe -arius dans les langues romanes*, diss., Uppsala, 1896. ¶ Related material.

1656. Staedele, A., "Bildung des Hauptworts durch Ableitung in der Mundart von Stahringen Kreis Konstanz (Baden)," *Teuthonista* 6 (1929) 108 ff. ¶ I., from nouns; II., adjectives, III., from verbs, with *i*-stems.

[1657. ——, "Zur Wortbildung der Stahringer Mundart," *Mein Heimatland* (1929) 86 ff.]

[1658. Stahl, Hannelore Eleonore, "Studien zum Problem der sprachlichen Neuschöpfungen bei Shakespeare. Die Suffixbildungen," diss., Freiburg, 1953.]

1659. Stahre, N. G., "Om fornnordiska verb med substantivisk förled," *Arkiv* 73 (1958) 71–96.

1660. Stakelkamp, Chr., "Het adjectief *weerzorig* en het Oud-Germ. suffix *-ôdi*," *Leuvense Bijdragen, Tijdschrift voor moderne philologie* 39 (1949) 79–91.

1661. Stang, Chr. S., "Zum indoeuropäischen Adjektivum," *Norsk Tidsskrift for Sprogvidenskap* 17 (1954) 129–145. ¶ Adjective formation, suffixes, compounding.

1662. Stanzel, Franz, "Zur Herkunft des Rhyming Slang," *Die Sprache* 3 (1956) 193–202.

1663. Stark, Franz, *Kosenamen der Germanen*, Wien, 1868. [K. G. Andresen, *ZfvglSpr.* 18 (1869) 216.] ¶ Kosenamen of one and two stems; general formation with emphasis on diminutives; supplement on *-bold* (*-bald*) (*-bod*), *-bert*, *-old* (*-wald*), *-met*, *-môt*, *-(g)er(d)*, *-hard* (*-hert*), *-wart* (*-wert*), *-rîk*, *-wolf*, *-brand*.

1664. Staub, F., and Tobler, L., *Schweizerisches Idiotikon*, Vols. 1 ff., Frauenfeld, 1889 ff.

[1665. Staverman, W. H., "Diminutivitis Neerlandica," *De Gids, Algemeen Cultureel Maandblad* (Utrecht) 2e haalfjaar (1953) 407–418. ¶ Abuse of the diminutive in contemporary Du.]

1666. ——, "Over rauwkost en sneltreinen, groothandelaren en kleinkinderen," *De Nieuwe Taalgids* 33 (1939) 29–34. ¶ Compounds of the type *groothandel*, etc.

1667. Steadman, J. M., Jr., "*Basketeria* and the Meaning of the Suffix *-teria*," *AmSp.* 5 (1929–1930) 417–418.

1668. Steglich, Wilhelm, "Über die Ersparung von Flexions- und Bildungssilben bei copulativen Verbindungen," *ZfdW* 3 (1902) 1–52. ¶ "in der alt- und neuen Zeit; kein Kummer- noch Trauerniss."

1669. Steiner, E., *Die französischen Lehnwörter in den alemannischen Mundarten der Schweiz. Kulturhistorisch-linguistische Untersuchung mit etymologischem Wörterbuch*, Wien, 1921. ¶ Chap. 17: wf; suffixes, paras. 316–326; "Falsche Rückbildung," 327; noun formation, 328–331; verbal formation, 332–340.

1670. Steinger, H., "Wortmischung mit fremder Betonung in deutschen Mundarten," *PBB* 53 (1929) 307 ff.

1671. Steinhauser, Walter, "Die althochdeutsche Vorsilbe *uo-* im Kreise ihrer Lautverwandten," *ZfdMdaf.* 27 (1961) 101–115.

1672. Steller, W., *Abriss der altfriesischen Grammatik*, Halle, 1928.

1673. Stene, Aasta, *English Loan-words in Modern Norwegian*, London, 1945. ¶ Chap. 10: wf, pp. 166–174; derivatives and compounds.

1674. Stern, Gustaf, *Meaning and Change of Meaning, with Special Reference to the English Language*, Göteborg, 1932 (= *Göteborgs högskolas aarsskrift* 38). ¶ Some mention of derivation in chap. 9; clippings, shortenings, omissions, chap. 10; Namengebung (new words), compounding, and derivation, chap. 11.

1675. Stertzing, G. Friedrich, "Einiges Bemerkungswerthes aus der hennebergisch-fränkischen Mundart. VI. Die Verba auf *-ern* nebst den Adjectiven und Adverbien auf *-erig*," *Fromanns Deutsche Mundarten* 2 (1855) 457–461.

1676. Stickelberger, H., "Die Deminutiva in der Berner Mundart," in *Festschrift für Eduard Sievers*, Halle, 1896, 319–335.

1677. Stiven, Agnes Bain, *Englands Einfluss auf den deutschen Wortschatz*, diss., Zeulenroda, 1936. ¶ Primarily loanwords.

1678. Stoett, F. A., "Het achtervoegsel *-baar*," *Noord en zuid* 18 (1895) 289–301.

1679. ——, "Het achtervoegsel *-lijk*," *Noord en zuid* 18 (1895) 422–429.

1680. Stoffel, C., *Intensives and Downtoners. A Study in English Adverbs*, Heidelberg, 1901 (= *Anglistische Forschungen* 1).

1681. Stolte, H., *Kurze deutsche Grammatik*, 2nd ed., Tübingen, 1951.

1682. Stoltenberg, Hans Lorenz, "Die Bezeichnung von Gruppen durch die Nachsilbe *schaft*," *Zt. für die gesamte Staatswissenschaft* 86 (1929) 136–142.

1683. ——, "Doppelzeitwörter—unmöglich?" *Muttersprache* 51 (1936) 392 f. ¶ Formations such as *stöhnschnappen, stampfschreitend*.

1684. ——, *Die Nachsilbe tum zur Bezeichnung einer geistigen Bewegung*, Tübingen, 1929.

1685. ——, "Der Wortstand auf *-tum*. Geschichte und Prüfung seines Gebrauchs," *Wissenschaftliche Beihefte zur Zeitschrift des deutschen Sprachvereins*, 7. Reihe, Heft 50 (1938) 116–132.

1686. ——, "Zeitwörter mit der Vorsilbe *be-*," *Muttersprache* 51 (1936) 345–346.

1687. Stoltz, G., "En flis av Bergensmaalet," *Maal og Minne* (1938) 137–140. ¶ LowGer. *-ert* in the dialect of Bergen.

1688. Stolz, Fr., "Zur mundartlichen Kurznamenbildung," *ZfhdMaa.* 2 (1901) 377 ff. ¶ Back-formation from verb.

1689. ——, "Zur Wortzusammensetzung," *Wiener Studien* 23 (1902) 312–314. ¶ Theoretical.

1690. Stone, Ruth M., *Studien über den deutschen Einfluss auf das amerikanische Englisch*, diss., Bochum-Langendreer, 1934. ¶ Loan translations, cf. *beergarden, and how*; often derivatives and compounds of such: *dumb, dumbbell, rumdumb*.

1691. Stopp, F. J., "Indirectly Compounded Verbal Forms in Present-Day German," *MLR* 53 (1957) 355–362.

1692. Storch, Theodor, *Angelsächsische Nominalkomposita*, Strassburg, 1886. ¶ Copulativa; Initialdeterminativa, Finaldeterminativa; reinnominale Composita.

1693. Storfer, Adolf Joseph, *Im Dickicht der Sprache*, Wien, 1937. ¶ Discusses "mehrgliedrige Zusammensetzungen" under "Aristophanische Zusammensetzungen," pp. 256–279.

1694. Stosch, Johannes, "Müdling," *ZfdW* 3 (1902) 128–129.

1695. Stosch, S. J. E., *"Aebtissin,"* No. 10 in *Kleine Beiträge zur näheren Kenntniss der deutschen Sprache*, Vol. I, Berlin, 1778, 27–28. ¶ *-inn, -sche* (fem. nouns).

1696. ——, "Ueber die mit *Stein, Stock* und *Blut* zusammengesetzte Wörter," No. 17 in *Neueste Beiträge zur näheren Kenntniss der deutschen Sprache*, Berlin, 1798, 104–114 (= *Kleine Beiträge zur näheren Kenntniss der deutschen Sprache*, Vol. IV).

1697. ——, "Ueber die Wörter Dummerjahn, Lami und Hosen," No. 7 in *Neueste Beiträge zur näheren Kenntniss der deutschen Sprache*, Berlin, 1798, 36–40 (= *Kleine Beiträge zur näheren Kenntniss der deutschen Sprache*, Vol. IV). ¶ *Dummerjahn*, pp. 36–37.

1698. ——, "Ursprung der Verkleinerungssilben *chen* und *lein*," No. 2 in *Neueste Beiträge zur näheren Kenntniss der deutschen Sprache*, Berlin, 1798, 25–28 (= *Kleine Beiträge zur näheren Kenntniss der deutschen Sprache*, Vol. IV).

1699. ——, "Von deutschen Wörtern mit fremden Endungen," No. 40 in *Kleine Beiträge zur näheren Kenntniss der deutschen Sprache*, Vol. III, Berlin, 1782, 120–123. ¶ *Blumist, -iren (-ieren)*.

1700. Strachan, L. R. M., "'Al,' Noun Suffix: 'Disallowal,' 'disallowance,'" *Notes and Queries* 7 (1913) 267, 414.

1701. Stratmann, F. H., "Altenglisch *-ere (-ære, -are)*," *Engl.Stud.* 3 (1880) 273 ff.

1702. Streitberg, Wilhelm, "Die Abstufung der Nominalsuffixe *-io-* und *-ien-* im Germanischen und ihr Verhältnis zu der des Indogerm.," *PBB* 14 (1889) 165–231.

1703. ——, *Die germanischen Komparative auf -ôz-*, Freiburg (Switzerland), 1890.

1704. ——, *Gotisches Elementarbuch*, Heidelberg, 1920.

1705. ——, "Perfective und imperfective Actionsart im Germanischen," *PBB* 15 (1889) 70–177. ¶ *ga-* in the past participle, pp. 170 ff.

1706. ——, *Urgermanische Grammatik*, Heidelberg, 1943.

1707. Strickland, Walter W., *How Foreign Words are Welcomed and Transfigured. A Brief Study in a Neglected Branch of Word Derivation*, New York, 1931. ¶ Borrowing and analogy.

1708. Stroebe, Lilly L., *Die altenglischen Kleidernamen*, diss., Borna-Leipzig, 1904.

1709. Stroh, F., *Handbuch der germanischen Philologie*, Berlin, 1952.

1710. ——, *Probleme neuerer Mundartforschung*, Giessen, 1928 (= *Giessener Beiträge zur deutschen Philologie* 24). ¶ Esp. pp. 45 ff.

1711. Strong, H. A., "Austral English and Slang," *The University Extension Journal* 3, 23 (1898) 70–71. ¶ Some effects of the native substratum (Australia) on Eng.

1712. Strothman, F. W., "Influence of Aspect on the Meaning of *nomina agentis* in Modern German," *JEGP* 34 (1935) 188 ff.

1713. Sturtevant, Albert Morey, "Certain Old Norse Secondary Formations," *Language* 28 (1953) 26–33. ¶ Includes the prefix *ga- > g-*.

1714. ——, "Certain Old Norse Suffixes," *Mod.Phil.* 26 (1928–1929) 149–159. ¶ *-(n)skja, -und, -aldi, -átta, -orð*.

1715. ——, "Certain Old Norse Suffixes," *Mod.Phil.* 26 (1928–1929) 467–476. ¶ *-ð, -endis, -yfli, -mund, -s, -k, -la, -kk-*.

1716. ——, "The Confusion of the Neuter *ia*-Declension with the Feminine *in*-Declension in Old Norse," *Language* 12 (1936) 45–47. ¶ *-læti, -ræði, -lyndi, -leysi* (neut.).

1717. ——, "The Genesis and Inflection of the Element *-fǫðr* in Old Norse Compounds," *JEGP* 53 (1954) 91–92.

1718. ——, "Miscellaneous Gothic Notes," *GR* 26 (1951) 50–59. ¶ No. 6 concerns the suffix *-arja*.

1719. ——, "Notes on Certain Variations and Forms in the Old Germanic Dialects," *MLN* 66 (1951) 300–304. ¶ Among others, the Gmc. suffix *-ar: -er* < PGmc. **-ar* or **-er*; the shift of **-er* to *-ar*; the split between *-ar* and *-er* in WGmc.

1720. ——, "Notes on Gothic Forms," *Language* 30 (1954) 448–452. ¶ No. 4, the suffix in *mannisk-odus*.

1721. ——, "Notes on the *j*-Suffix for the *v*-Suffix in the Old Norse Verb," *SSN* 10 (1928) 25–30.

1722. ——, "Old Norse Etymologies," *JEGP* 33 (1934) 89–97. ¶ *-la* (fem.), *-ill* (masc.).

1723. ——, "Regarding the Connective Vowel -*i*- in Old Norse Compounds," *SSN* 11 (1931) 125–127.

1724. ——, "Regarding the Prefix *ý* in Old Norse *ý-miss*," *MLN* 59 (1944) 175–176.

1725. ——, "Some Adverbial Formations in Old Norse," *Mod.Phil.* 25 (1927–1928) 137–147. ¶ Derivatives and compounds.

1726. ——, "Some Old Norse Etymologies," *JEGP* 25 (1926) 216–226. ¶ -*uðr* (masc.), -*ull* (masc.).

1727. ——, "The Suffix -*erni* in Old Norse," *SSN* 9 (1927) 267–270.

1728. ——, "The Suffix *-ōn-i* > -*an*, -*on*, -*un* in Old Norse Feminine Verbal Abstracts," *Arkiv* 67 (1952) 48–53.

1729. ——, "The Suffix -*sk*- in Old Norse *elska*," *AJPh.* 49 (1928) 188–195.

1730. ——, "Zum Fugenvokal in westgermanischen Kompositis," *MLN* 41 (1926) 188–193.

1731. Sütterlin, Ludwig, *Die deutsche Sprache der Gegenwart*, Leipzig, 1923. ¶ Part II, pp. 101–184, wf.

1732. ——, *Geschichte der Nomina Agentis im Germanischen*, Strassburg, 1887.

1733. ——, "Weiteres zum Praefix germ. *f*- < *py*-," *PBB* 18 (1894) 260.

1734. ——, *Werden und Wesen der Sprache*, Leipzig, 1913.

1735. Sundén, Karl F., *Contributions to the Study of Elliptical Words in Modern English*, Uppsala, 1904.

1736. ——, *A New Etymological Group of Germanic Verbs and their Derivations. A Study in Semantics*, Göteborg, 1943 (= *Göteborgs kungl. vetenskaps och vitterhetssamhälles handlingar* Följd 6, ser. A, 1, 3). [G. Stern, *SN* 16 (1943–1944) 286–296; F. R. Schröder, *GRM* 31 (1943) 63.] ¶ Primarily chaps. 1 and 2 dealing with derivation.

1737. ——, "On the Origin of the Hypochoristic Suffix -*y* (-*ie*, -*ey*) in English," in *Sertum philologicum Carolo Ferdinando Johansson oblatum. Festskrift tillegnad Karl Ferdinand Johansson paa hans 50-aarsdag den 16 sept. 1910*, Göteborg, 1910, 131–170.

1738. Suolahti (Palander), Hugo, "Die althochdeutschen Deminutivbildungen auf -*inkilîn*," *ZfdW* 9 (1907) 170 ff.

1739. ——, *Die deutschen Vogelnamen*, Strassburg, 1909.

1740. ——, "Drei Fragezeichen im mittelhochdeutschen Wörterbuch," *Neuphil.Mitt.* 45 (1944) 97–103. ¶ *grisenier, lobderanz, zwiserat.*

1741. ——, "Etymologien," *Neuphil.Mitt.* 19 (1918) 16–22. ¶ NHG *Windhund,* Eng. *kipper.*

1742. ——, "Der französische Einfluß auf die deutsche Sprache im 12. Jahrhundert," *Mémoires de la Société Néophilologique* 3 (1901) 77–204.

1743. ——, *Der französische Einfluß auf die deutsche Sprache im 13. Jahrhundert,* 2 vols., Helsinki, 1929 and 1933 (= *Mémoires de la Société Néophilologique* 8 and 10.)

1744. ——, "Mundartliche Nachklänge der alten Diminutivbildungen auf -inkilín," ZfdW 10 (1908–1909) 253 ff.

1745. ——, "Verba auf -(l)ieren," Neuphil.Mitt. 39 (1938) 1–17.

1746. Sverdrup, Jakob, "De gammelnorske adjektiver paa -ligr og adverbier paa -liga, -la," Arkiv 27 (1911) 1 ff., 140 ff.

1747. Swaay, H. A. J. van, "De 'Actionsart' en de Prefixen I," Taal en Letteren 13 (1903) 511–528.

1748. ——, Het prefix ga-, gi-, ge-, zijn geschiedenis, en zijn invloed op de "Aktionsart" meer bijzonder in het Oudnederfrankisch en het Oudsaksisch, Utrecht, 1901. [R. Wustmann, AfdA 29 (1904) 187.]

1749. Sweet, Henry, "Disguised Compounds in Old-English," Anglia 3 (1880) 151 ff.

1750. ——, The History of Language, London, 1900. [U. Lindelöf, Neuphil. Mitt. 3 (1901) 26.]

1751. ——, New English Grammar, Oxford, 1891. ¶ Vol. 1, paras. 63 ff., general compounding; 69 ff., general derivation; 444 ff., compounding (Eng.); 450 ff., derivation (Eng. and foreign).

1752. Swenning, Julius, "Tvenne ordbildningsfraagar i de nordisk fornspraaken," Arkiv 23 (1907) 1–35. ¶ -ligr, -liga.

1753. Sykes, Frederick H., French Elements in Middle-English. Chapters Illustrative of the Origin and Growth of Romance Influence on the Phrasal Power of Standard English in its Formative Period, Oxford, 1899. ¶ Nominal compounds and phrases, sec. 4.

1754. S[ytstra], O. H., "Wirdfoarming," Fryslân 12 (1931) 92–95. ¶ Nominal suffixes -me and -te, etc., compounding.

1755. Szadrowsky, Manfred, Abstrakta des Schweizerdeutschen in ihrer Sinnentfaltung, Frauenfeld, 1933 (= Beitr. z.schweizerd. Grammatik 8).

1756. ——, "Germanisch halljō(n)- im Deutschen," PBB 72 (1950) 221.

1757. ——, Nomina agentis des Schweizerdeutschen in ihrer Bedeutungsentfaltung, Frauenfeld, 1918 (= Beitr. z.schweizerd. Grammatik 12). [O. Behaghel, Literaturblatt (1921) 154 f.]

1758. ——, "Eine romanisch-deutsche Suffixverbindung," Teuthonista 5 (1928–1929) 201–208. ¶ Alemannic diminutive suffixes -etli, -elti, -ti from Romance -ett, -etta.

1759. ——, "Über sogenannte Abstrakta," PBB 51 (1927) 41–79.

1760. ——, "Widersprüche in der mundartlichen Wortbildung und Wortfügung," Muttersprache 40 (1925) 294–297. ¶ -los; un-, ent-, ab-.

1761. ——, "Zur deutschen Wortbildung," Teuthonista 3 (1926–1927) 2 ff. ¶ Suffix -i.

1762. ——, "Zusammenhänge zwischen Adjektiv- und Verbalabstraktion," PBB 52 (1939) 1 ff.

1763. Tamm, Fredr., Om afledningsändelser hos svenska substantiv, deras his-

toria och nutida förekomst, Uppsala, 1897 (= *Skrifter utgifna af k. humanistiska vetenskaps-samfundet i Uppsala* 5, 4 and 6, 8).

1764. ——, *Om ändelser hos adverb och arkaiskt bildade prepositionsuttryck i svenskan,* Uppsala, 1899 (= *Skrifter utgifna af k. humanistiska vetenskaps-samfundet i Uppsala* 6, 9).

1765. ——, *Om fornnordiska feminina, afledda paa* ti *och paa* iþqa, Uppsala, 1877 (=*Uppsala universitets aarsskrift, Festskrifter* 9).

1766. ——, *Tränne tyska ändelser i svenskan,* Göteborg, 1878 (= *Göteborgs kungl. vetenskaps- och vitterhets-samhälles handlingar,* ny tidsföljd 16, 8). ¶ Abstract substantives in *-ande, -ende;* nouns in *-else;* adverbs in *-ligen.*

1767. Taylor, Walt, *Arabic Words in English,* London, 1933 (= *SPE* Tract 38). ¶ Lists over 1,000 words in Eng. with some commentary on adaptation of Arabic suffixes, etc., in Eng.

1768. Teall, Francis Horace, *The Compounding of Words in Funk and Wagnalls' Standard Dictionary of the English Language; Containing a Brief Statement of the Principles that Govern the Compounding of Words, with a Comprehensive Alphabetical List of 40,000 Terms to which these Principles are Applied,* New York, 1892.

1769. ——, *The Compounding of English Words. When and Why Joining or Separation is Preferable, with Concise Rules and Alphabetical Lists,* New York, 1891.

1770. ——, *English Compound Words and Phrases. A Reference List, with Statement of Principles and Rules,* New York, 1892 and 1899. ¶ Particularly pp. 9–14.

1771. Tegnér, Esaias, "Om elliptiska ord," in *Forhandlinger paa det andet nordiske filologmøde, Aug. 10–13, 1881,* Kristiania, 1883, 46–78.

1772. ——, *Ur spraakens värld III,* Stockholm, 1930. ¶ Elliptical words; student jargon; wf in *-is.*

1773. Teichert, Fr., *Über das Aussterben alter Wörter im Verlaufe der englischen Sprachgeschichte,* Kiel, 1912.

1774. Terner, Emil, *Die Wortbildung im deutschen Sprichwort,* diss., Gelsenkirchen, 1908. ¶ Primarily formations by analogy, e.g., "gibt Gott kein Tischbier, so gibt er Fischbier."

1775. Tesch, A., *Fremdwort und Verdeutschung,* Leipzig and Wien, 1915.

1776. Teuchert, Hermann, "Mudding 'Mütterchen.' Die Herkunft des mecklenburgisch-vorpommerschen *-ing,*" *ZfMdaf.* 21 (1953) 83–101.

1777. ——, "Niederfränkisches Sprachgut in der Mark Brandenburg," in *Festschrift Friedrich Kluge zum 70. Geburtstage am 21. Juni 1926 dargebracht,* Tübingen, 1926, 145–154. ¶ Etymologies with comments on suffixation.

1778. ——, "Slawische Lehnwörter in ostdeutschen Mundarten," *ZfMaa.* 26 (1958) 13–31.

1779. ——, *Die Sprachreste der niederländischen Siedlungen des 12. Jahrhunderts,* Neumünster, 1944. ¶ Pp. 453 ff., wf: diminutives, suffixes.

1780. Teut, H., "*-en* statt *-ing,*" *NdKbl.* 53 (1940) 27.

1781. ——, "Hauptwörter auf *-els,*" *NdKbl.* 51 (1938) 37.

1782. ——, "Wörter auf *-aftig* und *-haftig,*" *NdKbl.* 53 (1940) 25.

1783. ——, "Wörter auf *-wies,*" *NdKbl.* 53 (1940) 41.

1784. Thiel, Elis, *Das Verbum substantivum im Dialektgebiet des deutschen Reiches,* diss., Marburg, 1917.

1785. Thiele, Otto, *Die konsonantischen Suffixe der Abstrakta des Altenglischen,* diss., Darmstadt, 1902. [W. Heuser, *Anglia Beibl.* 14 (1903) 213.]

1786. Thielke, Karl, "Das ne. Suffix *-ese* im Dienste der Stilcharakterisierung," *Die Neueren Sprachen* N.F. 2 (1953) 504–506.

1787. ——, "Neuenglische Kose- und Spitznamen auf *-s,*" *Engl.Stud.* 73 (1939) 315–316.

1788. Thierfelder, Franz, "Die Ismen," *Muttersprache* (1952) 323–325.

1789. Thors, Carl-Eric, "Om sammansatta verb i svenskan," in *Nutidssvenska,* ed. Carl-Eric Thors, Stockholm, 1965, 23–42.

1790. ——, *Substantivering av adjektiv i fornsvenskan,* Helsinki, 1949 (= *Studier i nordisk filologi* Vols. 36/38; also *Skrifter utg. av svenska litteratursällskapet i Finland* 322).

1791. Thun, Nils, *Reduplicative Words in English. A Study of Formations of the Types* tick-tock, hurly-burly *and* shilly-shally, Stockholm, 1963.

1792. Thyagaraja, A. F., "Germanic *AB- and its Verbal Derivatives," *JEGP* 47 (1948) 179–181.

1793. Tobler, Ludwig, "Die Lautverbindung *tsch* in schweizerischer Mundart," *ZfvglSpr.* 22 (1874) 133–141.

1794. ——, "Über die Bedeutung des deutschen *ge-* vor Verben," *ZfvglSpr.* 14 (1865) 108–138.

1795. ——, "Über die sogenannten Verba Intensiva im Deutschen," *Germania* 16 (1871) 1–37.

1796. ——, "Über die verstärkenden Zusammensetzungen im Deutschen," *Fromanns Deutsche Mundarten* 5 (1858) 1–30, 180–201, 302–310.

1797. ——, *Über die Wortzusammensetzung nebst einem Anhang über die verstärkenden Zusämmensetzungen. Ein Beitrag zur philosophischen und vergleichenden Sprachwissenschaft,* Berlin, 1868. ¶ Theoretical.

1798. Tobler, Titus, "Das anscheinende Abfallen des Vorlings *ge-* der Partizipien," *Fromanns Deutsche Mundarten* 2 (1855) 240–241.

1799. Törnqvist, Nils, "Zum Wortbildungstyp *Wagehals, Taugenichts,*" *Neuphil.Mitt.* 60 (1959) 12–28.

1800. Toit, S. J. du, "Abstrakta op *-ering* (*-iering*) teenoor dié op *-asie,*"

Tydskrif vir Wetenskap en Kuns, nuwe reeks 14 (1954) 57–61. ¶ Afrikaans. Abstract nouns in *-ering* (*-iering*) vs. nouns in *-asie*.

1801. ——, "Vreemde woorde met die agtervoiegsels *-(i)eel* en *-(i)aal*," *Tydskrif vir Wetenskap en Kuns*, nuwe reeks 15 (1955) 37–43. ¶ Afrikanns.

1802. Torp, Alf, "Gamalnorsk ordavleiding," in Marius Haegstad and Alf Torp, *Gamalnorsk ordbok med nynorsk tyding*, Oslo, 1909, 20–63.

1803. Tourbier, Richard, *Das Adverb als attributives Adjektiv im Neuenglischen*, diss., Weimar, 1928. ¶ Words passing into other classes, e.g., "our sometime sister."

1804. Trager, Edith C., "Superfix and Sememe. English Verbal Compounds," *General Linguistics* 2 (1956) 1–14.

1805. Trager, Felicia Harben, "English *-sion, -tion* Nouns," *Canadian Journal of Linguistics* 7 (1962) 86–94.

[1806. Trnka, Bohumil, "K staronagnlické deminutivní příponě *-incel*," *Časopis pro Moderní Filologii* 38 (1956) 1–5. ¶ OE diminutive suffix *-incel*; Eng. summary.]

[1807. Tschentscher, Christhild, "Geschichte der germanischen Bildungssilbe *tum*," diss., Erlangen, 1958.]

1808. ——, "Geschichte der Silbe *tum* im Deutschen," *Muttersprache* 72 (1962) 1–8, 39–47, 67–78.

1809. Twaddell, W. Freeman, "Graphical Alternation in Old Saxon Suffixes," *Monatshefte* 55 (1963) 225–228.

1810. Uhlenbeck, C. C., "Etymologica," *IF* 25 (1909) 143–146. ¶ *-ull* (masc.).

1811. Uhler, Karl, *Die Bedeutungsgleichheit der altenglischen Adjektiva und Adverbia mit und ohne -lic (-lice)*, Heidelberg, 1926 (= *Anglistische Forschungen* 70).

1812. Uhrström, W., *Pickpocket, Turnkey, Wrap-rascal, and Similar Formations in English*, Stockholm, 1918.

1813. Uitman, G. J., "Woordvorming in ambtelijke taal," *Levende Talen* (1958) 340–342.

1814. Ulvestad, Bjarne, "The Norwegian Masculines with the Suffix *-ert*," *GR* 30 (1955) 301–306. ¶ *-ert* from MDu. or MLGer.

1815. Valk, Melvin, E., "The Meaning of the Verbal Prefix *ge-* in Gottfrieds *Tristan*," *University of Wisconsin Summaries of Doctoral Dissertations* 2 (1939) 336–338.

1816. Van Beek, Peter, "The Prefix *be* in King Alfred's Translation of the *De Consolatione Philosophiae*," [University of Iowa] *Programs Announcing Candidates for Higher Degrees* (1933) [no pagination]. ¶ Abstract of diss.

1817. Varming, L., "Om endelsen *-er* i danske navneord," *Tidskrift for philologi og pædagogik* 6 (1870) 313 ff.

[1818. Vasil'eva, I. G., "Glago'nye obrazovanija tipa *afskære, skære af* v sovremennom datskom jazyke (strukturnye i semantiĕskie osoben-nosti)," *Vestnik Moskovskogo Universiteta. Serija 7: Filologija* 17 (1962) 34–45. ¶ Verbal formations of this type in modern Danish.]

1819. Veit, F., "Zur Diminutivbildung im Schwäbischen," *PBB* 35 (1909) 181 ff.

1820. Vendelfelt, E., "Ordsammansättningar av typen 'sötsur,' " *Nysvenska studier* 26 (1946) 96–110.

1821. Verdam, J., "Over het voorvoegsel *ont*," *Tijdschrift* 19 (1900) 245–260.

1822. ——, "Over werkwoorden op *-ken* en *-iken (eken)*," *Tijdschrift* 16 16 (1897) 175–211.

1823. Verdam, M., "Over *lijk* en *like* in Mnl. voornaamwoorden," *Taalkundige Bijdragen* 2 (1879) 220–226.

1824. Verdenius, A. A., "Adverbia van graad op *-e*," *De Nieuwe Taalgids* 33 (1939) 361–368.

1825. ——, "Composita bestaande uit eigennamen + waarderingselement," *De Nieuwe Taalgids* 34 (1940) 167–173. ¶ Deals with Du. compounds like *Thomasvaer.*

1826. ——, "De ontwikkelingsgang der Hollandsche voornaamwoorden *je* en *jij*," *Tijdschrift* 43 (1924) 81–104. ¶ As suffix or enclitic.

1827. Villiers, M. de, "Daar is geen verskil tussen *-tjie* en *-kie* nie," *Tydskrif vir Geesteswetenskappe* 1 (1961) 54–58. ¶ No difference between the two suffixes.

1828. Vogt, Richard, *Das Adjektiv bei Christopher Marlowe*, diss., Berlin, 1908. ¶ Part I, chap. 2, Wortbildungslehre (prefixes, suffixes, compounding).

[1829. Voicikaité, G. A., "Zametki po nemeckomu slovosloženiju (Verdeutlichende Zusammensetzungen)," *Kalbotyra: Lietuvos TSR Aukštųjų Mokyklų Mokslo Darbai* (Vilnius. With Russian summaries) 12 (1965) 55–58.]

1830. Voitl, Herbert, *Neubildungswert und Stilistik der Komposita bei Shakespeare*, diss., Freiburg, 1955.

1831. Vonbun, J., "Mundartliches aus Vorarlberg," *Fromanns Deutsche Mundarten* 3 (1856) 297–305. ¶ 2. diminutive verbs, pp. 301–303; 3. verbs in *-ela* and the adjectives and adverbs in *-elig*, pp. 303–305.

1832. Vonhof, Richard, *Zur Entwicklung der germanischen echten Verbalcomposita im Altwestnordischen*, diss., Bremen, 1905. ¶ Part I, general; Part II, prefixes (*and-, at-, bi-*, etc.): *echt* means that the verb is a "true" compound of unstressed prefix + verb.

1833. Vooys, C. G. N. de, "Mnl. *ontdiepen*," *Tijdschrift* 20 (1901) 248. ¶ *ont-, gront-, in-*.

[1834. Voroncova, G. I., "Ob imennom formante *'s* sovremennom anglijskom jazyke," *Inostrannye Jazyki v Škole* 3 (1948) 31–37, 4 (1948) 6–18. ¶ The nominal suffix *'s* in contemporary Eng.]

1835. Vreese, W. de, *Gallicismen in het Zuidnederlandsch*, Gent, 1899.

1836. Vries, Jan de, "Das Königtum bei den Germanen," *Saeculum* 7 (1956) 289–309. ¶ WGmc. *kuningaz:* suffix *-ing/ung* (later differentiated), pp. 291–292.

1837. ——, "Das *-r-* emphaticum im Germanischen," in *Mélanges de linguistique et de philologie Ferdinand Mossé in memoriam*, Paris, 1959, 467–485.

1838. Vries, M. de, "Bladvulling: I. Het voorzetsel *ob, of*," *Tijdschrift* 2 (1882) 75–77.

[1839. Vries, W. de, "Iets over Woordvorming," in *Verhandeling behoorende bij het Programma van het Gymnasium der Gemeente Groningen, vor het jaar 1920–1921. id. voor het jaar 1921–1922*, Groningen, 1922.]

1840. ——, "Nog iets over die noordoostlike Verkleinuitgangen," *Tijdschrift* 46 (1927) 88 ff. ¶ *-je.*

1841. ——, "Over deminutiva in en nabij Overijsel," *Tijdschrift* 51 (1932) 34–48.

1842. ——, "*Ponstghen*; en nog iets over *-tgijn* enz.," *Tijdschrift* 45 (1926) 45–49.

1843. ——, "*tj < tk*," *Tijdschrift* 61 (1942) 133. ¶ Diminutive suffix.

1844. ——, "Die verkleinuitgangen in de Nederlanden," *Tijdschrift* 43 (1924) 105–122. ¶ All the diminutive suffixes discussed.

1845. ——, "De Verkleinuitgangen (Nalesen)," *Tijdschrift* 49 (1930) 277 ff. ¶ *-je*, etc.

1846. ——, "Zijn de verkleinuitgangen met *j* en met *ie* uit Holland naar elders gekomen?" *Tijdschrift* 44 (1925) 21–43.

1847. Wackernagel, J., "Sprachtausch und Sprachmischung," *Nachrichten von der königlichen Gesellschaft der Wissenschaften zu Göttingen, geschäftliche Mitteilungen* (1904) 90–113. ¶ General; *-ei, -er*, etc.

1848. Wackernagel, Wilhelm, "Die deutschen Appellativnamen," in *Kleinere Schriften*, Vol. III: *Abhandlungen zur Sprachkunde*, Leipzig, 1874, 59 ff.

1849. ——, "Über Conjugation und Wortbildung durch Ablaut im Deutschen, Griechischen und Lateinischen," *Seebodes Archiv für Philologie und Paedagogik* 1 (1830) 17–50. (Also *Supplementband zu Seebodes und Jahns Neues Jahrbuch für Philologie und Paedagogik* 1 (1831) 17–50.)

1850. ——, "Die Umdeutschung fremder Wörter," in *Kleinere Schriften*, Vol. III: *Abhandlungen zur Sprachkunde*, Leipzig, 1874. ¶ Pp. 317–320, Ableitung; pp. 320–324, Umdeutschung durch Zusammensetzung; pp. 324–330, appellativa; pp. 330–333, Eigennamen.

1851. Wadstein, Elis, *Friesische Lehnwörter im Nordischen*, Uppsala, 1922 (= *Skrifter utg. af K. Humanistiska Vetenskaps-Samfundet i Uppsala* 21, 3). ¶ Brief mention of compound and derivation in discussion of shape of loanwords.

1852. ——, "Nordische Bildungen mit dem Präfix *ga-*," *IF* 5 (1895) 1–32.

1853. Waentig, K., *Die Self-Komposita der Puritanersprache*, diss., Leipzig, 1932.

1854. Waitzenböck, Georg, "Neugebildete Hauptwörter auf *-ler*," *Zdallgd-Sprv.* (1905) 235–238.

1855. Waldherr, Fredrich, *Die durch Ableitungssuffixe gebildeten Verba der schwachen Konjugation im 16. Jahrhundert*, diss., Darmstadt, 1906.

1856. Walker, James Albert, "Adjective Suffixes in Old English," diss., Cambridge, Mass., 1948.

1857. ——, "Gothic *-leik* and Germanic **lik-* in the Light of Gothic Translations of Greek Originals," *Philological Quarterly* 28 (1949) 274–293.

1858. Wall, Arnold, "A Contribution towards the Study of the Scandinavian Element in the English Dialects," *Anglia* 20 (1898) 45–135.

1859. Wallas, Graham, "Notes on Jeremy Bentham's Attitude to Word-Creation, and Other Notes on Needed Words," *SPE* 31 (1928) 233–234. ¶ *Methodization, meliorability, forthcomingness.*

1860. Walther, C., "Das Adjectiv *Bremeren* im Mndd. Wörterbuch," *Nd-Kbl.* 33 (1912) 13–14.

1861. ——, "Mit *ê-* gebildete Zusammensetzungen," *NdKbl.* 30 (1909) 60–61.

1862. ——, "Niederdeutsche Adjektive auf *-ern*," *NdKbl.* 31 (1910) 38–39.

1863. ——, "Plattdeutsche Adjektive mit hochdeutschen Endungen, in Verbindung mit Substantiven Haüser- und Straßennamen bildend," *NdKbl.* 19 (1896–1897) 25–26. ¶ *-er, -ener.*

1864. Wanner, Emma, "Wortbildung und Syntax der Zaisenhäuser Mundart," *ZfdMaa.* (1908) 345–348. ¶ Adj.: *-ǝt, -lect, -ic*; nouns in *-ǝr* from verbs; epenthetic *t*; feminines in *-ǝ*; collectives in *-ic*; *-werik-*compounds; *-k(ǝ)*; diminutive suffix *-lǝ*.

1865. Warnke, Carl, *On the Formation of English Words by means of Ablaut*, diss., Halle, 1878. ¶ Pure roots, words with suffixes *-lc, er.*

1866. Wasserzieher, Ernst, "Tautologien," *ZfddtU* 7 (1893) 606–608.

1867. ——, *Woher? Ableitendes Wörterbuch der deutschen Sprache*, 14th ed., Bonn, 1959. ¶ Part A: chap. 3, loanwords; chap. 4, foreign words; Part B.

1868. Watts, Thomas, "On the Anglo-Saxon Termination *-ing*," *Proc.Phil. Soc.* 4 (1848) 83–87.

1869. Weber, Albert, *Zürichdeutsche Grammatik*, Zürich, 1948. ¶ Part 5: Von der Bildung der Wörter, paras. 359–432: A. Zusammengesetzte Wörter, B. Abgeleitete Wörter, C. Umgebildete Wörter.

1870. Wedgwood, Hensleigh, "On Onomatopoeia," *Proc.Phil.Soc.* 2 (1844–1846) 109–118.
1871. Wegener, Wilhelm, *Abhandlung über die englische Verbalform auf* -ing, Königsberg, 1872 (= *Programm der städtischen Realschule zu Königsberg*, 1872). ¶ Part 3: ing- forms as verbal substantives.
1872. Wehrhan, K., "Nickköppen und Verwandtes," *NdKbl.* 31 (1910) 46. ¶ Compound verbs from a verb stem + name of a part of the body.
1873. Wehrle, Otto, *Die hybriden Wortbildungen des Mittelenglischen (1050–1400): Ein Beitrag zur englischen Wortgeschichte*, diss., Freiburg, 1935.
1874. Weick, Friedrich, *Das Aussterben des Präfixes ge- im Englischen*, diss., Darmstadt, 1911.
1875. Weidmann, Karl, *Der Einfluß des Französischen auf Fischarts Wortschatz im Gargantua*, diss., Giessen, 1913. ¶ II B. Umbildung mit Eindeutschung; III. Neubildungen durch reines Spielen mit dem Wortklang in Anlehnung an französischen und deutschen Sprachstoff; IV. Übersetzung; V. Mischungen.
1876. Weidmann, Robert, "Nominal Compounds in Middle High German Based on a Study of the Manesse Manuscript," *JEGP* 40 (1941) 349–359.
1877. ——, "A Study of Nominal Compounds in Middle High German, Based on the Manesse Manuscript," *University of Wisconsin Summaries of Doctoral Dissertations* 3 (1938) 344–346.
1878. Weijnen, A., "Structuren van Nederlandse voorzetsels," *Tijdschrift* 80 (1964) 116–132. ¶ Eng. summary.
1879. ——, "Stuiptrekkende categorieen van werkwoorden die met *ont*-beginnen," *Taal en Tongval* 9 (1957) 62–65.
1880. Weinhold, Karl, *Alemannische Gramatik*, Berlin, 1863.
1881. ——, *Bairische Grammatik*, Berlin, 1867.
1882. ——, *Deutsche Frauen in dem Mittelalter*, 3rd ed., Wien, 1897. ¶ Vol. I, pp. 12 ff., attempts to determine meaning of compound personal names.
1883. ——, *Mittelhochdeutsche Grammatik*, Paderborn, 1877.
1884. ——, *Über deutsche Dialectforschung. Die Laut- und Wortbildung und die Formen der schlesischen Mundart mit Rücksicht auf Verwandtes in deutschen Dialecten*, Wien, 1853. [Fr. Pfeiffer, *ZfvglSpr.* 3 (1854) 144.]
1885. Weise, Oskar, *Die Altenburger Mundart*, Eisenberg, 1889.
1886. ——, "Beiträge zur niederdeutschen Wortbildung," *NdJb.* 46 (1920) 28–40. ¶ Ablaut (*u:a*); onomatopoetic verbs in -*eien*, -*auen*; diminutive in -*ken*; verbs in -*stern*; nickköppen; reversal of order of elements.
1887. ——, "Firlefanz, Quirlequitsch, Tripstrille," *ZfdW* 3 (1902) 280 ff.
1888. ——, "Kateiker = Eichkatze und Verwandtes," *NdKbl.* 31 (1910) 32–33. ¶ Transposition of members of compound.

1889. ——, "Kinderlitzen und andere Deminutiva auf -*litz*," *ZfdW* 10 (1908–1909) 56–60.

1890. ——, "Nickköppen und Verwandtes," *NdKbl.* 31 (1910) 30–32. ¶ Compound verbs made from verb stem + name of a part of the body.

1891. ——, "Das Suffix -*s* in mitteldeutschen Mundarten," *ZfhdMaa.* 3 (1902) 280 ff. ¶ 1. Personenbezeichnungen, 2. Thätigkeitswörter, 3. Breiartige Massen.

1892. ——, "Über eingedrunge *r* und *n*," *ZfhdMaa.* 2 (1901) 244–246. ¶ Addition of *r*, *n* in loanwords and foreign words.

1893. ——, "Der Übergang von *s* in *z*," *ZfdMaa.* (1908) 193–197. ¶ E.g., *Zote, zimperlich*, etc.

1894. ——, "Der Übergang von *sch* in *tsch*," *ZfdMaa.* (1908) 197–200.

1895 ——, *Unsere Mundarten, ihr Werden und Wesen*, 2nd ed., Leipzig, 1919. ¶ Paras. 64–87, Wortbildung; 112–125, Fremdwörter; 126–131, Lautmalerei.

1896. ——, "Die Wortdoppelung im Deutschen," *ZfdW* 2 (1902) 8–24. ¶ *Fitzfatz, gigetehogete*, etc.

1897. Weisemann, Ewald, *Form und Verbreitung des Compositionsvokals in Nominalcompositen bei Notker*, diss., Nürnberg, 1911. ¶ Part I includes a list of compounds; Part II discusses the form and spread of the vowel in Gothic and Notker.

1898. Weisgerber, Leo, "Vierstufige Wortbildungslehre," *Muttersprache* 74 (1964) 33–43.

1899. Weiss, Walter, "Die Verneinung mit *un-*. Ein Beitrag zur Wortverneinung," *Muttersprache* 70 (1960) 335–343.

1900. Weitnauer, K., "Die Bildung des Eigenschaftswortes in der Allgäuer Mundart von Kempten und Umgebung," *Teuthonista* 6 (1929–1930) 118 ff. ¶ Suffixes primarily, some compounding; miscellaneous topics.

1901. Weitzenböck, Georg, "Neugebildete Hauptwörter auf -*ler*," *Zdallgd-Sprv.* (1905) 235–238.

1902. Wellander, Erik, *Die Bedeutungsentwicklung der Partikel ab in der mittelhochdeutschen Verbalkomposition*, diss., Uppsala, 1911.

1903. Wells, John Corson, "The Origin of the German Suffix -*heit*," in *Festschrift Taylor Starck*, ed. Werner Betz, Evelyn S. Coleman, Kenneth Northcott, The Hague, 1964, 51–55.

1904. ——, "The Suffix -*heit* in Old High German and Old Low German: its Origin and its History to 1100 A.D.," diss., Cambridge, 1952.

1905. Wendler, Wilhelm, *Zusammenstellung der Fremdwörter des Alt- und Mittelhochdeutschen nach sachlichen Kategorien*, Zwickau, 1865.

1906. Wennerberg, John, "De dubbelt sammansatta orden i svenskan," *Nysvenska studier* 41 (1961) [1962] 5–54. ¶ Double compounds in Sw.

1907. Wennström, Torsten, *Svenska spraakets historia*, Stockholm, 1941. ¶ Sec. 13: vocabulary and wf.

1908. Wentworth, Harold, "The Allegedly Dead Suffix *-dom* im Modern English," *PMLA* 56 (1941) 280–306.

1909. ——, "Blend-Words in English," diss., Ithaca, N.Y., 1934.

1910. ——, "The Neo-pseudo-suffix *-eroo*," *AmSp.* 17 (1942) 10–15.

1911. ——, " 'Sandwich' Words and Rime-caused Nonce Words," *West Virginia University Studies* 3 (1939) 65–71.

1912. Werbow, Stanley, N., "Zusammengesetzte Konjunktionen, Grammatisch-stilistische Mode," in *Donum Natalicium G. A. von Es*, Groningen, 1954, 125–141.

1913. Werner, Otmar, "Die Substantiv-Suffixe *-es/-as* in den ostfränkischen Mundarten," *ZfMdaf.* 30 (1963–1964) 227–275.

1914. Wessén, Elias, *Svensk spraakhistoria. II. Ordbildningslära*, Stockholm, 1943. ¶ OSw.; derivation and compounding.

1915. ——, *Zur Geschichte der germanischen* n-*Deklination*, Uppsala, 1914 (= *Uppsala universitets aarsskrift* 1914). ¶ *-n* suffix.

1916. Westergaard, Elisabeth, "Masked Germanic Suffixes in Lowland Scotch," *Anglia* 46 (1922) 344–346.

1917. ——, "Præfix *un* i engelsk rigssprog og engelske dialekter," *Nordisk tidsskrift*, Ser. 4, 8 (1919) 41–49.

1918. Western, Aug., "Lidt om verbene paa *-na, -ne*," *Den høiere skole* (Oslo) (1938) 214–215.

1919. ——, "Om nominalkomposita i Germansk, særlig i Norsk," *Maal og Minne* (1929) 45–76. ¶ Copulative compounds, determinative compounds, bahuvrîhi compounds.

1920. ——, *Om sprogriktighet og sprogfeil*, Oslo, 1931. ¶ In the appendix elements of wf are dealt with: *-ing, -ning, -en, -else, an-, be-, er-*.

1921. Westlake, John S., "2. Old Germanic Suffix *īn*," *Trans.Phil.Soc.* 33 (1907–1910) 282–284.

1922. Weyhe, H., "Beiträge zur westgermanischen Grammatik," *PBB* 30 (1905) 55–141. ¶ Pp. 76–83: OE *-weard (-wærd)/-ward (-word)*.

1923. ——, *Zu den altenglischen Verbalabstrakten auf* -nes *und* -ing, -ung, Habilitationsschrift, Halle, 1911.

1924. Wheatley, Henry B., *A Dictionary of Reduplicated Words in the English Language*, London, 1865 (= Appendix to the *Trans.Phil.Soc.* 1865).

1925. Wheeler, G. H., "The Method of Formation of Old English Placenames in '-hāēme,' '-sætan,' '-tūningas,' " *MLR* 11 (1916) 218–219.

1926. Whitman, Charles H., "The Birds of Old English Literature," *JEGP* 2 (1898) 149 ff. ¶ Etymological; compounds and derivatives.

1927. ——, "The Old English Animal Names: Mollusks, Toads, Frogs, Worms, Reptiles," *Anglia* 30 (1907) 380–393. ¶ Primarily etymological; some compounding.

1928. ——, "Old English Mammal Names," *JEGP* 6 (1906–1907) 649–656.
¶ Etymological; some compounding.

1929. Wick, Ph., *Die slawischen Lehnwörter in der neuhochdeutschen Schrift-sprache*, diss., Marburg, 1939.

1930. Wickberg, Rudolf, *Om genitivsuffixet -sja i de germanska spraaken*, Lund, 1878–1879 (= *Acta univ. Lundensis* 15, 3).

1931. Widding, Ole, "Endelserne -semd og -semi i norrønt sprog," *Maal og Minne* (Oslo) (1953) 23–31.

1932. Wiener, Leo, "French Words in Wolfram von Eschenbach," *AJP* 16 (1895) 326–361.

1933. ——, "German Loan-Words and the Second Sound Shifting," *MLN* 10 (1895) 10 ff.

1934. Wieselgren, Per, "Naagra smaa ordförklaringar," *Studia Germanica* (1934) 346 349. ¶ -ingr (masc.).

1935. Wiesner, Johann, *Deutsch Wortkunde, 1. Wortbildung, 2. Wortbedeutung und Wortvorrat*, Wien and Leipzig, 1922 (= *Lehrerbücherei* 17 and 18).

1936. Wilhelmsen, L. J., *On the Verbal Prefixes for- and fore- in English*, Oslo, 1938 (= *Avhandlinger utgitt av Det Norske Videnskaps-Akademi i Oslo, II. Hist.-filos. klasse* No. 2).

[1937. Willert, H., "Reimende Ausdrücke im Neuenglischen," in *Festschrift Adolf Tobler zum siebzigsten Geburtstage dargebracht von der Berliner Gesellschaft für das Studium der neueren Sprachen*, Braunschweig, 1905, 437–458.]

1938. ——, "Vom substantivischen Infinitiv," *Engl.Stud.* 48 (1914–1915) 246–250.

1939. Williams, Fred C., "Gangway for the -furter," *AmSp.* 27 (1952) 153–154.

1940. Williams, R. F., "Die deutsche Zusammensetzung," *ZdallgdSprv.* (1909) 360–362.

1941. Williams, Theodore, "On the -ness Peril," *AmSp.* 40 (1965) 279–286.

1942. Wilmanns, W., *Deutsche Grammatik*, Vol. II *Wortbildung*, Strassburg, 1899; 2nd ed., Berlin and Leipzig, 1930. ¶ Standard work.

1943. Windisch, E., "Zur Theorie der Mischsprachen und Lehnwörter," *Ber. der Kgl. Sächs. Ges. der Wsch. zu Leipzig, phil.-hist. Klasse* 49 (1897) 101–126.

1944. Winkel, J. te, "Geschiedenis der Nederlandsche taal (Vervolg), IV: Woordvorming door afleiding," *Noord en zuid* 18 (1895) 517–541.

1945. Winkel, L. A. te, "Over het woord *doem* en de zamengestelde woor-den, die op *dom* uitgaan," *Archief voor nederlandsche taalkunde* 1 (1847) 297–392.

1946. Winteler, J., "Über die Verbindung der ableitungssilbe got. -atj-, ahd.

-*azz*- mit guttural ausgehenden Stämmen resp. Wurzeln," *PBB* 14 (1889) 455–472.

1947 Wipf, Elisa, *Die Mundart von Visperterminen im Wallis*, Frauenfeld, 1910 (= *Beitr. z. schweizerd. Grammatik* 2). ¶ Part IV, Zur Wortbildung, pp. 162–178.

1948. Wis, Marjatta, "Fremdes *sk* im Frühneuhochdeutschen," *Neuphil. Mitt.* 65 (1964) 54–70.

1949 ——, *Ricerche sopra gli italianismi nella lingua tedesca*, Helsinki, 1955 (= *Mémoires de la Société Néophilologique* 17).

1950. ——, "Weinnamen bei Ottokar von Steiermark," *Neuphil.Mitt.* 59 (1958) 99–109.

1951. Wissler, H., *Das Suffix* -i *in der Berner resp. Schweizer Mundart*, diss., Bern, 1891.

[1952. Wissmann, Wilhelm, *Die ältesten Postverbalia des Germanischen*, Habilitationsschrift, Göttingen, 1938.]

1953. ——, "Die Bildungen auf '-lih' von Partizipien und der Abrogans," in *Festgabe für Ulrich Pretzel zum 65. Geburtstag dargebracht von Freunden und Schülern*, ed. Werner Simon, Wolfgang Bachofer, and Wolfgang Dittmann, Berlin, 1963, 308–315.

1954. ——, *Nomina postverbalia in den altgermanischen Sprachen*, I, Göttingen, 1932 (= *Ergänzungsheft zur ZfvglSpr.* 11). ¶ Deverbative ð-verbs.

1955. Withington, Robert, "More 'Portmanteau' Coinages," *AmSp.* 7 (1931–1932) 200–203.

1956. ——, " 'Portmanteau' and Pseudo-'Portmanteau' Words," *Notes and Queries* 157 (1929) 77–78. ¶ *Coxcomical, smackerel,* etc.

1957. Wittman, Elizabeth, "Clipped Words: A Study of Back-Formations and Curtailments in Present-Day English," *Dialect Notes* 4 (1913–1917) 115–145. ¶ Essentially classification and examples of the various types.

1958. Wittmann, Henri, and Fischer, Heins, "Die Verteilung des diminutivierenden /šə/ und /jə/ im Mittelfränkischen (Aschaffenburg, Neuwied)," *Études Germaniques* 19 (1964) 165–167.

1959. Wölcken, Fr., "Entwicklungsstufen der Wortbildung aus Initialen," *Anglia* 75 (1957) 317–333.

1960. Wölfflin, Ed., "Reduplikation in der Kindersprache," *ZfdW* 1 (1901) 263–264.

1961. Woeste, Fr., "Verba mit *af* zusammengesetzt," *NdKbl.* 1 (1876) 31.

1962. Woeste, J. F. L., "Mundartliches (Süderland) 1. Weibliche Geschlechts-Suffix *te*," *Herrigs Archiv* 10 (1852) 114.

1963. Wolf, Arthur, *Das Präfix uz- im gotischen und im deutschen Verbum*, diss., Breslau, 1915.

1964. Wolff, [J.], "Epithetisches *t*," *Siebenbürgisches Korrespondenzblatt* 4 (1881) 4–6, 13–18, 37–40.

1965. Wolfgang, Meid, "Das Suffix -no- in Götternamen," *Beiträge zur Namenforschung* 8 (1957) 72–108.

1966. Wood, F. T., *Word-Formation in German*, Charlottesville, Va., 1948.

1967. Wood, Francis Asbury, "The IE Base **ghero-* in Germanic," *Mod. Phil.* 1 (1903–1904) 235–245. ¶ Derivatives of the base.

1968. ——, *Indo-European* a^x; a^{x}i; a^{x}u. *A Study in Ablaut and in Word-formation*, Strassburg, 1905.

1969. ——, "Indo-European Root-Formation, I," *JEGP* 1 (1897) 280–308; "II," *JEGP* 1 (1897) 442–470. ¶ Suffixes.

1970. ——, "Iterative, Blends, and 'Streckformen,' " *Mod.Phil.* 9 (1911–1912) 173–194.

1971. ——, "Kontaminationsbildungen und haplologische Mischformen," *JEGP* 11 (1912) 295–328. ¶ Three types with more than 100 examples.

1972. ——, "The Origin of Color-Names," *MLN* 20 (1905) 225–229.

1973. ——, "Some English Blends," *MLN* 27 (1912) 179.

1974. Wood, R. S., *Word Building, Derivation and Composition* (Books 1–7), London, 1885–1899. ¶ Textbook type.

1975. Woods, Frank L., "Nominal Compounds of the Old High German Benedictine Rule," *JEGP* 56 (1957) 42–51. ¶ Types and examples (list).

1976. Wossidlo, Richard, "Der Gebrauch des Infinitivs im Mecklenburger Platt," *NdKbl.* 17 (1893) 64. ¶ Part V: infinitives in -ent.

1977. ——, *Imperativische Bildungen im Niederdeutschen*, Waren, 1890 (= *1. Jahresbericht des städtischen Gymnasiums in Waren*).

1978. ——, *Imperativische Wortbildungen im Niederdeutschen*, Leipzig, 1890.

1979. ——, "Niederdeutsche Adjektiva auf -ern," *NdKbl.* 32 (1911) 19.

1980. Wrede, Ferdinand, *Die Diminutiva im Deutschen*, Marburg, 1908 (= *Deutsche Dialektgeographie* 1).

1981. ——, "Sprachliche Adoptivformen," in *Beiträge zur germanischen Sprachwissenschaft. Festschrift für Otto Behaghel*, ed. Wilhelm Horn, Heidelberg, 1924, 83–91. ¶ Explains "sprachliche Doppelformen."

1982. Wülfing, J. Ernst, "Neue und seltene Wörter auf -ling," *ZfdW* 2 (1902) 300–301.

1983. Wundt, Wilhelm, *Völkerpsychologie*, Vol. I *Die Sprache 1. Teil*, 2nd ed., Leipzig, 1904. ¶ Chap. 5, Die Wortbildung: theoretical; deals with the conditions attendant upon origin of compounds in general; maintains that compounding is psychological not logical in nature.

1984. Wustmann, Rudolf, *Verba Perfektiva namentlich im Heliand*, diss., Leipzig, 1894. [V. E. Mourek, *AfdA* 21 (1895) 195–204.] ¶ I. Prefixes: *gi-, ge-, a-, for-, far-, af-, ant-, an-, bi-, be-, ti-, te-, thurh-, undar-, uuidar-*; II. Aspect of the verb in the *Heliand*; III. Syntactical relationships.

1985. Wyld, H. Cecil, "Old English 'gefyrhþe' and 'frið' and the Latin Suffix '-ētum,'" *MLR* 5 (1910) 347–348.

1986. Zachrisson, R. E., "The Suffix *-ingja* in Germanic Names," *Herrigs Archiv* 133 (1915) 348–353. ¶ Claims most Eng. place names and names ending in -inge are to be considered tribal names with *ja*-derivation; other Gmc. dialects included.

1987. Zandvoort, R. W., *A Handbook of English Grammar*, 2nd ed., London, 1962. ¶ Part IX: wf: 1. composition, 2. derivation, 3. miscellaneous.

1988. Zatočil, Leopold, "*Ge-* bei den sogenannten perfektiven und imperfektiven Simplizien," *Sborník Filozofickej Fakulty Univerzity Komenského, Philologica*, 8 A7 (1959) 50–64.

1989. Zieglschmid, A. J. F., "Englisch-amerikanischer Einfluß auf den Wortschatz der deutschen Sprache der Nachkriegszeit," *JEGP* 34 (1936) 24–33.

1990. Zimmer, H., "Keltische Studien. 4. Kosenamen und Deminutivbildung," *ZfvglSpr.* 32 (1893) 174–190. ¶ Deals with the Eng. suffix -ock, pp. 188–190.

1991. ——, *Die Nominalsuffixe a und â in den indogermanischen Sprachen*, Strassburg, 1876 (= *Quellen und Forschungen* 13).

1992. Zimmer, Karl E., *Affixal Negation in English and Other Languages: An Investigation of Restricted Productivity*, London, 1964 (= *Supplement to Word, Monograph* No. 5).

1993. Zimmermann, A., "Zur Entstehung des Ausdrucks Schubjack," *ZfdW* 10 (1908–1909) 47 ff.

1994. Zimmermann, Emil Rudolf, *Die Geschichte des lateinischen Suffixes -arius in den romanischen Sprachen*, diss., Darmstadt, 1895. ¶ Contains excellent summaries of theories concerning reflexes of *-arius*, of general interest and significance for Ger., Eng., etc.

1995. Zindler, Horst, "Anglizismen in der deutschen Presse nach 1945," diss., Kiel, 1959.

1996. Zingerle, J. V., "Einiges über *tsch* im Meraner Dialecte," *Die deutschen Mundarten: eine Monatsschrift für Dichtung, Forschung und Kritik* 3 (1856) 8.

1997. Zirker, Otto, *Die Bereicherung des deutschen Wortschatzes durch die spätmittelalterliche Mystik*, Jena, 1923 (= *Jenaer germanistische Forschungen* 3).

1998. Zuiden, Jozef van, *Die Verba auf -igen im Deutschen*, Maastricht, 1934.

1999. Zupitza, Julius, "German Words in Middle English," *The Academy* 827 (1888) 170 ff.

2000. Zwitzers, A., "Was ist rechtens in unserer Substantivkomposition?" *ZfddtU* 10 (1896) 124–133.

INDEXES

NOTE: The numbers refer to the numbered entries in the main body of the bibliography.

The user should keep in mind that the indexes are intended as locator aids, not as exhaustive summaries of information on prefixes, suffixes, grammatical categories, etc. It would not have been feasible to include, for example, every prefix and suffix included in the larger works which generally have extensive index material.

ABBREVIATIONS

adj.	adjective	nd.	niederdeutsch
adv.	adverb	NGmc.	North Germanic
ae.	altenglisch	nhd.	neuhochdeutsch
AE	American English	Nor.	Norwegian
ahd.	althochdeutsch	ODan.	Old Danish
Alem.	Alemannic	OE	Old English
Bav.	Bavarian	OEFr.	Old East Frisian
Dan.	Danish	OF	Old French
Du.	Dutch	OFr.	Old Frisian
E	English	OHG	Old High German
EME	Early Middle English	OIcel.	Old Icelandic
ENHG	Early New High German	OLowFranc.	Old Low Franconian
		OLowG	Old Low German
ESw.	East Swedish	ON	Old Norse
Fin.	Finnish	OS	Old Saxon
F	French	OSw.	Old Swedish
Fr.	Frisian	OWN	Old West Norse
G	German	PennG	Pennsylvania German
Gk.	Greek	PN	Proto-Norse
Gmc.	Germanic	RF	Rhine Franconian
Go.	Gothic	Rom.	Romance
HG	High German	Scand.	Scandinavian
Icel.	Icelandic	Scot.	Scottish
IE	Indo-European	Sil.	Silesian
It.	Italian	Skt.	Sanskrit
Lat.	Latin	Sp.	Spanish
Lith.	Lithuanian	subst.	substantive
LowG	Low German	Sw.	Swedish
masc.	masculine	Swab.	Swabian
MDu.	Middle Dutch	Westf.	Westfalian
ME	Middle English	wf	word formation
Meckl.	Mecklenburg(isch)	WGmc.	West Germanic
mhd.	mittelhochdeutsch	wk.	weak
MHG	Middle High German	WNorse	West Norse
MLowG	Middle Low German	Yid.	Yiddish

I. DICTIONARIES

II. WORDS, PHRASES, AND ETYMOLOGIES

Trabant, G, 867
treinbotsing, Du., 1308
Tripstrille, G, 1887
-tümlich, G, 605
Tumeigen, G, 605
Turnkey, E, 1812
twist, E, 477

un, MHG, 663
Unende, G, 663
ungesühte, MHG, 663
Ungewitter, G, 201
Unlust, G, 201
Unmut, G, 201
up-and-down, AE, 903
urtümlich, G, 605

vandblœss, Nor., 1252
vandgœfr, Nor., 1252
Vergissmeinnicht, G, 695
Viadukt, E, 477
vil, MHG, 646
vinnr, Nor., 1252
violoncel(lo), 1164
vlees, Du., 268
vrîbære, MHG, 1408

waac, E, 1328
Wagehals, G, 1799

wan, MHG, 663
wastine, OF, 107
we service, E, 1387
wedlock, E, 464
weerzorig, Du., 1660
weʒ . . . lā, OE, 157
weʒ . . . la . . . weʒ, OE, 157
wei . . . la . . . wei, ME, 157
wið, OE, 658
wiederkäuen, G, 1237
Wiesbader, G, 544, 827
wilhelminisch, G, 29, 515, 628, 717
wilhelmisch, G, 29, 515, 628, 717
Windhund, G, 1741
withdrawal, E, 1077
wrap-rascal, E, 1812

Yankee, E, 574
ý-miss, ON, 1724

Zeitvertreib, G, 170
zien, Du., 556
zimperlich, G, 1893
Zionismus, G, 109
Zirlin-mirlin, G, 1521
Zote, G, 1893
zurück, G, 1292
zwiserat, MHG, 1740

III. GRAMMATICAL CATEGORIES

Adjective: Bav., 1032; E, 11, 90, 223, 563, 834, 1008, 1101, 1366, 1414, 1467, 1535, 1803; Franconian, 1675; F, 1499; G, 29, 149, 183, 218, 243, 515, 516, 517, 564, 615, 628, 717, 1067, 1206, 1306, 1477, 1499, 1576, 1652, 1654; Gmc., 8, 616, 798; Go., 252, 1551; IE, 68, 1661; Jutlandish, 1188; LowG, 1171, 1862, 1863, 1979; ME, 1535, 1537; MHG, 683, 1433; MLowG, 1860; Nor., 1593; OE, 677, 1256, 1510, 1540, 1583, 1811, 1856; OHG, 82; OIcel., 271; ON, 874, 1746; OS, 1439; OSw., 1, 610, 1790; Rappenau, 1129; RF, 724; Sp., 1499; Swab., 1900; Sw., 117, 388, 1625; Swiss, 1149; Valdres, 701; Vorarlberg, 1831
Adjective, compound: E, 937; G, 715; Valdres, 701

IV. LANGUAGES

(The order of the entries for the Germanic languages follows that of the *Bibliographie linguistique des années* . . . , Utrecht, 1939 ff., published under the auspices of the Permanent International Committee on Linguistics.)

1139, 1145, 1149, 1153, 1154, 1155, 1156, 1157, 1167, 1179, 1188,
1191, 1194, 1198, 1199, 1202, 1206, 1207, 1208, 1209, 1210, 1212,
1217, 1218, 1228, 1235, 1237, 1242, 1245, 1258, 1259, 1262, 1263,
1264, 1265, 1270, 1279, 1281, 1284, 1285, 1286, 1287, 1288, 1289,
1290, 1291, 1292, 1293, 1294, 1297, 1302, 1303, 1304, 1306, 1310,
1311, 1315, 1317, 1320, 1321, 1322, 1323, 1329, 1331, 1332, 1334,
1337, 1344, 1348, 1349, 1351, 1352, 1357, 1365, 1368, 1369, 1371,
1389, 1390, 1391, 1394, 1400, 1401, 1402, 1404, 1407, 1411, 1413,
1418, 1419, 1420, 1421, 1424, 1427, 1429, 1430, 1432, 1435, 1437,
1447, 1448, 1449, 1453, 1458, 1459, 1463, 1464, 1465, 1475, 1483,
1496, 1497, 1498, 1499, 1500, 1507, 1508, 1509, 1517, 1519, 1520,
1521, 1526, 1534, 1538, 1539, 1542, 1543, 1549, 1556, 1558, 1559,
1560, 1564, 1565, 1572, 1573, 1576, 1589, 1590, 1592, 1608, 1609,
1610, 1617, 1637, 1641, 1647, 1652, 1654, 1668, 1677, 1681, 1682,
1683, 1684, 1685, 1686, 1688, 1689, 1690, 1691, 1693, 1694, 1695,
1696, 1697, 1698, 1699, 1712, 1731, 1734, 1739, 1741, 1745, 1756,
1758, 1759, 1761, 1762, 1774, 1775, 1788, 1794, 1795, 1796, 1798,
1799, 1808, 1847, 1848, 1849, 1850, 1854, 1855, 1866, 1867, 1875,
1887, 1889, 1892, 1893, 1894, 1896, 1898, 1899, 1901, 1903, 1912,
1929, 1933, 1935, 1940, 1942, 1949, 1950, 1960, 1963, 1966, 1971,
1980, 1981, 1982, 1988, 1989, 1993, 1995, 1997, 1998, 1999, 2000

Early New High German, 61, 492, 548, 549, 550, 626, 800, 1948

Middle High German, 15, 16, 17, 58, 204, 253, 370, 376, 412, 580, 646,
659, 663, 667, 683, 724, 726, 792, 793, 794, 1013, 1018, 1079, 1104,
1120, 1121, 1166, 1177, 1189, 1195, 1247, 1251, 1266, 1267, 1271,
1272, 1276, 1277, 1278, 1280, 1283, 1289, 1290, 1302, 1304, 1314,
1321, 1330, 1408, 1409, 1430, 1433, 1460, 1461, 1462, 1552, 1553,
1554, 1561, 1592, 1600, 1740, 1742, 1743, 1815, 1876, 1877, 1882,
1883, 1902, 1905, 1932, 1997

Old High German, 82, 142, 143, 158, 180, 208, 209, 210, 229, 246, 286,
294, 320, 341, 349, 434, 435, 440, 450, 479, 512, 533, 539, 547, 629,
667, 724, 785, 804, 805, 806, 807, 968, 976, 1017, 1018, 1035, 1057,
1125, 1130, 1137, 1146, 1213, 1239, 1257, 1304, 1313, 1321, 1398,
1412, 1430, 1431, 1456, 1481, 1514, 1577, 1592, 1600, 1638, 1671,
1738, 1897, 1904, 1905, 1946, 1953

German (Low), 56, 76, 141, 174, 178, 377, 378, 426, 478, 532, 545, 546, 567,
586, 674, 733, 734, 736, 783, 795, 891, 914, 960, 963, 964, 965, 966,
1033, 1042, 1053, 1135, 1138, 1139, 1168, 1169, 1170, 1171, 1172,
1173, 1174, 1175, 1244, 1501, 1555, 1568, 1570, 1584, 1585, 1586,
1587, 1634, 1649, 1650, 1687, 1780, 1781, 1782, 1783, 1814, 1861,
1862, 1863, 1872, 1886, 1888, 1890, 1961, 1977, 1978, 1979

V. TOPICAL

1205, 1232, 1674, 1987; G, 94, 553, 800, 912, 1206, 1212, 1589, 1850;
ME, 981; ON, 1802; OS, 1439; OSw., 1914; Swiss, 1869
Derivation, adj., Swiss, 1149
Derivation, allusive, E, 767
Derivation, regressive, Du., 1442
Derivation, subst., OS, 703
Derivation, suffixes, Nagu, 406
Derivation, syllables: Gmc., 1333; OHG, 1137
Derivation, terms for, 4, 758
Derivation, verb, Sw., 269
Derivation, vocalic, OE, 872
Dialects, G, 1167, 1179
Diminutive: Afrikaans, 812, 1144, 1148; Alem., 89, 1758; Amrum, 1031;
    Austrian, 1231; Bentheim, 1406; Bern, 1676; Cattenstedt, 325; Dan., 1185;
    Du., 72, 255, 293, 304, 354, 685, 818, 819, 847, 1011, 1339, 1605, 1665,
    1840, 1841, 1843, 1844, 1845, 1846; ENHG, 548, 549, 550; East Du., 848;
    E, 295, 749, 822, 1000, 1468, 1469; Flemish, 1339; Föhr, 1031; F, 431;
    Franconian, 1958; Fr., 249, 288; G, 38, 314, 431, 455, 1051, 1056, 1111, 1348,
    1349, 1369, 1390, 1610, 1698, 1744, 1880, 1889; Gmc., 930, 1107; Hanau,
    790, 791; Handschuhsheim, 1347; IE, 230; Lat., 561; Lötschental, 633;
    LowG, 273, 964, 1174, 1568, 1585, 1886; Meckl., 91; MDu., 1779; ME,
    665, 1468; MHG, 580, 793, 1266; Nidwalden, 1261; North Brabant, 772;
    North Fr., 673; Oberschopfheim, 1579; OE, 367, 1468, 1806; OHG, 1738;
    PennG, 1591; Pommeranian, 961; Rappenau, 1127; RF, 724; Rom., 561;
    Swab., 1819; Sw., 579; Unterzips, 522; Westfalian, 1246; WGmc., 1362,
    1363; Yid., 951; Zaisenhaus, 1864
Diminutive, elliptical, Du., 558
Diminutive, pejorative, Dan., 1530
Diminutive suffixes: Fr., 674; IE, 486; LowG, 674
Dissimilation, G, 669, 692, 1652
Domestic animal names, Nor., 279
Domestic tool terms, G, 1289
Double suffixes, E, 11
Doublets: E, 90, 750, 906, 1360; G, 1981; OE, 189
Doublets in compounds, G, 927
Doubling: Afrikaans, 1148; E, 838; G, 1896; IE, 655
Downtowners, E, 1680
Dutch influence on E, 287, 339

Elements, F > E, 468; Lat.-Rom. > OHG, 450
Ellipsis, 590
Elliptical words: E, 1735; Sw., 1771, 1772

Klammerformen, G, 1258
Kompositionsfuge: OHG, 533; OS, 533
Kosenamen: E, 1787; G, 38, 1458; Gmc., 1663
Kurzformbildungen, E, 1215
Kurznamen, G, 1688

Ländernamen, G, 1265
Lallwort, G, 1263
Language, origin, 656
Language names, E, 262
Latin elements in E, 624; in F, 624; in G, 345, 624; in MHG, 253
Latin influence on OHG, 143
Latin-Romance elements in Nassau, 55
Lautmalerei, G dialects, 1895
Lehnbedeutungen, OE, 506
Lehnbeziehungen, Fin., 1287; G, 1287
Lehnbildungen, 145; G, 144; OE, 506; OHG, 142, 294, 479
Lehnprägung: Du., 1275; OHG, 1125; PennG, 1504
Lehnübersetzung, G, 57
Lehnwort, G, 1294
Linguistic borrowing, 344, 585
Liquid suffixes, Swiss, 542
Loan formations: G, 399; OHG, 1577
Loan influence, G, 400
Loan suffixes: G, 1290; Sw., 1625
Loan translation: G, 502; OE, 1606
Loanwords, 1943; Alem., 1669; AE, 903, < Gaelic, 711, < G, 258, 881, 1437,
    1543, < Norse, 437; American Swedish < AE, 768; Baltic-G, 27; Dan.,
    1103, < Du., 565, < E, 348, < F, 1326; Du. < F, 1490; East G dialects <
    Slavic, 1778; E, 416, 593, 1098, 1598, < Anglo-French, 487, < Arabic,
    1767, < Celtic, 442, < Du., 339, 1028, < F, 176, 336, 934, 975, 1443, < G,
    20, 259, 261, < Norse, 160, < North Great Britain, 307; Esse < AE, 28,
    < E, 28; Fr., 491; G, 172, 221, 418, 1024, 1279, 1465, 1500, 1592, 1867,
    1892, 1933, < E, 41, 476, 477, 915, 1677, < F, 457, 696, < Gk., 350, < It.,
    445, 1949, < Lat., 345, < Polish, 782, < Scand., 1538, < Slavic, 1929;
    Go., 394; Gmc., 858, 1596, < Fin., 1182; Lat., 1176; Low Saxon < F, 1544;
    Lusern, 203; ME, 1423, < Lat., 335, < Rom., 1422, < Scand., 159; MHG,
    1592, < F, 794, 795, 1120, 1280, 1932, < OF, 1271, < Rom., 1177; MLowG
    < Rom., 1177; Norse < F, 1851; Nor., 281, < E, 1673, < G, 207, < ODan.,
    922; OE < F, 1620, < Gk., 1364, < Lat., 466, 1060, 1364, < Norse, 206, <
    Rom., 1364; OHG, 1592, < Gk., 246, < Lat., 1057, < Rom., 246; ON, 664;

Wortforschung, IE, 1342
Wortkonkurrenz G, 1212
Wortkreuzung, G, 1116, 1117
Wortmischungen, AE, 471
Wortschöpfung, G, 657, 1262
Wortschwund, E, 723
Wortstruktur, G, 536
Wortumdeutung, G, 657
Wortwahl, ENHG, 61
Wurzelerweiterung: G, 1475; IE, 1343
Wurzelvariation, IE, 1343

Zahlwörter, G, 554
Zwillingswörter, G, 100

VI. SPECIFIC PREFIXES, SUFFIXES, ETC.

Affixes beginning with æ, ə, š, ð, and þ are listed after z
a-: E, 834, 1015, 1238, 1358, 1414, 1622; OS, 1984
á-, Dan., 415
â-, Gmc., 991
*ā-, WGmc., 974
-a: G, 51; Gmc., 720, 872; IE, 1991; North Nor., 279; Sw., 124, 272
-â, IE, 1991
aan-, Du., 992
-aar, Du., 555
ab-: G, 1760; MHG, 1902
*AB-, Gmc., 1792
-ability, E, 1133
-able, E, 11, 329, 563
-ad, E, 275
-ade, E, 1082
af, Go., 710
af-: Du., 992; LowG, 1173, 1961; OS, 1984
-aftig, LowG, 1782
-ag: Gmc., 1529; OHG, 724
-age: AE, 903; E, 469

-agr, Gmc., 798
-agtig, Dan., 222
-ah, Gmc., 526
-ahs, Go., 1551
-aille, G., 1209
-aja-, Gmc., 1614
-aktig, Sw., 1625
al-, G, 831
-al, E, 1077, 1700
âl, LowG, 1053
-ala, Gmc., 720
-älde: Sw., 1012; WNorse, 1012
-ald: Sw., 1012; WNorse, 1012
-aldi, ON, 1714
-ali: Swiss, 543; Yid., 951
aller-, G, 831
-alo, ON, 414
-alôn, Gmc., 1367
an-: Nor., 1920; OS, 1984
-an: AE, 262; ON, 1728; OSw., 1043; Sw., 272
-ana, Gmc., 720
-ancy, E, 11
and-: Go., 1595; ON, 1832

-chenk, Unterzips, 522
-cide, E, 1133
-cillin, E, 1142
-cin, Du., 1011
-craft, E, 1383

-d, Sw., 272
-dage, OS, 676
-dara, Gmc., 720
de-, E, 904, 1088
der-, G, 13
-dey, LowG, 733
-ding, Sil., 357
dis-: E, 1088; Go., 1451
-dl, Yid., 951
-dom: Du., 1945; E, 247, 1383,
    1908
-dôm, OS, 676
du-, Go., 1451
durch-, G, 842, 1034
duþi, Go., 1151

-e-, G, 59
-c: E, 421; G, 615, 973;
    LowG, 1587; MHG, 1013;
    North Nor., 279; OSw., 664;
    Sw., 272; Upper Saxon, 449
-é, F, 1300
c̄: Gmc., 786; OHG, 1035
-ê-, LowG, 1861
-ec: MHG, 1032; OE, 367
-(e)de, G, 1285
-ede, LowG, 276
-ee: AE, 903; E, 570, 893, 904,
    1064, 1133, 1219, 1341, 1383
-eer, E, 1064
-eht, Rappenau, 1129
-ei: G, 299, 945, 1647, 1847;
    LowG, 478
-eie, MHG, 1554
-eien, LowG, 1886
-ēja-, Gmc., 1614

-eke, Halländsk, 1019
-eken, Du., 1822
-el: Du., 820; E, 1299; G, 519, 1209;
    LowG, 1585; OE, 367; Sw., 272
-el-: Du., 948; G, 1652; LowG, 966
-ela, Vorarlberg, 1831
-ele-, OE, 367
-elei, G, 945
-eler, Upper G, 241
-eles, G, 38
-elig, Vorarlberg, 1831
-eljoen, Du., 1224
-ell-, Lat., 1056
-els, LowG, 178, 545, 546, 567, 736,
    783, 1138, 1501, 1781
-else: Dan., 1193; East Norse, 876;
    LowG, 965, 1042; Norse, 1594;
    Nor., 47, 138, 1920; OSw., 1043;
    Sw., 272, 1766
-elska, ON, 1729
-elti, Alem., 1758
-en: E, 337, 740, 895, 1325;
    LowG, 1780; Nor., 1920;
    OE, 367, 1256
-ency, E, 11
-end: OE, 781; LowG, 1168
-e-nd, OE, 403
-ende: Sw., 270, 272, 958, 1766;
    Valdres, 701
-endis, ON, 1715
-ene: E, 275; Sw., 1346
-ener, LowG, 1863
-enez: Basel, 666; Swiss, 671
-ennes, Basel, 666
-en(n)es, Swiss, 671
-enq-, Lat., 1359
-ens, Fr., 288, 443
-ense, OFr., 1580, 1581
ent-, G, 1760
-ent, Sw., 1250
-enzen, G, 852
-eous, E, 11

1235, 1274, 1351, 1352, 1418,
1794, 1798, 1988; LowG, 1584;
MHG, 370, 1079, 1195, 1815;
MLowG, 1584; Nürnberg, 1476;
Oberschopfheim, 1579; OE, 112,
167, 642, 983, 1009, 1010, 1353,
1493; OHG, 349; OS, 133, 1984
-(g)er(d), Gmc., 1663
-gerðr, Gmc., 967
gi-, OHG, 968; OS, 1984
-gi: Du., 1748; OEFr., 614;
OHG, 320
-goed, Du., 503
gront-, MDu., 1833

-hāēme, OE, 1925
-haft: G, 439; Rappenau, 1129;
RF, 724
-haftig, LowG, 1782
-hard, Gmc., 1663
-hart, G, 1209
-hêd, OS, 676
-heid, Du., 888, 889, 892
hciðr-, Icel., 1318
-heim: Alem., 182; G, 54, 1637;
Sw., 1563
-heimer, AE, 1542, 1543
-heit: G, 1291, 1357, 1903;
MHG, 1409; OHG, 1904;
OLowG, 1904; RF, 725;
WGmc., 79
her-: Du., 557, 1569; G, 1317
-hert, Gmc., 1663
hin-, G, 1317
hinter-, G, 1034
-hövel, G, 51
-hof, G, 51
-holt, G, 51
-horst, G, 51
-huð, ON, 245
-hus, G, 51
-hûsen, OHG, 286

*-Xaiðuz, Gmc., 618

i-, ME, 1354
-i-: Norse, 413; ON, 1723
-i-, Gmc., 1163
-i: Alsatian, 1136; Bernese, 1951;
Gmc., 720, 872, 1184;
North Nor., 279; Rappenau, 1136;
Sw., 1250; Swiss, 1951
-î: G, 1291; WGmc., 79
-(i)aal, Afrikaans, 1801
-iär, Sw., 1249
-ian, G, 802, 1209
-ianus, G, 1209
-ible, E, 11, 329
-ic: AE, 262; E, 275, 329;
MHG, 1032; OE, 367;
Zaisenhaus, 1864
-ical, E, 329
-icge, OE, 1159
ich-, G, 361
-ich: G, 982; Rhenish, 980
-icht, Upper Saxon, 449
-ick, Rhenish, 980
-icus, G, 1209
-icze, OE, 1361
-id, E, 275
-id(a), OHG, 1285
-ida: G, 1291; OS, 676; WGmc., 79
-idi, OS, 676
-ie: Afrikaans, 1148; E, 1737;
F, 1647; OS, 676
-ie-, Du., 1846
-îe: G, 401; MHG, 1554
-(i)eel, Afrikaans, 1801
-ien, G, 401, 1265
-ien-, Gmc., 1702
-ier, MHG, 1276, 1462
-ieræere, MHG, 1276, 1462
-ieren, G, 521, 1076, 1293, 1464,
1699
-iering, Afrikaans, 1800

-ierre, MHG, 1276, 1462
-ig: E, 775; G, 243, 982, 1556, 1654;
    Nor., 1593; Rhenish, 980;
    Upper Saxon, 449; Valdres, 701
-îg: Gmc., 1529; OHG, 724;
    Rappenau, 1129
-igen, G, 1998
-iX, RF, 724
-iken, Du., 1822
-ikon, Alem., 179
-ila, Gmc., 720
-ile, E, 11
-ilioen, Du., 1224
-ill: Gmc., 1038; ON, 1722
-illi-: Lat., 1056; ON, 31
-ilo, ON, 414
-ilôn, Gmc., 1367
in-: G, 663; Gmc., 756;
    MDu., 1833
-in: ESw., 706; G, 333, 973, 1652;
    Valdres, 701
-în: G, 852; MHG, 724; OHG, 724;
    Rappenau, 1129; RF, 724
-īn: Gmc., 1921; OE, 367
-ina, Gmc., 720
-incel, OE, 367, 1806
-inde, ME, 423
-in(e), ME, 107
-ine, E, 11
-înez, Swiss, 671
-ing: Bav., 1616; Du., 1190;
    E, 23, 32, 193, 322, 932, 1454,
    1871; G, 50, 248, 630, 1459, 1556;
    Gmc., 598, 1618; LowG, 273,
    734, 1172, 1780; Meckl., 1776;
    ME, 423; Northwest Thuringian,
    631; Nor., 47, 1920;
    Oberschopfheim, 1579; ODan.,
    25; OE, 322, 367, 403, 916, 1868,
    1923; Sw., 272, 1346, 1563;
    WGmc., 1836
-inga, OS, 676

*-inga, Gmc., 1226
-ingen, Alem., 179
*-ingja, Gmc., 1986
-ingo-, Gmc., 1359
*ingō, Gmc., 322
-ingr: OIcel., 773; Sw., 1934
-injo, WGmc., 79
-inkil, WGmc., 1362, 1363
-inkilîn: G dialects, 1744;
    OHG, 1738
-inklîn, G, 852
-inn: G, 1695; ON, 414
-inne, Du., 821
-inôn, Gmc., 1367
-inski, G, 1209
-int, Valdres, 701
-iŋ, RF, 725
-io-, Gmc., 732, 1702
-ioen, Du., 1224
-ion, Sw., 1250
-ious, E, 11
-ir, ON, 414
-ire, OEFr., 622
-iren, G, 1699
-îrôn, Gmc., 1367
-is: Dan., 1530; E, 71; IE, 1638;
    Lat., 127; Sw., 1482, 1772;
    Swiss, 671
-iš, RF, 724
-isc, Rappenau, 1129
-isch: G, 243, 516, 517; MHG, 1032
-ise, E, 638, 989
-iser, F, 989
-ish: AE, 262; E, 275
-isieren, G, 989
-isk, Sw., 755
-iska, Go., 1151
-isla, E, 391
-isli, OS, 676
-islo, OS, 676
-ism: E, 496, 649, 1383, 1479;
    Sw., 1250

-ismus, G, 351, 684, 1788
-isôn, Gmc., 1367
-iss, F, 188
-ist: E, 275, 1383; G, 99, 1209;
    Sw., 1250
-ite: AE, 146; E, 275, 1383
-iteit, Du., 1471
-ithi, LowG, 377
-itis, E, 247, 1383
-itz, G, 852
-ive, E, 1082
-iveness, E, 1082
-ization, E, 1383
-ize, E, 329, 398, 638, 989, 1327
-iþa, OS, 676

-j-, Du., 1846
-j, ON, 1721
-ja: G, 1526; Gmc., 393, 872
-jär, Sw., 1249
-jan: G, 672, 802, 1209; Gmc.,
    1367; OHG, 1412
-jann, G, 802
-jas-, IE, 234
je-, Cattenstedt, 326
-je, Afrikaans, 1148; Du., 1840, 1845
-jə, Franconian, 1958
-joen, Du., 1224

-k: ESw., 707; G, 1641;
    Gmc., 409, 1162; Norse, 609;
    North Fr., 673; ON, 1715;
    Scand., 319
ka-, AE, 1484
-ka: Go., 1152; OSw., 664
-kaar, Du., 187
-kamp, G, 51
ke-, AE, 1484
-ke: E, 574; LowG, 426;
    Meckl., 91, Upper Saxon, 1211
-kêk(e), LowG, 1650

-ken: Du., 1822; LowG, 1174, 1886;
    Meckl., 91
ker-, AE, 1484
-ker, G, 51
-k(ə), Zaisenhaus, 1864
-kheit, RF, 725
-kie, Du., 1740
-kk-, ON, 1715
-ko, Gmc., 798
-kunds, Go., 252

-l-: Gmc., 1613; OE, 781; OS, 698,
    Swiss, 940
-l: ESw., 707; E, 438, 463, 769;
    G, 164; Gmc., 1162; IE, 1162;
    Norse, 609; Yid., 951
-ḷ, E, 769
-la: Faroese, 1112; Gmc., 720;
    OE, 367; ON, 875, 1715, 1722,
    1746; Sw., 272
lac, OE, 464
-læti, ON, 1716
-laga, Faroese, 1112
-lar: Du., 458; MHG, 1553
-laus, G, 620
-le: E, 1865; OE, 367
-leben, LowG, 76
-lcct, Zaisenhaus, 1864
-leg, Valdres, 701
-lega, OIccl., 271
-legr, OIcel., 271
-leht, Rappenau, 1129
-leik, Go., 1857
-lein, G, 485, 1698
-lek: Dan., 1192; Sw., 1192
-ler: AE, 146; G, 1209, 1401, 1854,
    1901; Upper G, 241, 242
-less, E, 1158
-let, E, 11, 295, 824
*leut-, Gmc., 928
-leysi, ON, 1716

-lə, Zaisenhaus, 1864
-lic, OE, 1606, 1811
-lice, OE, 1811
-lich: G, 243, 973, 1654;
    MHG, 1561
-lîch: MHG, 1552; Rappenau, 1129
-liche, E, 421
-lich(t), G, 1576
-(l)ieren, G, 1745
-lig, Nor., 1593
-liga: OIcel., 271; ON, 1746, 1752
-ligen, Sw., 1766
-ligr: OIcel., 271; ON, 875, 1746,
    1752
-lih, OHG, 1953
-lîh, OHG, 629
-liX, RF, 724
-lij, Du., 1470
-lijk: Du., 1679; MDu., 1823
-lik, Du., 1470
*-lik, Gmc., 1857
-lîk, Gmc., 1529
-lika, OSw., 1
-like, MDu., 1823
-liker, OSw., 1
-likin, OSw., 610
-lin: North Nor., 279; Swab.,
    1234
-ling: Du., 1642; E, 1204;
    G, 205, 332, 419, 1209, 1210,
    1400, 1565, 1608, 1609, 1982;
    OE, 367
-lings, G, 81
-lis, Fr., 288
*lit-, Gmc., 928
-litz, G, 1889
-lös, Sw., 1494
-logy, E, 576
-loht, Rappenau, 1129
-lon: E, 21; G, 51
-long, E, 1204
-loos, Du., 643, 1470

-los, G, 620, 1067, 1760
-lp, E, 463
-ly, E, 694, 1101, 1358, 1626
-lyndi, ON, 1716

m-, 744
-m, OE, 1583
-ma: G, 51; Gmc., 720
-mässig: G, 1588; Sw., 1624, 1633
-mann: G, 51; Sil., 357
-manship, E, 1478
-mat, G, 879
-matic, G, 879
-me, Fr., 1754
-menni, LowG, 378
-ment: AE, 833; E, 469, 1383
-met, Gmc., 1663
miss-: G, 730, 973; Gmc., 374
missa-, OHG, 1430, 1431
-mobile, E, 22, 1392
-môt, Gmc., 1663
-mp, E, 463
-mund, ON, 1715

-n-: Alem., 136; G, 1892
-n: E, 769; Gmc., 1915; ON, 414
-ṇ, E, 769
-na: ESw., 707; Gmc., 720;
    Nor., 1918
-nad, Sw., 272
-na(n): Go., 34; ON, 34
*-nassuz, Gmc., 618
-ne, Nor., 1918
near-, E, 1393
-nede, Du., 821
-nes, OE, 1923
-ness, E, 1941
-nesse, OFr., 1580, 1581
-ng, OHG, 1130
-ni: Go., 365; Nor., 47
-nik: AE, 1474; E, 1391; G, 1391

-ning: Nor., 47, 1920; OSw., 1043;
   Sw., 272, 1044
-nis: E, 775; RF, 725; WGmc., 79
-nisse, OFr., 1580, 1581
-nissi, OS, 676
-no-, Gmc., 1965
-(n)skja, ON, 1714
-nt-, IE, 839
-nt, IE, 1635
-n̥t, IE, 235
-ntie, G, 1076
-ntz, G, 1076
-nussi, OS, 676

ō, OS, 699
o-, Norse, 1455
ô-, Gmc., 599
*ō-, WGmc., 974
-o-, Norse, 413
-o, ON, 414
-ó, Icel., 770
ob-, Du., 1838
-oc, OE, 367
-ock, E, 1990
-od, OE, 367
-odi, WGmc., 79
-ôdi, Gmc., 1660
-odus, Go., 1720
oð-, OE, 1055
-öli, Swiss, 543
-öri, Swiss, 543
of, Norse, 321, 323
of-: Du., 1838; ON, 938
ofer-, OE, 1440
-og, Valdres, 701
-oh, Gmc., 526
-oht, Rappenau, 1129
-ol, OE, 1256
-old, Gmc., 1663
-oli, Swiss, 543
-ology, E, 576, 1383
-on: ESw., 706; E, 21; ON, 1728;
   Sw., 124, 1506
-ôn, Gmc., 1367
on(d)-, OE, 1055
*-ōn-i, Gmc., 1728
ont-: Du., 1821, 1879;
   MDu., 1273, 1833
-or, OE, 1583
-orð, ON, 1714
-ori, Swiss, 543
-ost, OE, 1583
-ot: OE, 367; Sw., 117
-ote, E, 275
-oþ, OE, 367
-ôz-, Gmc., 1703

para-, 649
por-, OF, 340
-pp, Gmc., 1225
py-: Gmc., 1301, 1733; Gk., 1301

-r-: G, 1892; Gmc., 1613, 1837;
   Swiss, 940
-r: ESw., 707; E, 463; Norsc, 609
-ra: Gmc., 720; OE, 1583; Sw., 272
-rád, OE, 195
-rade, LowG, 56
-ræði, ON, 1716
-rama: AE, 903; E, 1048, 1082,
   1480
-red, OE, 189
-rich, G, 1411, 1564
-rid, G, 1111
-rîk, Gmc., 1663
-rode, LowG, 56
rød-, Scand., 727
-roo, E, 1388
-ry, E, 11, 469
-rzen, MDu., 1039

s-: G, 844, Gmc., 679
-s-, G, 212, 441

-tschen, G, 197
-tsen, Du., 1309
-tsien, LowG, 1568
-tsier, LowG, 1568
-tum, G, 605, 1357, 1402, 1684,
   1685, 1807, 1808
-tūm, RF, 725
-tūningas, OE, 1925
-tuom, WGmc., 79
-type, E, 1604
-tz(-), G, 1076

u-, Valdres, 701
-u: Gmc., 872; Go., 771
-uc, OE, 367
ūð-, OE, 1055
-uð, ON, 245
-ūðigr, ON, 245
-uðr, ON, 1726
über-, G, 1034
-ug̊-, ON, 874
-ug, Gmc., 245
-ugr, Gmc., 798
-uh, Gmc., 526
-uhr, ON, 414
-ul, OE, 367
-ula, Gmc., 720
-ulf, OE, 189
-ull: Gmc., 1810; ON, 1726
-ulo, ON, 414
um: Norse, 323; ON, 321
um-, G, 1034, 1617
-um, Lat., 127
un-: E, 364, 836, 1088, 1158, 1219,
   1917; E dialects, 1917; G, 184,
   201, 751, 973, 1760, 1899;
   OE, 1607
-un, ON, 1728
-una, Gmc., 720
-uncel, OE, 367
-und, ON, 1714
undar-, OS, 1984

-ung: G, 697, 943, 973, 1150, 1618;
   LowG, 1172; Oberschopfheim,
   1579; ODan., 25; OE, 403, 1923;
   WGmc., 1836
*unga, Gmc., 1226
-unga, OS, 676
-unge, E, 421
-ungo-, Gmc., 1359
*-ungō, Gmc., 322
-ungr: Gmc., 1037; OIcel., 773
-unnjō, WGmc., 911
unter-, G, 1034
uo-, OHG, 1671
-ura, Gmc., 720
-uri, Swiss, 543
-urig, G, 1259
-urr, Gmc., 1038
us-, G, 708
-us: Basel, 666; G, 1209; IE, 1638;
   Lat., 127; Swiss, 671
-usta, OIcel., 757
-ut, Valdres, 701
uuidar-, OS, 1984
uz-: G, 1963; Go., 539, 1963;
   OHG, 539; OE, 974

-v, ON, 1721
-var, MHG, 204
-vas-, IE, 234
ver-: G, 634, 823, 988, 1264;
   Gmc., 987
-ville, E, 77
vol-, ENHG, 626
voll-, Gmc., 374
volle-, ENHG, 626
vollen-, ENHG, 626

-wærd, OE, 1922
-wald: Gmc., 1663; OE, 189
wan, Fr., 1373
-ward, OE, 1922
-wark, LowG, 963